THE IRONSIDES

A LIFETIME IN THE LEAGUE

Who's Who of Newport County

1912 -1989

A. K. Ambrosen

Published by:
Yore Publications,
12 The Furrows,
Harefield
Middx.
UB9 6AT

© A.K. Ambrosen 1991

British Library Cataloguing–in–Publication Data
A catalogue record for this book is
available from the British Library.

ISBN 0 9513321 7 1

Printed by:
BPCC Wheatons Ltd.,
Hennock Road,
Marsh Barton,
Exeter. EX2 8RP.

This book is dedicated

to my mother,

who never lived

to see it published

CONTENTS

Acknowledgements:

This book is the product of many years' work. While most of the effort has been put in by myself, many others have given considerable help. Much of the early assistance came from Richard Shepherd, who was happy to lend his copious notes on results and transfers. I should also particularly like to thank Richard for the loan of many of the photographs used. Over the last few years, Jim Creasy has given freely of his time in digging out old dates of birth, death and transfers. Doug Lamming, Ian Garland, Ceri Stennett, Michael Featherstone, David Howgate and too many members of the Association of Football Statisticians to name individually have also given useful information.

Help has also been received from old players and their relatives. Sadly Jack Evans, who played for the Club in the 1920's and supplied some useful material, died before the book was completed. I would also like to thank the staff of the Cardiff and Newport Reference Libraries for their help, together with the Football League plus Welsh and English Football Associations.

N ewport County made up a very large part of my life.

I was born only two streets away from the Somerton Park Ground, and my father played for the Club in its very first season.

My own debut, for the reserves, was at the tender age of 15, and my connection with the Club lasted until its end. I was involved with the County from my schooldays and knew many of the pre–war players, not to mention most of those since the War.

(Billy Lucas)

Like so many other people in the town I was very upset to see the Club close down after so many years' existence, but at least this book is a souvenir of better times and an acknowl-edgement of the hundreds of players who made their varying contributions to the County.................

Billy Lucas

FORMAT:

The players section of the book gives brief details of the player, followed by a 'Pen Picture'. As some yardstick was necessary, players with at least one full Football League appearance to their credit have been included.

The underlining of a player's christian name (or a name in brackets) refers to the popular name of that player, where the first given name is/was not relevant. A name in inverted commas, refers to the player's popular nickname. The dates of birth of some pre–war players have been extracted from Registers which only give three month periods, hence the reference to 'early', 'mid' and 'late'. Reference has also been made to height and weight, to add to the statistical information. Heights have been given to the nearest inch, but neither height or weight should be regarded as having medical accuracy, especially as most forwards 'lost' several inches on joining the Club!

The number of Football League appearances (without substitutions) and goals are then given, followed (in brackets) by the total number of first team appearances, including major Cup competitions etc., in order to provide a more detailed picture of that player's career. This is then followed by a list of the player's clubs', transfer dates, and where known, transfer fees'. With some players, especially pre–war and amateur, these are difficult to establish and any inaccuracy, that is subsequently revealed, is regretted. International appearances are included, with the number of appearances following the Country of representation, and period. Most abbreviations are self–explanatory, but to avoid confusion the following are used:

b.	Place, and date (or period) of birth.
cs.	Close season.
app.	Apprentice.
pro.	Professional.

THE IRONSIDES

In the early part of March 1989, Newport County A.F.C. which had been formed in 1912, was gradually wound up. The Club, which had previously been evicted from Somerton Park by the Borough Council before the start of the season, was once more evicted, and consequently expelled from the Vauxhall Conference.

The Club was used to struggle from the moment of its inception and had been on the brink of closure on numerous occasions. This book, however, is not about the trials and tribulations of the Club itself, but about the players, who have been the lifeblood of the Club. Although the trophy room has been sparsely furnished – as the mythical Irish burglar discovered – the players have been many, and often colourful. This book is about them and their contribution to the history of Newport County.

The lack of literature on Newport County has failed to reflect the impact of the Club on the town, for the Club's existence is well woven into the tapestry of Newport and Gwent. Trophies were few, but old supporters of all generations can relate stories of the players who sported what was normally the black and amber. My own Grandfather, who worked at Lysaght's, could recall the founding of the Club. My Father would fight with his brothers for a first look at the 'Football Argus', before the war, and I in turn sat on his shoulders to watch my early games. Generations have visited the little Ground, and on their lips are still the heroes and villains of many decades – Jimmy Gittins, Harry Duggan, Tom Johnston and the rest. Many are thankfully still with us, others have long passed on, but the tales and personalities will survive for generations to come.

NON-LEAGUE DAYS:

1912 – 1913.

On the 7th of September 1912, Newport County played their first competitive game, beating the Tonypandy side Mid–Rhondda 3–0 at Somerton Park. The line–up for that historic game consisted of:

> *Husbands, Lean, Taylor, Cox, Thornton, McDougall, Holt, Hall, Vowles, Fyfe and Westwood.*

There was a fair amount of experience in the side, which is illustrated by the fact most of the team remained as regulars throughout the season.

One of the first players signed was the goalkeeper, Teddy Husbands, a good honest professional, who had played in Cardiff City's first competitive match, two years previously, after previous service with Liverpool (1906) and Wrexham (1908). He had won Welsh Cup Winners medals in 1909, 1910 and 1912, and was to miss only two Southern League games during the season. Ted, who was born in Wrexham on the 29th of July 1885, was later with Mardy, and in the 1930's became the Clapton Orient trainer.

Glasgow born Louis Lean, who played right–back or centre–half, was an ex–goal scoring centre forward. He had appeared for Liverpool reserves, Third Lanark, and had two spells at Swindon, before arriving at Somerton Park, where he missed just one match during 1912/13. A dour Scot, Louis carried too much weight, but was a hard tackler, with a good shot and head. He played a few war–time games for County and afterwards signed for Caerphilly Town.

'Big Billy' Taylor was also a Scot, from Edinburgh, and was a regular at left back all season. He was a more artistic player than Lean, and had appeared for Airdrie, Gainsborough, West Ham, Newcastle, Croydon Common and Swindon.

Right–half Albert Cox played his last Southern League game against Aberdare on the 2nd of November, and then dropped into the reserves. He was a young, Bristol born, part–timer, signed from the Rovers.

Centre–half, and later at right–half, was Tommy Thornton, a product of the Birmingham League, who had had a couple of seasons with Aston Villa.

Left–half throughout the season, was Manager Davy McDougall, a sound player who scored a penalty in the first game.

Outside–right Andy Holt played in every match until his transfer to Cardiff on March the 5th, for the princely sum of £100. He had scored in the previous five games, and was eventually leading scorer for the season with eight. A former Schoolboy International, Andy was a speedy player, who had previously been with Kidderminster and Sheffield United, and later played for Exeter, Chesterfield, Gillingham and Mansfield. He was also a cricket pro. with the Oxcroft Club, and later the Sports Supervisor of a large industrial concern in West Wales.

Blackburn born Proctor Hall, played in every game at inside–right or centre–forward. Then in the veteran stage, he had been with Manchester United, Brighton, Luton Town, Bradford City and Preston, and in the close season of 1913 he signed for Mardy.

The slowish Bob Vowles from Worcester appeared in five different positions, and scored in the first match. His last appearance in the first team was versus Llanelly on 28.12.12. He had been signed from Chepstow Town, for he was living there at the time.

Scottish inside–left George Fyfe was the third player who scored in the first match. He was a ball juggler, who was at the end of his career, having previously been with Hibernian, Watford and Halifax Town. He afterwards played for Swansea and Barry. George was signed from the New Brompton Club, which was later to become 'Gillingham'.

During the course of the season others appeared:

J. Perry, an Eastern Valley product, was the regular right–back from September.

David Ewing, a left–back or left–half, came from Q.P.R., and had a run on ten consecutive first team games. He was a stocky player with a powerful shot, but was strictly left–footed. The previous season he had been with Machen.

One of the part–time pros. was Billy Bowdler, who played in any forward position. He came from Pontnewydd, and was afterwards with local teams such as Lysaght's and Alexandra Dock.

27 year–old William Albert 'Ike' Fyfe, who lived in Rogerstone, did not miss a game after arriving from Risca on the 7th of December. He had scored in the shortlived Newport F.C.'s F.A. Cup tie versus Frome, in 1906. 'Ike', whose brother was the Chairman of the Newport and District League, scored six Southern League goals, mainly from centre–forward. In the close season he joined Caerphilly, and after the War, Abercarn. He later owned a Garage and Private Hire business, and conducted the Bethesda Chapel Choir, and he died in 1961.

One of the most interesting characters was Ernie Hammett or (to give him his full title), Ernest Dyer Galbraith Hammett. He was born in Radstock, Somerset, on 15.10.1891, and died in Newport 23.6.47. He attended Crindau School, and was a good runner, attracting the interest of the soccer team Newport Barbarians. He afterwards joined Treharris, and in 1912 won a Welsh amateur cap. After playing for Newport Thursdays and Wolves, Ernie made his Newport County debut versus Llanelly 28.12.12., and was County Captain until World War 1. He was expected to rejoin County after the War, but took up rugby instead, becoming an England International.
He later went as Sports Master to a Public School in Sussex, becoming connected with Blackheath. He also played for Wales versus England at Lawn Tennis.

George Groves played three games at inside–left from the end of March, and 'Whiskey' Jones made three appearances in April.

Another interesting character, who made a couple of appearances, was William 'Ginger' Davies, a local from Robert St., who joined from Newport Barbarians. Although being gassed at Ypres, he returned to be captain, and later trainer of Lovell's Athletic, before dying in June 1937.

1913 –1914

Newport County started their second season in the Southern League with an almost entirely new staff. One or two of the old guard made appearances – Ernie Hammett scored 12 League goals, including four versus Treharris, and Ted Husbands was the reserve goalkeeper – but new faces predominated.

In goal was six foot Bob McLeod, who had played in the 1912 Scottish Cup Final for Raith Rovers, having joined them earlier from the 7th Scottish Rifles. He was an outstanding goalkeeper, and saved two penalties in a game at high flying Luton. At the end of the season Bob left the County for Q.P.R., and played for them in an important Cup–tie versus Everton. In 1921 he joined Armadale.

At full–backs, were the cool and resourceful Tom Spittle, who missed only two games, and the ever present Fred Flanders. Fred's career has been covered previously, but Tom's games for the County were restricted to the Southern League. He was a gentlemanly player, a good tackler and was well versed in the offside game. He joined the County from Glossop, having begun at Limehouse St.Peter's.

The ever smiling Haydn Green was a utility player and missed only three Southern League matches during the season. He was a classy player and had previously been with Aston Villa. At the end of the season he left and joined Reading. In 1930 Haydn became Ebbw Vale manager, before taking over this role at Torquay and Guildford City, the latter winning the Southern League in 1937/38.

Albert Edwards, the frail but cultured centre–half, had also been with Villa, but he had joined the County after playing four Division 2 games for Bristol City. With his deceptive raking stride and sound positional sense, Albert was a defender of undoubted ability, but sadly died during World War 1.

Another utility man was Alf Preece, who had joined the Club from Newport Thursdays. He was a young, lively player, who eventually turned professional, but his career was stopped by the War.

At inside or centre–forward could be found Frank Lindley, who won a Lanarkshire Cup Winner's medal with Motherwell, and who afterwards played for Sheffield Untied. He was a big, powerful player, but was wounded in the War.

Billy Matthews was a skilled player and captain of the side, missing only two games. He had played for Derby, Notts. County and Aston Villa, and was in fact, the first Notts. County player to score at Meadow Lane (versus Nottingham Forest 3.9.10). Billy was quick on the ball and good at combining with the other forwards. During the course of the second season he scored ten Southern League goals, two goals in the County's first F.A.Cup-tie (versus Mond Nickel Works) and a hat-trick versus Cardiff Corries.

Jack 'Jock' Butler, was a 12 stone centre-forward or right winger. When Sam Hollis took over at Bristol City in 1911, he signed six Scots, buying Butler from Motherwell, with Brand, for £90. He was a speedy player, who scored many goals through his forcing tactics, but was not a success at Newport until tried on the wing.

Ernie Hammett played in various positions.

On the left wing was Tom Tomlinson, who had a fine turn of speed. Tom, who was born in Sheffield in 1890, had played for Mexborough and Notts. County, although he was not a regular at Meadow Lane.

Jack Smart, a former Bristol Rovers player, was a regular at full-back or wing-half.

The County's big signing of the season was Joe Enright, an Irish International inside-left, who at £50, cost £5 more than the rest of the team put together. The Belfast born player was clever and fast having played for Shelbourne and Leeds City, the latter the forerunners of the United. He scored only five Southern League goals, the best being obtained against Stoke, in pouring rain. He was paid the maximum wage of £4 per week, and at the end of the season moved on to Coventry City. Ironically on the 28.11.14, he scored four goals in the City's 10-1 drubbing of County!

1914–1915

This season is very obscure, for it was played in war-time, and many thought it wrong to concentrate on entertainment when men were being mown down overseas. Consequently press coverage was thin, but County clearly had a settled side.

In goal was Harold Sedgeley, a close season signing from Barry, who was virtually an ever present. He was an excellent goalkeeper, and adept at saving penalties.

At right back was Arthur Cleverley who had come from Swansea after playing for Brentford. Jack Jarvis was a half-back or forward, but the rest of the defence – Flanders, Preece, Spittle and Edwards – had played for County the previous season.

At outside-right was Willie Messer, who was signed by Swansea as an amateur after a trial at Morriston in 1912, and returned to the Vetch after his spell at Somerton Park. George Groves was the regular inside-right and Ernie Hammett played centre-forward, scoring plenty of goals. Crad Evans, the brother of Birmingham's R.O.Evans and once on Arsenal's books, played at inside-left for the first half of the season. Tom Tomlinson was the regular left-winger.

....

Organised soccer closed down in the close season of 1915, the name of Newport County being kept alive by munitions workers, plus soldiers on leave, or stationed nearby. Friendlies were played to the end of 1915, and then the team operated in the South Western Combination until the close season. Amongst the players were a few familiar names, like Ted Husbands, George Groves and 'Whiskey' Jones. Only a few friendlies were played in the next two years, then regular friendlies began in December 1918, in preparation for the resumption of organised football. A few well known characters like Husbands, Groves and Flanders were still playing.

(Ted Husbands)

1919 – 1920

Before the War, County had played in the obscurity of the Southern League Division 2. Now, since there was a vacancy due to the resignation of Stalybridge Celtic – who joined the Central League – they were to play in Division 1, which the following season became Division 3 of the Football League. In their first match of 1919–20, versus Norwich City, the County team line–up consisted of:

> *Cooper, Barnacle, Collins, Brookes, Jones, Harris, Savage, Lockley, Dobson, Mann and Gaughan.*

Of these only Cooper, 'Whiskey' Jones, Dobson and Gaughan were to play for the Club in the Football League. Cooper, Dobson and Gaughan missed only a few games. Dobson scored 10 Southern League goals, 'Whiskey' Jones scored the first post–war goal versus Norwich, and Gaughan scored their last Southern League goal versus Portsmouth.

32 year old Dick Barnacle made his one and only appearance, versus Norwich. He was born in Coventry and made 129 Southern League appearances for Coventry City before World War 1. He joined them in 1908 from Foleshill St. George's, while he was working in the pits. In the War he served in the Royal Marines, spending 16 months in France. His vigorous style made him very popular with the Coventry fans, and he played in their 10–1 demolition of the County.

The bald–headed 'Pat' Collins normally played right–back, and only missed two matches during the season. He was a popular and consistent performer, and as well as playing for such outfits as Bilston United and Birmingham Veritas, had played for Wolverhampton (where he was born in 1882) and Port Vale. His main moment of glory came playing in the 1909 F.A. Cup Final. In 1918/19 he had been playing for Sunbeam Motors, for whom he worked. He was in his late 30's and did not remain with Newport when they entered the Football League because of accommodation difficulties (he travelled from Wolverhampton for matches). Instead he signed for non–League Hednesford Town.

Utility defender Arthur Brookes played only four matches. A Yorkshireman, born in Park Gates, he had been with Rotherham County for two years before joining Wolves. He had a useful kick with both feet.

13 stone Harry Harris, also a utility defender, had come from Bristol Rovers, after playing for Kidderminster. He was born in Oldhill, Staffs., and was the brother of George Harris of Aston Villa.

Bill Lockley, a winger, played in half the Southern League games, mainly in the first half of the season. He was born in Smethwick, and, after starting in the Birmingham League, had played for Reading. On the outbreak of the War he joined the 2nd Worcesters and on his demob., in 1919, played for Oldham, Preston and Aston Villa reserves. In 1920 he moved on to Darlaston Town.

Jackie Mann, normally an inside–left, played in more than 30 matches, and scored 7 goals. He was only 5'–4" tall, and was very fast. Born in Tipton, Staffs. in 1894, he had been with W.B.A., and was later to play for Walsall. Jackie, who had played in 3 Junior Internationals, used to travel down from West Bromwich, and, like Collins, left in the close season because of accommodation problems.

22 year–old George Savage, an outside–right or centre–forward with a good shot, missed only a few games and obtained 7 goals. Born in Birmingham c.1897, he had played for Birmingham reserves and Coventry.

Other players soon came into the team and became regulars. These played on into the Football League, and included Groves, Kelson Griffin, Devlin and Ernie Edwards. Jimmy Hindmarsh, later their long–serving manager, played a few games, normally at centre–half.

During the course of the season, various players came into the side for the odd few games. These included Billy Mayo, a diminutive but speedy winger, who had been with Hartlepools, Reading, Southend and Swansea, and had gone on a successful tour of South America.

Bert Evans was the reserve goalkeeper from Cardiff, and a young Jimmy Gittins appeared at inside–right. Billy Richards was a versatile, well built player who could operate at centre–half or centre–forward. Like others, he was born in Wolverhampton (c.1893), and joined the County from Lysaght's at the end of the War. He had been a schoolboy international, and in 1914 had served in France with the Dragoons, later joining the Machine Gun Corps.

In the match at Plymouth on April 14th, four of the players missed their rail connection because of the Cheltenham races. Manager Harry Parkes, trainer Fred Good and Tom Perry were seconded into the team, along with a Plymouth amateur, F.W. 'Wilf' Worden. Harry Parkes played a few reserve games the following season.

1931 – 1932

This season was unusual in so far as apart from players like Len Madley from Maindee – who came in for the odd game – all of the players appeared for County in the Football League. These included ever–presents Len Blakemore, Billy Bagley and Billy Thomas; Jimmy Gittins who scored 13 goals, including four versus Barry, and Frank Peed, who scored 23 including six versus Taunton.

Other regulars in the side were Billy Clarke, George Wheeler, Jack Clifford, Charlie Brittan, Ron Hugh, George Kitson and Bill Jones.

The end of the season saw a return to League Football.

1939 –1940

This was a strange season, for it began with three Football League matches and continued with a string of friendlies, followed by the Club's entry into the South Western Division of the War League. The situation was even odder than normal for Newport, as the County moved on to Rodney Parade and then Rexville, after Somerton Park had been taken over by the A.R.P.

28 games were played in the War League, and most of the performers had appeared for the County in League football. The defence comprised of six regulars; the ever–present goalkeeper Alex Ferguson, Jack Webb, Len Richards, W.M. Owen, Norman Low and Ernie Brinton. The forward positions were much more in doubt, however, as players enlisted either with the Armed Services, – bodies such as the A.R.P., or the Fire Service. Others returned home to other parts of the Country. Players like Duggan, Hickman and Hydes turned out only around half a dozen times, but Lance Carr managed 16 games on the left side of the attack.

Young players had opportunities because of the War situation. Ray Wilcox played nine times at left–half and Danny Newall played thirteen games on the wing. Ken Wookey appeared in fourteen matches and scored nine times. Others like Wilfred Hares, who had been signed from Tredegar in 1938, and Trevor Mead, who joined the R.A.F., came in for the occasional game.

The County's biggest signing was Walter Robbins. Walter, who was born in Cardiff 24.11.10, joined the City from Ely United in 1926 and proved to be a prolific scorer, notching five from the left–wing in a match against Thames. He was then transferred to W.B.A. in April 1932, and had a long spell at the Hawthorns before holding various staff positions in Welsh Soccer. Walter who died 7.2.79, played 22 games during his season with County and scored 17 goals. He had been signed in the close season for a substantial fee.

Tommy Appleby returned to the Club for the final 13 games and netted 16 goals.

Tommy O'Reilly, signed from Bohemians, played two games on the right wing, and Andy Higgins came in for four matches. Cardiff City players George Ballsom, Arthur Granville and the Amateur International Louis Ford made guest appearances.

In June 1940, the Club made it's final competitive appearance for five years. Lovell's took over the mantle of soccer in the town.

1945 –1946

The first season after County's resurrection was a very strange one. Many players were in the Forces and could make only a limited number of appearances. Many of the old players were 'over the top', and occasionally other teams' players turned out as guests. Despite this, it was in many ways a notable season, for the County played numerous First Division sides in the League (South), in front of large attendances. The Christmas games, for instance, were against Arsenal.

The team which kicked off at Brentford on August 25th was:

Ferguson, Webb, Warhurst, W.M.Owen, Low, Brinton, Derrick, Mogford, Appleby, Wood and Carr.

Only Frank Warhurst, a guest from Plymouth, who had played pre–war for Bristol Rovers, did not appear in the Football League for County, and considering the circumstances, a remarkable number remained regulars throughout the season. Norman Low was ever–present at centre–half and right–half W.M.Owen missed only one game. The veteran goalkeeper Alex Ferguson and left–half Ernie Brinton were regulars until April. Lance Carr played throughout the season, Jack Webb until November and Albert Derrick until his transfer to Swindon in January, after scoring 12 goals.

Tommy Wood played only three games before packing in, and after the early matches Mogford and Appleby did not turn out until March. Warhurst, on trial in August, played in the first team until November.

Many of the players appeared in the Football League for County before or after the War. These included regulars, such as Ken Wookey, Bill Roberts, Stan Batty and Freddy Leamon, plus others who played just a few matches – including

W.E.Owen, Ray Lawrence, Arthur Hydes and Charlie Turner. Some never appeared for the County in the Football League however. Some were locals, whilst others were guest players or servicemen stationed nearby. Gordon Newcombe was a local outside–left, who afterwards went to Exeter City and later held a Government post in Reading. Full–back Ralph Avery, whose brother, Arthur, was also on the County's books, was skipper of Merthyr Tydfil in their Southern League days, when they were the best team outside of the Football League. He scored against Arsenal at Somerton Park.

Forward Jimmy Pollard played for the reserves until leaving for Tranmere. Left–back Wilf Thomas was a local from the Army and Amateur International, Wayte, came from Tredomen. Ernie Shergold played two games at inside–right. The brother of the well known Billy, Ernie was a 'Bevin Boy', and later turned out for Senghenydd.

Syd Howarth (known as 'Tibby'), was born in Newport 28.2.23 and was the son of Tommy Howarth, a Bristol City centre–forward and later manager of the City and Lovell's. Syd's career started   started in Palestine with the R.A.F. and he became the costliest (to that date) Southern League player when he left Merthyr for Aston Villa for £6,500 in June 1948. In September 1950, he joined Swansea Town for £5,000, later moving on to Walsall. He has spent forty years in the licensing trade, starting with the 'Narrow Gauge', in the early 1950's and now ending up at the 'Brewer's Arms' in Dowlais.

A few Internationals appeared briefly on loan. Billy Lucas (with Swindon) played three games. Dougie Witcomb and Alex 'Sandy' McNab of W.B.A. also played.

Full–back Albert Goldstraw was stationed at Tenby and impressed with the Western Command X1. He was later with Worcester city. Forward, Eddie Boatright, had played in the Leyton side beaten in the 1937 Amateur Cup Final. Oakham born goalkeeper Bill Harris (W.B.A.) played twice and some reports credited him with scoring a goal at the other end of the pitch! He had been wounded in Normandy and later played 90 consecutive games for Oldham Athletic. Other guests who appeared were the Scottish centre–forward Robert Kinnell from Dunfermline, who was stationed at Cardiff and Jimmy Southam of W.B.A., who later joined County full–time before moving on to Birmingham City.

Considering the patchwork nature of the season and the standard of the opposition, County did reasonably well. At least they did not finish bottom, as they did in no uncertain manner the following season; and they suffered no 0–13 defeats!

1988 –1989

Newly installed manager John Mahoney performed wonders to put out teams in the Vauxhall Conference and Welsh Leagues on the first day of the season. The Club had been evicted from Somerton Park by the Borough Council, and it was only after this was overturned in the High Court that the Club was sure to commence the season. All of this happened a matter of days before County's initial match and only around half a dozen professionals remained on the books. Thus an unfamiliar team lined up at Stafford on the opening day of the season:

> *Bird, Abbruzzese, Sherlock, Hamer, Thompson, Peacock, Millett, Ford, Taylor, Morgan and Evans.*

Steve Morgan, along with Jim McLaughlin, who played in two games, arrived on trial from the Llanelli area and soon departed. Robbie Taylor, who had joined the Club in March 1987, also played just one game before moving on to Weymouth, as did Kevin Hamer to Merthyr Tydfil. Apart from these only Glynne Millett departed before the winding up of the Club. He played regularly in the first part of the season and made a dozen Vauxhall Conference appearances before returning to Abergavenny.

Tony Bird was the only ever present in the Vauxhall Conference, though he was due to be replaced by the newly signed Kenny Allen when the Club folded. There was a row with Cwmbran when he signed, for they claimed he had been approached illegally. He had earlier played for Ely Rangers and Cardiff Corries, and was 30 when he made his debut in the Vauxhall Conference. Cardiff born Tony runs his own contract cleaning business, and joined County on a non-contract basis, showing pretty consistent form for most of the season. In July 1989, he was persuaded to join Newport AFC, for whom he has played regularly.

Young David Abbruzzese stayed with the Club and played eight Vauxhall games before being dropped.

The very experienced Steve Sherlock missed only three of the twenty–nine games at left–back.

Left–back Darren Peacock, who had an eighteen month lay–off through a broken leg, returned to play 14 games, before he had another spell out of the team with badly broken fingers.

Liverpool born central defender Max Thompson made 15 appearances, though he was dropped because of his inconsistent performances. Max had played in the

Football League for Liverpool, Blackpool, Swansea, Bournemouth and Port Vale. In more recent times he had played for Baltimore Comets (U.S.A.), Northwich Victoria and Academica (Portugal) and signed on a non-contract basis for County.

Francis Ford, something of a utility player, made 16 appearances. he had played for Cardiff City and in the Welsh League, but joined the County from Hermes, the Second Division Cyprus team, as did Richard Evans.

Richard Evans is the son of the former Swansea International Brian Evans, who was once a County reserve player. Richard played 11 games as a striker, but found the net only twice. He was later with Newport AFC.

During the course of the season various County players reappeared. Some of them played regularly. David Withers appeared in 18 games, scoring four goals, and Phil Brignull played 13 times. Paul Sugrue made a much bigger impact than in his Football League stay. He played 13 Vauxhall Conference games and scored Cup hat-tricks against Bridgend, Caernarvon and Buxton. Shane Walker played two games and Graham Rogers four.

David Giles scored twice on his debut, versus Wycombe, and Roger Gibbins played two games, but would have played many more, having been signed just before the winding up. Others who came on as substitutes were Ryan Preece, Sean Mills and Sean Bennett.

Two players came on loan from the local side Albion Rovers. There was Gareth Jones, who had broken his leg twice in 1986, and Rovers' skipper, Dave Bickerton. Others who made odd appearances were Jamie King, Mark Gripton, the Cwmbran goalscorer, and the tall Boston born striker Mike Nuttell – on loan from Peterborough United. Assistant Manager A.M. Les Chappell, who had been with Rotherham in 1965, made one appearance in the Welsh Cup versus Caernarvon, becoming probably the oldest player to appear in the County first team. Dartford born Ian Thompson played only two Vauxhall games, but would have been a regular if the Club had continued. He had played over 100 Football league matches for Bournemouth, and had scored a cup goal against Manchester United. Ian had moved to South Wales to take up a teaching post, and has since scored regularly for Merthyr in the Vauxhall Conference.

Of the newcomers who played regularly, none made a bigger impact than Paul Sanderson. Born in Blackpool 16.12.66, he began his career with Fleetwood Town and as a Manchester City reserve, then played in the Football League for Chester, Halifax, Cardiff and Walsall. He played on both wings and in the centre during the season, showing speed and the ability to beat his full-back, and centre.

Phil Williams also made over 20 Vauxhall appearances, on the left side of midfield. He is a former Welsh Schools and Youth International, and has played for Swansea City in the Football League. In 1988 he had been sent off in a friendly at Somerton Park.

The sturdy Chris Banks is also a former Youth International. Born in Pwllheli 27.8.69, he spent three years with Bolton and is something of a utility player.

Chris Marustik showed touches of his vast experience in his games for County and also scored three goals. He has been capped six times for Wales and played 144 Football League matches for Swansea City, as well as 43 for Cardiff. The Swansea born defender Gary Richards played 14 Vauxhall games. He has played in the Football League for Swansea, Lincoln, Cambridge and Torquay, but suffered a knee injury in 1987–88. Swansea born winger Keri Andrews suffered from a broken ankle in the same season. A former Swansea player, he made his debut in a Welsh Cup semi-final versus Shrewsbury, at the age of 16, having won three Welsh Youth caps. Will Foley turned out in the Vauxhall Conference. He has played for Cardiff and Swansea and had most recently been with Point Chevalier in New Zealand.

During the crisis which came in February and March, the County continued signing players right to the end. Derek Dawkins, the coloured defender from Torquay, did not have time to make a Vauxhall appearance, and the veteran goalkeeper Kenny Allen did not even have time to come to Newport for training.

In the whole unsatisfactory chain of events, the most remarkable thing was the loyalty of the players. Around the time the Club was wound up, the only full-time professional to leave was Darren Peacock, who went to Hereford. Paul Sanderson turned down a £15,000 move to Yeovil in the hope that the Club could continue, and other players left only on a loan or non-contract basis. Players who found other clubs at the time of the crisis included Richard Evans (Port Talbot), Phil Williams (Cheltenham), Tony Bird (Cwmbran Town), Paul Sugrue (Kidderminster), David Withers (Barry Town), Will Foley (Brecon Corries), Roger Gibbins (Cardiff City), Kenny Allen (Torquay), Ian Thompson plus David Abbruzzese (Merthyr Tidfil), the latter after an unsuccessful trial with Torquay. David Giles and Phil Brignull went to Sully.

COUNTY MANAGEMENT:

In July 1912, Davy McDougall became the first County player/manager.....

David Mc Dougall, a Scot born around 1882, was a splendid player, who had enjoyed a very full career before arriving at Somerton Park. His previous clubs had included Rangers, Partick Thistle, Bristol City and the Irish clubs Portadown, Glentoran and Distillery. He had represented the Irish League versus the English and Scottish Leagues. In July 1910, he became the Cardiff City's first player/manager, but in May 1911 he was sacked from his managerial duties, although he continued as a player until joining the County. He was a very popular player, and voted Captain by the rest of the team. By the time he reached Somerton Park he had slowed down from outside–left to left–half. Davy was a sturdy player, 5'10" tall and weighing 12st.4lbs. Although engaged for the 1913–14 season, he left to become Steward of the Excelsior Club. By the 1920's he had become the proprietor of the 'Bunch of Grapes' in High Street, and was later the Landlord of the 'Duke of York' in Wellington Street, Cardiff. At the time County won promotion in 1939, Davy still used to pop over from Cardiff to watch the odd match.

July 1913 saw Sam Hollis appointed Manager.

Samuel W. Hollis was born in Nottingham around 1866, and died at the 'Rose and Crown' in Redcross Street, Bristol 17.4.42. Sam, who dressed immaculately and sported a bowler hat, gold watch and bristling black moustache, was in many ways the 'Billy Lucas' of Bristol City. From 1894 to 1897 he was the Trainer of Woolwich Arsenal. On 21.4.1897 he was first appointed Manager of Bristol City at £200 per annum. This was when the Club turned professional and joined the Southern League. He was given £30 to buy players, later coming back for another £10. He resigned 18.3.1899, partly because the Directors were pressing him to give up his pub, the 'Engineer's Arms', which adjoined the old St.John's Lane Ground. The Directors appointed Robert Campbell of Sunderland to run the City and Sam took over as Manager of neighbouring Bedminster. He lost the post when the two clubs merged, but he was then brought back in 1901, when the new Club was elected to Division 2 of the Football League. He left in March 1905, to run the 'Southville Hotel', but was re–appointed in 1911. He departed once more, in the close season of 1913, and took over at the County, staying until 1917.

He became the Chairman of the Bristol City Shareholders' Association in 1921, and retained an interest in the Club until his death. Sam's early working days had been spent in a Probate Office in Nottingham, followed by a spell with the G.P.O. He was also a keen cricketer, playing for Notts. Colts and coaching Oxford University for many years.

Harry Parkes became County's third Manager in June 1919.

Harry Arnold Parkes was born in Halesowen in July 1888. He was the Captain of Halesowen Grammar School's football and cricket teams. He began with Halesowen and moved on to W.B.A. in 1906. Lightly built Harry weighed only 9st.2lbs, and at the age of 18, played in an F.A.Cup semi-final. In December 1908, he left for Coventry City and played 161 Southern League games for them. For the period of the 1914-18 War, he was Assistant Manager of W.B.A., and was also a worker in munitions. He gave up playing because of a cartilage problem, and after a spell working for his father, in June 1919 he was appointed Secretary/manager of County. He had just two months to knock things into shape before the Club's first season in the Southern League Division 1. He resigned in the close season of 1922, and became the Manager of Chesterfield. He had five seasons there, and proved himself an exceptional Manager, for the team never finished lower than seventh. He moved on to Lincoln in the close season of 1927, and the team showed the same consistency, winning promotion in 1931-32. Harry was in charge at Mansfield from May 1936 until January 1938, and around the following December took over at Notts County, resigning in July 1939.

In many ways the most formidable of County's pre-war Managers was Jimmy Hindmarsh, who took over the reigns in May 1922.....

James Lyons Hindmarsh was born in South Shields mid-1886, and died in Luton 16.3.59. A centre-forward and later centre-half or full-back, he began his career with Whitburn Colliery moving on to Sunderland in September 1905. He joined Fulham in May 1906, Watford in 1907, and Plymouth one year later. Jimmy was sold to Stockport for £100 in 1910, leaving for Manchester City three years later. He was living in Newcastle in 1919 when signed by Harry Parkes the day before County were due to play Watford. He was so tired after the 18 hour journey, that he fell asleep in the dressing-room and missed the match!

He was at first just a player, then player/coach to the reserves. For thirteen years he fought hard to keep football going at Somerton Park, signing some useful players, although with little resources, and obtaining £20,000 in transfer fees. He worked hard to secure the Club's re-election to the Football League, and would ride his bike around local pitches trying to find players for the reserves. Jimmy, who turned down five offers to manage other clubs, finally resigned through ill-health 3.4.35 having devoted a great part of his working life to Newport County. He then obtained employment in Luton, and never had anything further to do with professional football.

In June 1935, the England International Louis Page became the Manager.......

Louis Antonio Page was born in Kirkdale, Lancashire 27.3.1899, and died in Birkenhead 11.10.59. An outside-left in his playing days, he was 5'8" tall and weighed 11st.9lbs. The first Catholic to play for Liverpool schoolboys, he later joined the Merchant Navy. In July 1915, he signed up for the Royal Navy, and two years later was torpedoed whilst on HMS 'Virginian'. Around the end of World War 1, he had three seasons with South Liverpool, before being sold to Stoke in the 1919 close season. Northampton brought him in the close season of 1922, and he remained there for three seasons. In May 1925, he joined Burnley, where he had his best seven years – scoring over 100 goals. Short spells at Manchester United (March 1932) and Port Vale (October 1932) then followed before he first became player/manager, and later Manager, of Yeovil and Petters, in 1933. In the 1934–35 season, the Club had a splendid F.A.Cup run, and Louis played in the third round defeat, despite a broken collar bone.

Coming to Somerton Park 12.6.35, he survived for two years before being suspended 8.9.37 in a row over team selection, and was then sacked. He took legal action over the matter, and won damages for wrongful dismissal. In December 1938, he became trainer/coach of Glentoran, and when War broke out he returned to work in Liverpool Docks, managing the amateur side Carlton in his spare time. He was the Swindon Town Manager from July 1945 to May 1953, and then had three seasons with Chester, leaving in June 1956, and becoming a Leicester City scout. One of four footballing brothers, Louis won seven England caps between 1926 and 1928. On 10.4.26, playing his first game at centre-forward, he scored a hat-trick in both halves for Burnley versus Birmingham. A quiet and self-effacing man off the pitch, he was a fast and elusive player and a powerful marksman. Louis was an all-round athlete, captaining the England baseball team, and his brothers were also Internationals.

Billy McCandless joined Newport County in September 1937, and became the first Manager to win promotion for the Club.......

William McCandless, more familiarly known as 'Billy Mac', was born in Belfast in 1894, and died in Swansea 18.7.55. 5'7" tall and weighing 11st., he was a left–back and won ten Irish caps, as well as playing twice for the Irish League. He began in the North Belfast Combination, then played for Ligoniel and Barn Athletic (in Carrickfergus) before signing for Linfield in 1914. In November 1920, he moved on to Glasgow Rangers for £2,500, an Irish record, and stayed for ten years before departing for Ballymena. From 1933 he had a four year spell as Manager of Dundee – whom he left in the April of 1937 – before arriving at Somerton Park as Secretary Manager 23.9.37. He won the Championship of the Third Division (South) in 1938–39, and carried on into the following War season, although on an unpaid, honorary basis. He was re–engaged 1.7.45 and 'resigned' 9.4.46. Billy had taken over a virtually derelict Ground, since it had been taken over by the A.R.P. for the duration of the War. In June 1946, he became the Cardiff City Manager, and in November 1947, was appointed Manager of Swansea Town, eventually dying the day before the players reported for training in 1955. Billy was associated with success throughout his career. As a player he won a Scottish League Championship medal eight times and reached two Cup Finals with Rangers, ending up with 42 medals. As Manager, he achieved an unparalleled success in guiding all three South Wales clubs to promotion. To commemorate this he was presented with a gold watch in August 1949, before the Cardiff versus Swansea game, in front of a crowd of 57,510. Billy was (according to some reports), teetotal and a non–smoker, his sole 'vice' being pigeon fancying; according to others, he was always accompanied by a whisky bottle and his black cat!

When League football returned in 1946–47, Tom Bromilow was in charge, having taken over in May.....

Thomas George Bromilow was born in Liverpool 7.10.1894 and died 4.3.59. He began with the United West Dingle Presbyterian Club, before becoming a late starter with Liverpool, due probably to the War. He was taken on trial in 1919, making his debut at Burnley in October, and stayed for another eleven years, winning five England caps between 1921 and 1926. He was a crafty and determined tackler, and always played the ball, showing style artistry and anticipation. He was in the Liverpool Championship side of 1921–22, and also represented the English League. He became the coach of Amsterdam in the close season of 1931, and in October 1932 became Manager of Burnley, where he signed Tommy Lawton. In July 1935, he became Manager of Crystal Palace, having two spells in charge, before moving on to Leicester City in July 1939. In May 1945, he went on to Holland, returning the following May to Britain, when he took charge of the County. Tommy was an old fashioned Manager who never took part in training, etc. He resigned in January 1950, and was a scout for Leicester City from July 1950 until his death.

In March 1950, Fred Stansfield took over as Manager, followed by Billy Lucas in December 1953. Billy became player/manager, and then Manager, having played his last game at 40. In May 1961, Bobby Evans was appointed player/manager. The team played some good football, but the results went against them, resulting in relegation, so Billy was recalled as Manager in March 1962. Eventually he left for the Vetch Field, and another former player, Les Graham, took over in February 1967, having previously been the Manager of Merthyr Tydfil. Later Trevor Morris was appointed to be General Manager along with Graham.....
(N.B. The careers of Fred Stansfield, Billy Lucas, Bobby Evans and Les Graham are all covered in the 'Players Section')

Trevor Morris O.B.E., D.F.M., was born in Gorslas, Carmarthenshire around 1920. He had been a wing–half, joining the new Football League entrants Ipswich Town from Caerphilly in August 1938. In May 1940, he moved on to Cardiff City, but his leg was broken in a war–time cup–tie with Bristol City in 1942 and his career was finished. In the War he flew on 40 missions over enemy territory. He was the pilot of the lead aircraft of a Lancaster Squadron on D Day. He was at first the Assistant, and later Manager, of Cardiff City (in April 1954), then in the close season of 1958 became the Swansea Town Manager. He stayed at the Vetch for 7 years, and took the Swans to the F.A.Cup semi–finals in 1963–64, but finally left when they were relegated. He then had a short spell as a journalist before having a brief stay at Somerton Park, where things did not really work out. He was out of football when shortlisted for the post of Assistant Secretary of the Football Association of Wales in June 1970, and on St.David's Day, 1971, he became Secretary. He was a member of a host of international committees, and was the only F.A. Secretary to be awarded the Football League's 21 year long service medal. He had to leave his post of Secretary after 11 years because of a heart complaint.

Bobby Ferguson became the Newport County Manager 23.7.69, having been signed from Barry Town, for the princely sum of £250! The County had a bad time, and after a catastrophic 1-6 F.A.Cup defeat at non-League Barnet, he was sacked 2.11.70, but continued with the Club as a player. Billy Lucas returned again, at first on an acting basis, and on 16.1.74. became the General Manager, so that his dissatisfied Assistant, Brian Harris, could become Manager. Harris eventually left, disillusioned, to become a publican. Lucas took over briefly and remained as General Manager until he retired 16.6.76. Dave Elliot came from Southend United as player/manager in April 1975, until his sacking on the 25th of February 1976. At this time, the well known player and manager, Jimmy Scoular, was appointed.....

(N.B. The careers of Bobby Ferguson, Brian Harris and Dave Elliot are all covered in the 'Players Section')

James Scoular was born in Livingston, Lothian 11.1.25. His father, Alec, had been a pre-war centre-forward with a string of lower division Scottish League sides, including Alloa, Stenhousemuir and Leith Athletic. Jimmy himself was a wing-half and something of an 'iron man'- hard and uncompromising – but nonetheless popular. While serving on H.M.S. 'Dolphin' during World War 2, he played for Gosport Borough. He joined Portsmouth around November 1945, and had the rare distinction of turning out for both Gosport and Pompey in the F.A.Cup during the same season. He played no less than 249 Football League games whilst at Fratton Park, and was part of the famous 1949 and 1950 Portsmouth Championship sides. In addition to this he won 9 Scottish caps between 1951 and 1953. In June 1953, he moved to Newcastle for a fee of around £25,000. There he played another 247 Football League games, and skippered the 1955 F.A.Cup Final team. In January 1961, he became player/manager of Bradford (Park Avenue), for a transfer fee of £1,300. He made 108 Football League appearances before being sacked in May 1964. He was then made Manager of Cardiff City, where he became something of a legend. The Club gave the impression of qualifying for the European Cup Winners' Cup every season, and they played in many notable games. The side failed to win promotion however, and in November 1973, he was sacked following a Club take-over. After scouting for Wolves and Aston Villa, he eventually became Manager of Newport County on 26.2.76., where he recruited many of his former Cardiff City players. The County was run on a shoestring at this time, and his duties included cutting the sandwiches before 'away' games! He resigned after 37 Football League matches, becoming a company rep. and Swansea scout. In the 1980's, Jimmy suffered a series of strokes, and retired to run a guest house with his wife.

In January 1977, Colin Addison became Manager of Newport County, bringing increased optimism to the Club .....

Colin Addison was born in Taunton 18.5.40, but moved to York at the age of 12. An able forward, he was signed by York City in May 1957 from the junior side Cliftonville. In January 1961, he was bought by Nottingham Forest for £12,000, and in the next six years made 160 Football League appearances. In September 1966, Arsenal paid out £45,000 for his services, but just over a year later he was on the move again, to Sheffield United, for £40,000. In October 1971, he moved on to Hereford for a few thousand pounds, and his career was finished when he broke his leg at Barnsley in November 1972. In his career he scored over 100 Football League goals. He took over from John Charles as player/manager at Hereford when the Club was in the Southern League. Hereford were promoted in his first season, but he was sacked in 1974. He managed Durban City (South Africa) in January 1975, and was appointed Coach to Notts County in December 1975, resigning in October 1976. He was appointed Manager of Newport County 19.1.77, and stayed until the end of May 1978. He managed to infuse some new enthusiasm into the Club and was aware of the value of good public relations. At the end of his stay, he was sought by other clubs, and he was made Assistant Manager of W.B.A. In July 1978, Colin became Manager of Derby County, being eventually sacked 27.1.82. He was then appointed Manager of the County for the second time, when Ashurst was sacked 8.2.82. After three years (23rd of May 1985), Colin was sacked to save money, being reputedly on a salary of £20,000 per year, and after being absent from the Ground for some time with 'nervous exhaustion'. He then found work in Kuwait, Qatar and Spain (Real Celta and Vigo). He returned to W.B.A., 3.9.87, as Assistant Manager to Ron Atkinson. They later left for Atletico Madrid, but Atkinson was sacked after three months. Addison took over control, in January 1989, but later became Assistant again, and finally left in the close season of 1989. He returned to take over Cadiz 11.3.90., but in July of that year he rejoined Hereford, only to announce his resignation from the post in May 1991. In April 1986, Colin had a street named after him in Hereford.

In June 1978, Len Ashurst became Manager. His impact on the Club can only be classed with that of McCandless. He was only the second Manager to obtain promotion for the Club, and the only one to win the Welsh Cup......

Leonard Ashurst first saw the light of day in Liverpool 10.3.39. He started as an amateur with Liverpool and Wolves, and joined Sunderland from Prescot Cables 27.12.57. He was a talented left–back and played over 400 Football League games for the Roker Park Club. He had been a Youth international, and won an England Under–23 cap against West Germany in 1961. In March 1971, Len became Hartlepool's player/manager. He was appointed Gillingham Manager in June 1974, and was in charge of Sheffield Wednesday from October 1975 to October 1977. He turned down the chance to manage Sunderland in June 1979, a few weeks after signing a four  year contract with Newport. His time at Newport was highly successful, with the Club receiving wide publicity for it's achievements in European games. He made many good signings, but things began to go wrong with the unsuccessful transfers of Alan Waddle (£80,000) and Jeff Johnson (£60,000). He was sacked in February 1982, after having applied unsuccessfully for the Bristol City job. He replaced Richie Morgan as the Cardiff City manager 3.3.82., the night after his County benefit match versus Manchester City. He achieved promotion for Cardiff, then moved on to Sunderland in February 1984, taking them to the Milk Cup Final. He was sacked when they were relegated, and has since worked in such places as Kuwait, Qatar, and sunny Blackpool, at the latter becoming Assistant Manager. More recently, Len was managing the financially struggling Cardiff City, until his sacking in May 1991. Like Mark Aizlewood, Len had the distinction of having a racehorse named after him.

After Addison's dismissal, Bobby Smith, who had acted as Manager, took over in a full–time capacity......

Robert W.Smith was born in Prestbury 14.3.44. A solid and reliable half–back, he won six England Schools caps, and later had six years with Manchester United. He played no first team matches for them, but appeared in 200 reserve team games. As a player he was then with Scunthorpe, Grimsby, Brighton, Chester and Hartlepool. In August 1973, he joined Bury as player–coach, becoming Manager in the October. The Club won promotion under him, but he was later sacked. In November 1977, he was appointed Manager of Port Vale, and in May 1978 of Swindon. The team reached the Football League Cup semi-finals, but he was dismissed in October 1980. He was Assistant Manager at Blackpool when joining County early in July 1982. He became acting Manager at the end of 1984, and full-time from 23.5.85. He resigned 10.3.86 after the team's fourth successive defeat to give someone else a chance. He was afterwards on the staff of Cardiff City, leaving in July 1990, and at Hereford United. In March 1991 he joined Swansea City, and shortly afterwards saw them win the Welsh Cup.

After Smith's resignation, John Relish was persuaded to act as player/manager. Because of his popularity, the struggling side made an all out effort to stave off relegation. He was not interested in the full-time post however, and stepped down at the end of the season to take up a post with the P.F.A. Jimmy Mullen came from Cardiff City as player/manager, a fee of £1,500 being imposed later by a Tribunal. After quite a short time, he left to join his friend Ian Porterfield at Aberdeen. At this time the club was in a financial crisis. The Administrator on 20.2.87 appointed the senior professional, John Lewis to run the club as player/manager. He had no money to spend on players, and the team had poor results. In the October, he was dismissed in an atmosphere of some acrimony, by Chairman Darlow, who brought in Brian Eastick on 8.10.87. ......
(N.B. The careers of John Relish, Jimmy Mullen and John Lewis are covered in the 'Players Section').

Brian Eastick was born in Balham, London, in 1949. A goalkeeper, he was a young pro with Crystal Palace, and had 18 months with Plymouth, but spent his career in the Football Combination. He was Q.P.R. Youth team Coach from 1975, and had four years with Chelsea. After this he had spells with Brighton, the Sporting Club of Kuwait and Charlton. He suffered from two major drawbacks on being made County Manager. The first related to the Club that was in a financial crisis with the possibility of folding at any time. The second disadvantage was that he was an 'unknown', and his presence had all the impact of a lead balloon! Nevertheless he impressed with the dignity and integrity he showed in trying circumstances. The team rallied, to some extent, when Bodin and Carr were bought, but they were sold after a few weeks. He was dismissed 11.3.88 because the Club could not afford to pay him, and he agreed not to seek compensation in case it bankrupted the County. He later joined the staff of Orient, and in December 1990, became the reserve team chief at Coventry City.

David Williams was Manager for some time, but later stepped down to be Trainer again, because of the uncertainty of the situation and the difficulty of finding out exactly what was happening. Eddie May was appointed 7.7.88. and became the Manager who never saw a game, for he resigned less than a month later because of the financial situation......

Edward C. May is a native of Epping, born 19.5.43. A solid, useful defender, he began with Dagenham, then played in the Football League for Southend, Wrexham and Swansea, making well over 500 appearances in total. He saw Wrexham promoted from Division 4, winning the Welsh Cup twice, and appearing in the European Cup Winners' Cup quarter-final in 1975–76. Swansea were also promoted when he was there, and he then became Coach of Leicester City, where the team won the Second Division Championship in 1980–81. He was afterwards Assistant Manager of Charlton Athletic for three years before coaching in Kenya and Qatar. Just before joining the County, Eddie had been in charge of KS (Iceland) for six matches. He quickly left the County and was soon Assistant Manager of Lincoln City. More recently he joined the Cardiff City staff, and in July 1991 was appointed first team coach.

On Eddie May's resignation, John Mahoney, who had arrived as his assistant 13.7.88. became Manager. The Club was evicted from Somerton Park, and its participation in the Vauxhall Conference was in doubt until the last minute......

John F. Mahoney was born in Cardiff 20.9.46. A talented and tenacious midfield player, he played three Under–23, and fifty–one full Internationals, for Wales, from 1968 to 1983. He joined Crewe Alexandra from Ashton United in March 1966. In March 1967, he was bought by Stoke for £20,000 and stayed with the Club for ten years, making 272 Football League appearances. Middlesbrough brought him for £90,000 in August 1977, and two years later Swansea paid out £100,000. Swansea were promoted during his three years at the Vetch. He was later Manager of Bangor City, who played in Europe under him. Bangor suffered from similar financial problems as County, and he resigned in October 1987. John endured the eviction from Somerton Park stoically, and performed miracles to put out Vauxhall Conference and reserve teams on the first day of the season, for things were in doubt until the last minute. He signed some useful players, although results were poor. John is now back as Manager of Bangor City.

Although the Club had been in a critical situation at the start of the season, it was still a great shock when it folded, because of reassurances in the Press that the Directors had sufficient funds to meet the Club's debts, and the fact that new players were being signed right up to the last minute. Newport County was gradually wound up from St.David's Day 1989, and John Mahoney became the first County Manager not to be sacked, or resign, but to be liquidated!

COUNTY TRAINING

Trainers have been the unsung heroes at Somerton Park, as the 'magic sponge' has persuaded many a wounded soldier to return to the fray! The first to hold the position was Fred Good.....

Frederick Good had been the Assistant Trainer at Cardiff City. In April 1912, he was appointed Trainer at the newly formed County side, and remained there for the first ten years of the Club's existence. When players failed to turn up, he was even pressed into service in the team. He was a talented physiotherapist, and could repair breaks and strains without the aid of a doctor. In the close season of 1922 he resigned, in order to set up his own business as a masseur in the Western Mail Chambers, Cardiff.

From 1919, Fred had the assistance of Enoch Thomas. Enoch seemed to go on forever, staying as Assistant until 1939, after the team had won promotion. On one occasion, Enoch, who was also a member of the Fire Brigade, turned out for the team and managed to fracture his leg. In 1922, Fred Good's place was taken by the well known former player Bob Chatt.....

Robert S. Chatt, who was born in Barnard Castle in August 1870, had enjoyed a successful career in football before joining the County. He had begun with Stockton and the shortlived Middlesbrough Ironopolis, before arriving at Aston Villa in August 1893. He played fairly regularly at Villa for five years. His main moment of glory came in the 1895 Cup Final. He was credited at first with scoring a goal in the first minute, but apparently his shot rebounded off the goalkeeper, and was put in by Devey. He won League Championship medals with Villa in 1896 and 1897. In 1898, he returned to Stockton, where he played in their side which won the Amateur Cup Final and later moved on to South Shields. In 1904, he became Trainer of Doncaster Rovers – and in 1906 at Manchester City where he spent ten years. He was on the staff of South Shields before joining the County in the 1922 close season. He was on the Somerton Park staff for nine years, but was released when the Club failed to secure re-election in 1931. Bob died around 1935.

When Newport County rejoined the Football League in 1932, the Trainer appointed was Tommy Gibbon.....

It was from the North–east that Thomas Gibbon hailed, being born in Sunderland. He was a goalkeeper in his playing days. 5'10" tall and weighing 11st.7lbs. he had a long reach and was a bold and resourceful 'keeper. He played for Northampton, and then Merthyr in 1919. From there he went North to Dundee for a season, where he was an ever present. He then joined Luton Town for three seasons, followed by Q.P.R. (close season of 1924). After that he was on the staff of Norwich City, Southampton and the ill-fated Thames. He was a businesslike trainer, with energy and enthus- asm. After leaving the County, he found employment in Luton, along with Jimmy Hindmarsh and Bobby Anderson.

June 1935 saw the appointment of Charlie Bates.....

It is with Burnley that Charles Bates will always be associated. A Scottish Junior International, he joined the Turf Moor Club from Darlington in 1910, as a 22 year-old inside-right, and became the reserve team Trainer before being called up, in 1914. Although he made only a a few Football League appearances, he had a very long stay as Trainer, being at Turf Moor for no less than 24 years, and was with the team which went a record number of Football League games without defeat. But he was finally sacked in 1934 after his side had had a bad season. He was appointed by Louis Page on 22.6.35., but resigned after a few months (8.11.35.)

November 1935 saw the arrival of the former England International Harry Martin......

Harry Martin was born in Selston, Notts. 5.12.1891. He was an outside-left, and one of the most consistent players that Sunderland ever had. He made his debut in the 1911-12 season, after arriving from Sutton Junction. Despite the intervention of World War 1, he managed to notch up over 200 Football League appearances during the next ten years. Although 5'10" tall and weighing 12st.4lbs., he was a flier on the wing, with amazing pace and the ability to place his centres on Charlie Buchan's head. He received a piece of shell in his right side during the War, but gradually regained his footballing form. He won a full England cap in 1914, was capped in the war-time Victory Internationals, and also represented the Football League. At Roker Park, a League Championship medal was won, and he appeared in the 1913 F.A.Cup Final. In May 1922, Harry moved on to Nottingham Forest, where he spent three years before departing to Rochdale for a four year spell as a player. He became their Trainer in the 1929 close season, and was Manager at Mansfield from December 1933 to March 1935. His stay at Somerton Park was a short one, for he left in the summer of 1936, to join Swindon Town, where he was still coaching in the 1940's, and kept goal in a Wartime game in May 1940.

Stan Bowsher was made Trainer in 1936, a post he held until October 1937, when Bill Poyntz took over.....

William Ivor Poyntz was born in Tylorstown, Rhonnda on 18.3.1894, and died in Leeds on 5.4.66. An able forward, after World War 1 he was playing for

Llanelly, and joined Leeds United in May 1921. He then moved to five Clubs in rapid succession, spending roughly a year with each (Doncaster, Northampton, Bradford P.A., Crewe and Hartlepool). One of his claims to fame was scoring a hat–trick for Leeds (versus Leicester 20.2.22), three hours after getting married. On leaving Hartlepools he was Coach at Bury, and was then on the staff at Leeds for nine years. He brought on a number of Internationals at Elland Road, and was an able trainer, having completed a five year course at Leeds Infirmary.

September 1939 saw the start of World War 2, and the disorganisation of professional football, though Bill Poyntz stayed as the County trainer. The Club did not play from 1940 to 1945, the flag being kept flying in the town by Lovell's Athletic, and in July 1945 Stan Bowsher was appointed Trainer, as the team prepared for the transitional League (South). Twelve months later Jimmy Marshall became the new trainer as the team re–entered League football.....
(The career of Stan Bowsher is covered in the 'Players Section')

James H. Marshall was born at Peterhead in Scotland. He was a well–built, but speedy forward, 5'11" tall and weighing 12st.5lbs. he began with Partick Thistle and joined Bradford City in the 1914 close season. The War obviously marred his career, and in the 1919/20 season he suffered from injuries. He joined Oldham Athletic in the summer of 1920, and spent three seasons at Boundary Park, before a lengthy period in Holland, as Trainer and Coach. He was made County Trainer in July 1946, and stayed until the 14.5.48.

In late June 1948, Ray Lawrance was appointed to the Trainer's post. He was 'part of the furniture' by the time he left in March 1958, to manage Abergavenny Thursdays. Walter Robbins had an exceedingly short spell with the sponge, leaving in September 1958. The evergreen George Kitson , who had been Assistant since 1946, took over, and later the long serving Ray Wilcox became involved, the two being more or less joint Trainers. This continued until the 30.6.67. when George Kitson was released, since there was considered to be no post left for him. Ray himself left in February 1970, and Ken Burfitt of Barry stood in until the close season. The the well known former Cardiff City player Ron Stitfall then took over.....
(The careers of Ray Lawrance, George Kitson and Ray Wilcox are covered in the 'Players Section')

Ronald F. Stitfall is a native of Cardiff, having been born there on 14.12.25. He was a talented full–back, one of three footballing brothers who were on the books of Cardiff City. A Welsh Schools International, developed by Moorland School and Cardiff Boys, he played in the war–time City team at a very young age. After four years in the Army, during which time he played for the Combined Services team, he returned to Ninian Park in 1947, and had a notable career, making over 400 Football League appearances for the Bluebirds and winning two Welsh International caps, in 1953 and 1957. He retired from playing in 1965, and being an F.A. Coach, he eventually became the County Trainer in August 1970, staying until 14.5.76. He is now employed in the National Sports Centre, Cardiff, and is also the Welsh team trainer.

As Ron Stitfall left, so another old City player, Ronnie Bird, took over......

Ronald P. Bird was born in Erdington on 27.12.41. Although he was never a top flight player, he was popular with the fans. An England Youth International, he began with Birmingham in january 1959, and then in June 1961 he moved on to Bradford (Park Avenue), where he made over 100 appearances and played under Jimmy Scoular, then a player/manager. After a short spell with Bury (commencing October 1965), he joined cardiff (February 1966), again under Scoular. He had quite a successful time at Ninian Park before ending his career with a season at Crewe (1971–72). Although owning a hairdresser's business, he stayed in football with Bridgend, and then became the County Trainer/Coach on 31.5.76., staying until 1987. He had a brief spell as County reserve Trainer before returning to Bridgend, when he was sacked as Bridgend Manager in October 1990, which resulted in many of the players walking out.

In January 1979, Jimmy Goodfellow joined Len Ashurst at County.....

Born in Bishop Auckland 16.9.43., James Goodfellow began with Crook Town and Bishop Auckland, winning an Amateur Cup Winners medal with Crook. As a professional, he played for Port Vale (June 1966), Workington (July 1969), Rotherham (January 1974) and Stockport (August 1978), retiring though injury in January 1979. Jimmy was a midfield player, and made well over 400 Football League appearances. After being Trainer/Coach and Ashurst's Assistant at County (sacked 25.11.81), he joined him at Ninian Park in July 1982, after a stay in the U.S.A. He had a short time in charge after Ashurst's departure from 4.5.84, to his sacking on 27.9.84. After coaching Plymouth Argyle, he returned to Ninian Park as physiotherapist in 1986.

The long–serving David Williams held various posts at Somerton Park from July 1980. These included Coach, Trainer and Acting Manager. he was still Trainer with the Club when it was wound up in March 1989 (His career is covered in the 'Players Section'). After 30 years with the County, he went to start work at the Orb Steelworks, where many of the County personalities had begun...............

ABBRUZZESE, David.

b. Aberdare 8.10.69. 5'6" 10st.7lb.
24–0 (41–1)
Npt. (Reserves, YTS Aug.1986, pro 1988)
Torquay Utd. (Trial Mar. 1989) Merthyr T.
(Mar.1989) Barry T. (Nov.1989)

David was a promising right–back, developed by the Club. A product of the Mountain Ash school team, he was capped several times by the Welsh Youth team. Although not very big, he was a tough tackler, with a strong shot and centre. Later made a full professional, he was one of the few County players to stay with the Club into the Vauxhall Conference. Once County were wound up he moved into non–League football.

AINGE, Ronald P.

b. Pontardawe 5.8.20. 5'10" 11st.6lb.
5–0 (5–0)
Llanelli. Npt. (Oct. 1946) Llanelli (at first on loan, Dec.1946) Retired May 1955.

A left winger who had a short stay at Somerton Park just after World War 2. Ron was selected for an Amateur International in October 1946, but signed professional for the County instead. He soon returned to Llanelli, where he had another nine seasons, and in 1949, won a Welsh Cup run-ners–up medal. Retired through ill health in 1981. Lives in Pontardawe.

AIZLEWOOD, Mark.

b. Newport 1.10.59. 6'0". 12st. 8lb.

35–2 (43–2) (Wales 25, 1986 to date, 2 U–21 1979 –81)
Cromwell F.C. Npt. (Amateur early 1975, app. 1975–76, pro Oct.1977). Luton T. (Apr. 1978 £50,000) Charlton Ath. (Nov. 1982 £50,000). Leeds Utd. (Feb. 1987 £200,000). Bradford C. (Aug. 1989 £200,000). Bristol C. (Aug. 1990 £125,000).

A Welsh schoolboy International, and Youth team Captain, who turned down Arsenal for the County. Mark is a tall, very talented defender or midfielder, with a defence splitting crossfield pass. He lived just a few hundred yards from Somerton Park and was even younger than his elder brother Steve, when making his County debut. As an eighteen year old he became a record sale for the Club and has since been a regular Football League player at the highest level. A late starter at International level, he has since established him-self in the Welsh side. He is an all-round athlete, good at baseball, cricket and golf.

AIZLEWOOD, Steven.

b. Newport 9.10.52. 5'11" 12st.6lb.
191–18 (223–19) (Wales Under 23 5 1972–76)
Npt. (schoolboy 1966 pro Oct 1969) Swindon T. (Mar.1976 £13,500). Portsmouth (June 1979 £45,000). Waterlooville (1984–85)

Tough and resolute central defender, who made his debut as a 16 year old, whilst at Hartridge School.
Steve gave years of good service to County, but through financial necessity became a Club record sale in 1976. He afterwards made over 100 appearances for both Swindon and Portsmouth, whom he captained. A gifted header of the ball, he scored over 40 Football League goals in his career. He took a Polytechnic course after retiring and is now a valuation surveyor, having gained a B.Sc. in Estate Management.

ALDRIDGE, John W.

b. Liverpool 18.9.58 5'11" 10st. 4lbs.
159–69 (213–88) (Eire 39 1986 to date)
Cheshire Lines (1977) South Liverpool (cs 1978) Npt (Apr.1979 £3,500) Oxford Utd. (Mar 1984 £70,000) Liverpool (Jan. 1987 £750,000) San Sebastian (Sept. 1989 £1,100,000. Tranmere (June 1991 £250,000)

One of the most famous players developed by County. An apprentice toolmaker with British Leyland, he was spotted by Len Ashurst's brother and signed for a meagre fee after turning down Tranmere. John soon established himself as a prolific scorer in County's promotion and European campaigns. Having decided to leave he brought the Club's record fee and created an Oxford record with 30 goals in 1984–85. He won a Division II Championship medal with them and helped them win the Milk Cup in 1986. He was then signed as a replacement for Liverpool's Ian Rush and scored in his first eleven full League games. Although he created an unfortunate record by missing a penalty in the 1988 F.A. Cup Final, he won a League Championship medal. He threatened to give up football after the Hillsborough tragedy, but went on to score the first goal in the 1989 F.A. Cup Final. Moving on, he became the first Real player to score in six consecutive games. John qualified to play for Eire through a tenuous link and uncharacteristically failed to score in his first 18 games, despite often playing well. He netted twice, however, versus Malta (Nov. 1989) to take Eire to the World Cup Finals for the first time.

ALLEN, Brinley W.

b. Gilfach Goch 28.3.21 5'8" 10st. 01lbs.
26-8 (29-9) (Wales 2 1951)
Manchester Utd. (pre-war) Swansea T. (c 1939) Gilfach (1939-40) Cardiff C. (guest 1944, pro. Dec 1945) Npt (Oct 1947 £5,000) Cardiff C. (Aug 1948 p/exch.) Reading (May 1949 fee) Coventry C. (Feb 1950 fee) Hereford Utd. (Aug.1952) Barry T. (July 1953) Haverfordwest (1957-58)

Clever, constructive inside-forward. Bryn was a leading light in Cardiff's 1946-47 promotion side, scoring 17 goals. He was the County's record signing when he arrived at Somerton Park, but soon returned to Ninian Park in exchange for Reg Parker. After winning a few caps Bryn drifted back into non-league soccer and worked as a postman in Swansea. He now lives in Tonyrefail.

AMPHLETT, Raymond Henry.

b. Manchester 25.9.22 5'8" 10st 01lbs
Guildford C. (amateur) Cardiff C. (Feb 1948) Npt. (Apr 1949) Headington Utd. (Mar 1950) Stockport Co. (trial Aug.1950)

A full-back who never realised his potential in the League. He had good positional sense, a strong kick and a tenacious tackle. Ray was dropped after one bad game and later asked for a transfer because of accommodation difficulties. He moved on to Headington, who later became Oxford United.

ANDERSON, Robert.

b. Ardrossan 5'-6" 10st-10lbs
137-0 (147-0)
Ardrossan Winton Rovers Luton T. (July 1923) Npt. (June 1926) Lincoln C. (July 1930-32)

Bobby was the smallest right-back in Division III, but one of the best. After making 75 Football League appearances for Luton, he was a regular for County for four years and did not miss a game for two seasons, making over 100 conexcutive appearances. Afterwards he moved on to Lincoln C. with Jimmy Maidment. In the mid 1930's he was working in Luton, along with Jimmy Hindmarsh and Tommy Gibbon.

APPLEBY, Thomas Alexander.

b. Wolverhampton 5.10.16 d. Newport 26.5.77
5'9" 10st 7lbs
14-4 (31-21)
Beechwood Corries (c 1932) Windsor Juniors Npt (amateur 1934, pro Oct 1935) Yeovil (Jan 1938) Folkestone (1938-39) Southport (Aug 1939) Tranmere R. Npt (guest Feb 1940) Merthyr T.

Winger or centre-forward, very much a local product. Tommy scored plenty of reserve team goals at Somerton and found the net 32 times for Folkestone in 1938-39. He was with Southport for one month when the War broke out. Then returned to Newport, guesting for County. He scored 12 goals in their last five war-time games.

APSEY, Thomas Leonard.

b. Ynyshir 11.2.10 d. Caerphilly 24.5.67
2-0 (2-0)
Trethomas Bluebirds Npt. (Sept 1930) Burnley (Jan 1931) Arsenal (trial Aug 1931) Porth (mid 1930's)

Len was signed as an amateur by County, then released, giving him no chance to establish himself. He went straight from junior football into Division III, where he made two appearances. A strong, vigorous leader, who had trials with Burnley and Arsenal and was still scoring goals in local Welsh football five years later.

ARCH, William Henry (Harry).

b. Tipton, Staffs 29.11.1894 d. Stourbridge late 1978 5'7" 11st 2lbs
29-0 (32-0)
Great Bridge Celtic (1910) Pensnett (1912) W.B.A. (pro Mar 1919) Npt. (May 1921) Willenhall (es 1922) Grimsby T. (June 1923) Hartlepools Utd. (July 1926-27) Bilston Utd.

A tough-tackling right-back with a hefty kick. Harry did not make the W.B.A. first team, but played fairly regularly in his one season with County and later made over 90 Football League appearances for Grimsby T.

ARMAND, John Edward (Jack "Snowy")

b. Sabathu, India 11.8.1898 d. Grimsby mid 1974 5'7" 11st 0lbs
3-1 (4-1)
West Stanley Leeds Utd. (Dec 1922) Swansea T. (May 1929) Ashton National (July 1931) Southport (Aug 1932) Npt (Aug 1932- 1933)

Versatile forward who, despite making only a handful of appearances for County, had spent seven seasons with Leeds and played over 50 games for Swansea. He had scored 48 goals for Ashton National in non-League football before arriving at Somerton Park.

ARMSTRONG, Keith T.

b. Corbridge 11.10.57 5'8" 11st 5lbs
3-0 (4-0)
Sunderland (juniors, pro. Jan 1975) Npt. (loan Aug 1978) Scunthorpe Utd. (loan Oct.1978) Oulu Palloseura (Finland) Newcastle Utd. (June 1979) Hong Kong (winter 1979) Oulu Npt. (Oct 1980) Workington (Nov 1980) Oulu

Winger with the ability to beat a man, but who failed to stay with any team for long. When first coming to Somerton Park Keith was signed on loan, but Sunderland refused to extend the period. Later he had a trial here, but this was terminated after three weeks. He helped Oulu to win the Finnish League Championship and played in their 10-1 European Cup defeat by Liverpool.

ASHTON, Royston W.

b. Llanidloes 16.8.21 5'9" 12st 10lbs
11-0 (11-0)
Wrexham (war-time) Cardiff C. (amateur, pro. Apr 1948) Bath C. (c 1949) Npt. (Dec 1949) Merthyr T. Npt. (Dec 1950) Milford Utd. (Oct 1951) Headington Utd. Barry T. (c 1952)

Goalkeeper who made more reserve than first team appearances for County. Roy had been reserve to Danny Canning at Ninian Park and played in the last Football League game of the 1947-48 season. Later he starred for Barry T., but broke his leg in late 1952.

ASTON, Alfred John.

b. Newport 29.7.30 5'6" 11st 0lbs
6-1 (7-1)
Newport YMCA (1946-47) Npt. (amateur, pro Apr 1948) Senghenydd (1950) Abergavenny Th. (1952)

A stylish outside-left, a product of local schools and youth football. John's career was interrupted by National Service in the R.A.F. and most of his games were for the reserves. He was an electrician by trade.

BAGLEY, William.

b. Wolverhampton mid 1909 d. Lake District c. 1975 5'7" 10st 7lbs
71-11 (107-20)
Newport Excelsior Npt. (amateur early 1929, pro Feb 1930) Portsmouth (June 1933, Fee – retired c 1940)

Billy lived in nearby Magor St., where his mother's ganders were a familiar sight and went to Corporation Road School. He worked for Lovells for five years, but strangely never played soccer for them. After winning a reserve team place early in 1929–30, he made his first team debut versus Brentford 1.2.30, signing professional four days later. A quick, ball playing inside–left he was considered by Hindmarsh to be the club's best forward and was inevitably sold. He was unlucky to play in every round of Portsmouth's F.A. Cup winning season (1938–39) apart from the final. He died on holiday in the Lake District.

BAILEY, Neil.

b. Billinge, nr Wigan 26.9.58 5'9" 11st 4lbs
136–8 (184–11)
Burnley (App 1974, pro July 1976) Ashton Utd. (1978) Npt. (Aug 1978, full-time Sept 1978) Wigan Ath. (Oct 1983) Stockport Co. (July 1986) Npt. (loan Mar 1987)

Neil began with Wigan Boys, joining Burnley straight from school. An able midfield player in County's European and promotion side, he arrived on trial after two years as a regular Burnley reserve. He returned

North in 1983, but had a brief spell back on loan during the relegation season of 1986–87.

BAKEWELL, Herbert.

b. Barnsley 8.3.21   8–0 (8–0)
Barnsley (pre-war reserve) Npt. (Oct 1946 to May 1947)

A goalkeeper who made his Football League debut in the same game as Eddie Carr and Ray Wilcox, during the club's only Division II season. He spent most of his time in the reserves and was released at the end of the season.

BARKLAM, Horace.

b. Newport 18.2.12 d. Newport 11.6.84 5'7"
10st 7lbs
3–1 (3–1)
Hiswerry Juniors Somerton Park F.C. Npt. (1931, pro July 1933) Newport Rangers

A fast, old–fashioned winger, a good dribbler who loved to hug the touchline. Horace was mainly a reserve and his career was cut short at its start due to a heart condition. For fifty years afterwards he worked at Henry Cordy outfitters in Newport.

BARRATT, Peter.

b. Edinburgh 5'7" 11st 0lbs
18–4 (20–5)
East Fife Npt. (July 1927) Dundee (May 1928 to 29)

Scheming inside–forward, who during the previous season had appeared in the Scottish Cup Final for East Fife, having played in every round. Peter scored on his debut versus Q.P.R. 27.8.27, but despite finding the net a few times was allowed to leave at the end of the season.

BARTHOLOMEW, Henry (Harry).

b. Motherwell 18.1.20 5'10" 12st 0lbs
3–0 (3–0)
Motherwell Exeter C. (May 1947) Bournemouth (Aug 1949) Npt. (1950 £400) Ilfracombe (Aug 1951)

Scottish half–back, who had been captain of Exeter C. Harry only had a brief spell here, mainly in the reserves, and his contract was cancelled by mutual consent. Now living in Ilfracombe.

BARTON, Douglas John.

b. Islington 31.7.27 5'9" 10st 8lbs
23–0 (24–0)
Guildford (1946–47) Fords Sports Reading (Feb 1949) Npt. (Jan 1953) Dartford (July 1954) Romford (July 1959)

Full–back who had quite a short spell at Somerton. Dougie had previously been a reserve at Reading, where he had made ten Football League appearances.

BATTY, Stanley G.

b. Tottenham 14.2.17 5'11" 11st 8lbs
60–3 (91–9)
Finchley (pre–war) Tottenham H. War guest for Luton T. Birmingham C. & Walsall Ashton Villa Npt. (guest Dec 1945 full-time July 1946) Hereford Utd. (guest 1945–46) Worcester C.

Solid half–back or inside–forward who played in County's immediate post–war team. He was acting Manager for a month when Billy McCandless left. Eventually he refused terms and moved on. Stan is now living in Torquay.

BEATTIE, George.

b. Aberdeen 16.6.25 5'7" 11st 6lbs
113–26 (130–34)
Rosemount Southampton (1944) Gloucester C. (Dec 1948) Npt. (Sept 1950 £2,000) Bradford P.A. (July 1953 £3,000) Tonbridge July 1955)

George was a regular centre or inside–forward with the County in the early 1950's. He began in Aberdeen schools football and spent three years on a fishing trawler before joining the Royal Navy on the outbreak of war. His career did not continue for long after he left the County and he returned to Newport to run a successful coal business. George, who still lives locally, is the father of Alex, who has played for Newport AFC, and Andy, who won a Welsh Cup Winner's medal with Merthyr (after beating the County) and played in Europe.

BEDDOW, Harry.

b. Rogerstone early 1901 d. ?Auckland, New Zealand 13.5.72 5'10" 10st 10lbs
1-0 (1-0)
Bassaleg Npt. (1922-23)

A quick amateur fall-back or winger, a club product who made one Football League appearance versus Merthyr 21.10.22. He played 15 reserve team games that season. Harry is believed to have emigrated to New Zealand.

BEECH, Cyril.

b. Tamworth 12.3.25 5'9" 11st 6lbs
39-8 (43-9)
Merthyr T. (1947) Swansea T. (Aug 1949 – with his brother Gilbert for £6,000) Worcester C. (1954) Npt. (July 1955) Hereford Utd. (Mar 1957) Merthyr T. (Aug.1960) Brierley Hill.

An experienced winger or centre-forward with an explosive shot who was over 30 when arriving at Somerton Park. Cyril had spent 5 years in Division II with the Swans, for whom he made over 100 Football League appearances. These days Cyril who lives in Merthyr, is still involved in Soccer, scouting for Luton Town.

BEER, Walter John ("Dollar").

b. Bideford 10.5.1900 d. Penarth 31.3.81 5'8" 10st 7lbs
1-0 (1-0)
Cardiff Bohemians Chepstow Npt. (May 1922) Lovells Ath.

Clever amateur inside-forward who was a regular Welsh League player in 1922-23, playing over 30 games and scoring 18 goals, but made only one first team appearance versus Aberdare 27.1.23. Walter played for Lovells in the Welsh Amateur Cup Final of 1923-24.

BELL, Gareth.

b. Halesowen, nr Stourbridge 4.4.47 5'7" 11st 3lbs
126-5 (143-6)
Halesowen (1963) W.B.A. (amateur) Lower Gornal Ath. (pro) Cardiff C. (Feb 1966 £750) Hereford Utd. (loan Mar 1974) Npt. (loan Apr 1974, full-time Jan 1975 £2,000) Gloucester C. (1978) Bridgend T. (June 1979) Caerau (p/manager) Ebbw Vale (Sept 1986, p/coach)

Gary started as a winger, but developed into a very polished and professional full-back, with a telling cross into the goalmouth. His pro. career was delayed by a dispute with W.B.A., but a long stay with Cardiff followed, despite a 1-7 start at Wolves. Gary then gave the County four years solid service before returning to non-League football. He won three Welsh Cup Winner's medals during his spell at Ninian Park.

BELL, John James.

b. Dundee 1891 5'9" 11st 4lbs
21-9 (22-9)
Dundee (c 1913) Albion R. (July 1922, p/exchange) Npt. (July 1923) Watford (July 1924) Arbroath (cs 1926)

Johnnie was a hard–shooting centre–forward, a clever dribbler and a good distributor of the ball. In 1913–14 he amassed 27 goals in 27 games for Dundee. He was exchanged for George Greenshields, but made little impact with Albion Rovers. During his season with County he scored a few goals, but then he moved on to Watford, where he was converted to an inside–right.

BENNETT, Sean.

b. Newport 3.9.70
4–0 (6–0)
Leeds Utd. (App cs 1986) Npt (YTS Jan 1988)

A young player thrust into the County's disastrous side of 1987–88. Sean was the captain of the Gwent Schools side. He showed some ability in his few games at left–back and made the odd appearance in midfield for the Vauxhall Conference team, before leaving after a row with Glyn Jones. He went to work for the Civil Service.

BERRY, Steven A.

b. Liverpool 4.4.63 5'7" 11st 0lbs
60–6 (78–8)
Gosport Borough Portsmouth (App 1979, pro 1981) Aldershot (loan Mar 1983) Sunderland (July 1984) Npt. (Nov 1985 £5,000) Swindon T. (Mar 1987 £12,500) Aldershot (loan, full–time Oct 1987) Northampton T. (Oct 1988)

Steve arrived at Somerton Park as a midfield player of some potential, with good balance and the ability to

round a goalkeeper. Before joining the County he had been a first team regular at Sunderland and appeared in the 1985 League Cup Final. His form deteriorated somewhat during his stay and he was allowed to move on for a relatively modest fee. He later scored the Northampton goal which knocked Coventry out of the F.A. Cup 6.1.90.

BESWICK, Keith.

b. Cardiff 3.2.42 6'2" 13st 2lbs
58–0 (62–0)
Cardiff Corries Swindon T. (amateur) Millwall (Jan 1962) Npt. (Aug 1964) Barry T. (July 1987) Cwmbran T.

A somewhat unorthodox goalkeeper, who had been kept out of the Millwall side by Alex Stepney. Despite the presence of Len Weare, Keith managed to make a fair number of appearances in the County first team dropping down into non–League football.

BIRCH, Clifford.

b. Crumlin 1.9.28 5'7" 10st 8lbs
143–28 (163–31)
Treowen Stars (1946) Cardiff C. (amateur 1946) Ebbw Vale Norwich C. (July 1946, pro Dec 1946) Npt. (Oct 1950) Colchester Utd. (June 1954 £500) Spalding Yarmouth Gorleston Retired 1958

Cliff was an elusive, thrustful right–winger, who looked like the County's answer to Denis Compton. He began in the Welsh Boy's Club team in 1946 and went to Norwich, where his progress was interrupted by National Service. He was signed by Newport after their earlier capture from Norwich, George Morgan, proved unfit and for four years became a fixture in the first team, being selected to play for the Welsh League in 1951. Later he settled in Norwich, where he still lives.

BIRD, Anthony.

b. Dublin c 1910 5'11" 12st 0lbs
29-16 (31-17)
Richmond Utd. (junior) Dundalk (c 1928) Bray Unknowns (Irish Free State League 1928) Plymouth A. (Oct 1930) Npt. (June 1934) Tranmere R. (Aug 1935) Boston T. (Oct 1935)

An accomplished tactician, who started as an inside–forward, but was tried as a centre–forward in a Plymouth injury crisis. Tony was never a regular first–teamer in Devon, but he stayed there for four seasons and won two Southern League winner's medals. After scoring freely with the County he lost form and was allowed to go North at the end of the season. He never made Tranmere's Football League side, however.

BIRD, John Francis.

b. Cardiff 21.11.40 5'8" 11st 2lbs
276-3 (322-5)
Npt. (amateur, pro Nov 1957) Swansea T. (July 1967) Hereford Utd. (cs 1968) Merthyr T. (1971)

Useful full–back, who had been a Schoolboy International. In 1957 he cancelled a trial with Wolves and County stepped in, thus starting a ten year stint at the club for Johnny. He made his Football League debut at sixteen and was a regular for eight seasons, amassing many appearances and playing in the beaten Welsh Cup team of 1963, but his season at the Vetch was less successful. He has since worked for British Rail.

BISHOP, Raymond J.

b. Hengoed 24.11.55 5'7" 10st 0lbs
8-2 (23-3)
Bargoed Y.M.C.A. Merthyr T. Tredomen Ton Pentre (cs 1975) Cheltenham T. Brighton (Dec 1976) Cheltenham T. Cardiff C. (Jan 1977 £1,000) Npt. (Feb 1981 £10,000) Torquay Utd. (Aug 1982)

Small inside–forward, who had spent much of his career in non–League football. Ray was a G.P.O. engineer when joining the County, where he had few opportunities to establish himself in the first team, despite displaying some ability. He soon moved on for a brief spell at Torquay.

BLACK, James.

b. Scotland
3–0 (4–0)
Arbroath Ardenlea Npt (Dec 1924) Forfar Ath. (cs 1925)

A Scottish wing–half or inside–right, who made just a handful of first team appearances, before returning North of the border. He did however, manage to score 14 reserve team goals.

BLAKEMORE, Leonard.

b. Wheatley Hill late 1904 5'9" 11st 6lbs
73–0 (108–0)
Washington Colliery Fulham (cs 1926) Npt. (Aug 1927) Hereford Utd. (Aug 1932 to circa 1938)

A North–easterner who had made no first team appearances for Fulham, where he played centre–forward in the Combination. Len was the County's reserve goalkeeper at first, but eventually established himself in the Football League side. He had a strong kick and played one game at centre–forward versus Crystal Palace in 1929. He once missed a game because his brother had died playing football in Durham in September 1930.

BLOTT, John P.

b. Middlesbrough 26.2.65 5'11" 12st 2lbs
1–0 (1–0)
Manchester C. (Sept 1982) Carlisle Utd. (Nov 1984) Scunthorpe Utd. (1985–86) Mansfield T. Npt. (Mar 1987, non–contract)

John was a goalkeeper who was with the club for a very short time. He played only one game in the first team and was given a free transfer after a couple of months.

BLOTT, Samuel Prince.

b. London Jan. 1886 d. Southend 1.1.69 5'9" 12st 0lbs
16–1 (18–1)
Southend Athletic (amateur) Bradford PA (cs 1907) Southend Utd. (May 1908) Manchester Utd. (cs 1909 £600) Plymouth A. (May 1913) Npt. (June 1920 to 1921 £225)

Prinnie was a versatile player, a beautiful dribbler and passer with an excellent centre. He enjoyed an extensive pre–war career, including four seasons as a reserve at Old Trafford. He represented the British Army five times whilst serving in Egypt. He was a wing–half or winger for the County. His career was virtually ended by a thigh injury versus Swindon, following which he was out for three months with an operation and signed on temporary contracts. An easy–going personality, Prinnie returned to live in Southend, working on the seafront or pier.

BODIN, Paul J..

b. Cardiff 13.9.64 5'10" 10st 11lbs
6-1 (6-1) (Wales 7 1990 to date, Wales Under 21 1 1983)
Chelsea (associated schoolboy) Npt. (app. 1981, pro Jan 1982) Cardiff C. (Aug 1982, at first on trial) Merthyr T. (Aug 1985) Bath C. (Aug 1985, at first on trial) Npt. (Jan 1988 £16,000) Swindon T. (Mar 1988 £25,000+) Crystal Palace (Mar 1991 £550,000)

A skilful, versatile player, who was recommended to the County by Harold Joy after not being offered apprentice terms by Chelsea. He had played for Llanrumney School and won 7 Wales Youth caps. He made his County debut in a friendly versus Manchester City, but was later released. Paul was a regular of the Cardiff side promoted to Division II in 1982-83. A penalty taker, he scored 16 goals for Bath City in 1986-87 and was signed by Eastick with money provided by Brian Stent. He had to be sold at a profit a few weeks later to prevent the club from folding. Shortly afterwards he appeared for Swindon Town in the semi-final of the Simod Cup and has recently become a member of the Welsh team – laid on goal versus Germany, 1991. Paul also played baseball for Tavistock.

BOLTON, Anthony G.

b. Newport 15.1.68 5'7" 11st 4lbs
6-0 (10-0)
Charlton Ath. (app. 1984, later pro) Npt. (Aug 1986) Radstock Bridgend Ton Pentre

A midfield player, who was given a few chances in the County's relegation side of 1986-87, but failed to impress and was given a free transfer at the end of the season.

BONSON, Joseph.

b. Barnsley 19.6.36 6'0" 12st 6lbs
83-47 (101-59)
Wolverhampton W. (Juniors 1953) Cardiff C. (Nov 1957 £5,500) Scunthorpe Utd. (June 1960 p/exchange) Doncaster R. (Feb 1962) Npt (June 1962 £3,000) Brentford (June 1964 £6,000) Lincoln C. (Jan 1966) Hednesford (cs 1967) Lower Gornal (1967-68)

Joe was a goal scoring forward, who had been a schoolboy sprint champion and first featured in Wolves F.A. Youth Cup winning side of 1957. He helped Cardiff City win promotion to Division I and had two successful seasons with the County, scoring hat-tricks in the League, League Cup and Welsh Cup. He found the net with great regularity at Somerton Park, often through headers, and had a good partnership with Ralph Hunt.

His 100th Football League goal was versus Lincoln City 22.4.64. He was later allowed in join Brentford.

BOOTS, George Horace.

b. Newport 5.5.11 d. Port Talbot 5.8.71
3-0 (3-0)
Somerton Park Juniors Npt. (Sept 1930)
Lovells Ath. (cs 1934)

Although he was the club's reserve goalkeeper for a few seasons, George's first team opportunities were almost non-existent due to the remarkable consistency of players like Blakemore and Emery. A steel-worker, he later moved to Port Talbot with Lysaght's along with the Wheelers.

BOUGHEN, Dean.

b. Hemsworth 25.7.71
1-0 (1-0)
Npt. (YTS Aug 1987) Bristol R. (trial)
A youngster who made his debut at the tender age of 16 in the County's last ever Football League game versus Rochdale. He did not let the side down.

BOWEN, Thomas Henry ("Toddy").

b. West Bromwich 21.8.24 5'10" 10st 12lbs
37-6 (41-6)

Radcliffe W.B. Athletic W.B.A. (Oct 1941) Npt. (July 1946) Npt. Walsall (July 1950 £1,750) Hereford Utd. (Aug 1953) Brierley Hill (July 1953)

Outside-right who spent much of his time in the reserves despite being a constructive, two-footed player. Toddy scored a hat-trick versus Bristol C. 31/12/49. A part-time pro who worked in a Midlands steel plant, he only saw his team-mates on match days. He trained with Walsall, for whom his father had played.

BOWLES, John Charles (Jack).

b. Cheltenham 4.8.14 5'11" 11st 6lbs
4-0 (6-0)
Cheltenham T. Npt. (June 1937) Accrington S. (June 1937) Stockport Co. (cs 1938 to 1953) Watford (war-time)

After short spells with the County and Accrington, Jack established himself as the regular Stockport goalkeeper before and after World War II (he played one war-time game for Watford). In the first four post-war seasons he only missed six games. He had been pushed into the County first team too soon and improved with experience.

BOWMAN, Andrew.

b. Pittenweem, Fifeshire 7.3.34 5'7" 11st 6lbs
69-7 (79-8)
Chelsea (Juniors 1949, pro June 1951) Hearts (Aug 1955) Npt (Aug 1961) Tonbridge (Aug 1963) Hamilton Acs. (Aug 1965) Stenhouse-muir (1967-68)

Fiery wing–half, known for his tough tackling and thunderbolt shot. A Scottish schoolboy international, he made just one First Division appearance for Chelsea before winning two Championship medals with Hearts. Andy impressed with County and was reputedly the highest paid Third Division player at £40 per week. Later he moved back to Scotland and became a Derby County scout.

BOWSHER, Stanley James.

b. Newport 3.10.1899 d. Newport 14.12.68
5'6" 11st 0lbs
125-3 (141-4) (Wales 1 1929, Wales Amateur 1923-24)
Lovells Ath. Npt (cs 1925) Burnley (Jan 1929 £500) Rochdale (Mar 1933) Npt (July 1933 to 1934)

Local half–back, who was a resolute defender and accurate passer. Stan went on the Welsh tour of Eire in 1927 and was reserve for the Wales verus England game in 1929. He was selected for the Ireland game,

being sold to Burnley shortly before the match. He became County captain when he returned in 1933, but only played five Football League games. He was appointed trainer in July 1936, resigning in September 1937 and had another spell in 1945. He was also at one time the Welsh baseball captain. Later Stan kept the "Windsor" club, where he eventually collapsed and died.

BOYD, John Robertson ("Jock").

b. Bo'ness 7.3.26 5'11" 12st 0lbs
1-0 (2-0)
Bo'ness Juniors Npt. (Feb 1947) Chippenham T. (Dec 1948 to 1954)

"Jock" was a Scottish wing–half, who played almost 50 Welsh League games for County in two seasons.

BOYLE, Terence D.J.

b. Ammanford 29.10.58 5'10" 12st 8lbs
166-9 (208-13) (Wales 2 1981, Wales Under-21 1 1982)
Tottenham H. (App. Nov 1975) Crystal Pal. (Jan 1978) Wimbledon (loan Oct 1981) Bristol C. (Oct 1981 p/exchange) Npt. (Nov 1982) Cardiff C. (Aug 1986 £22,000) Swansea C. (Aug 1989 £11,000) Merthyr T. (cs 1990)

During his spell at Somerton, Terry was the County captain, a classy central defender and inspirational figure on the pitch. He was the first pupil of Llanelli Grammar School to win a Welsh Schoolboy cap and later scored on his debut for the Welsh senior team. County were lucky to obtain his services on a free transfer when struggling Bristol City were getting rid of their high earners. He only missed one Football League game in three seasons, but then decided to leave. Birmingham City could not afford the fee fixed by a Tribunal and he joined Cardiff City instead. When he afterwards moved on to the Vetch the fee was again decided by a Tribunal.

BRADFORD, Lewis.

b. Ashby–de–la–Zouch 24.11.16 5'9" 12st 0lbs
24–0 (31–0)
Preston N.E. (c 1934) war–time games for Rochdale, Southport, Carlisle Utd., Blackburn R. & Burnley Kilmarnock (1945) Bradford C. (Oct 1946) Npt. (Nov 1948) Trowbridge (Aug 1949) Bath C. (Aug 1950)

A solid, hard tackling full–back who joined Preston before World War II at the age of 17. After a varied war-

time career Lew joined Bradford City and later had one season at Somerton Park. He is always remembered as a member of County's famous F.A. Cup side of 1948–49. After leaving Bath, returned to Preston to look after their junior sides.

BRADSHAW, Paul W.

b. Altrincham 28.4.56 6'3" 13st 4lbs
23–0 (27–0) (England Under–21 4 1977–78)
Blackburn R. (App July 1973) Wolverhampton W. (Sept 1977) Vancouver Whitecaps W.B.A. (Apr 1985) Bristol R. (Mar. 1987, non–contract) Npt. (July 1987, non–contract) W.B.A. (1988) Peterborough Utd.

Paul is a very tall and impressive goalkeeper, who has been sadly prone to injury. He won England Youth and Under 21 caps and has enjoyed a long career. During his spell with County he suffered from a dead leg and was out of action for months, something which contributed to the club's exit from the Football League. He later rejoined W.B.A., for whom he appeared in an F.A. cup tie versus Everton, when Naylor was injured.

BRIGGS, Arthur Lionel.

b. Newcastle–on–Tyne 27.5.1900 5'11" 12st 10lbs
40–0 (42–0)
Jesmond Villa (Newcastle) Walker Celtic Hull C. (May 1921) Manchester C. (trial June 1924) Tranmere R. (Aug 1924) Ashton National (July 1932) Swindon T. (Feb 1933) Npt (June 1935 to May 1936)

Arthur was a very competent goalkeeper, who could boot the ball a tremendous distance. He was capped as an amateur by Cumberland and went on to understudy Billy Mercer at Hull. He became virtually an institution at Tranmere, where he missed only four Football League games in one four year stretch and was only out of the first team for two matches during his season at Newport. His trade was motor mechanic.

BRIGNULL, Philip Arthur.

b. Stratford 2.12.60 6'0" 11st 2lbs
3–0 (21–2)
West Ham (App. 1976, pro Sept 1978) Bournemouth (Aug 1981) Wrexham (loan Dec 1985) Cardiff C. (loan Feb 1986, full-time Mar 1986 £9,000) Npt. (July 1987) Merthyr T. (cs 1988) Npt. (non-contract Sept 1988) Sully (Mar 1989) AFC Cardiff Weymouth (Nov 1989)

A very cool and polished central defender, good with his head, who had been an England Schools international. In his first season at Dean Court Bournemouth were promoted and won his Associate Member's Cup. Phil was the County captain at the start of the 1987–88 season, but a bad knee injury forced him to retire prematurely from League football and helped towards the club's exit from the Football League. He started playing again with Merthyr but soon returned to Somerton Park on a non-contract basis. A sales representative for Allied Dunbar. Phil is a cousin of David Webb.

BRINTON, Ernest James.

b. Bristol 26.5.08 d. Bristol 17.9.81 5'7"
10st 10lbs
73–3 (150?–12)
Russian Oil Products Avonmouth T. Bristol C. (1928, pro Feb 1930) Npt. (June 1937) Bristol C. (war guest) Aldershot (Aug 1946) Street Chippenham T. (1949–50)

One of the most stylish half-backs in Division III. A hard working player with good ball control, Ernie had played well over 200 games for Bristol City before arriving at Somerton Park. At County he formed part of the impressive Owen-Law-Brinton half-back line and was a regular during the promotion season. He went to work at Bristol Aerodrome in 1939 and played for City for most of the War. Ernie carried on at a local level into his forties. A "gentle man with a big heart", to use his brother's words, he passed away after a heart attack in 1981.

BRINTON, John Victor (Jack).

b. Bristol 11.7.16 5'7" 10st 6lbs
6-0 (11-3)
Shellmex and B.P. Avonmouth T. Bristol C.
(1936) Npt. (July 1937) Derby Co. (Jan 1938
£1,000 plus a friendly) Stockport Co. (July
1946) Leyton O. (Aug 1948) Street Chippenham T. (Sept 1949)

An inside- or outside-left, the younger brother of Ernie. He scored after five minutes of his Bristol debut in April 1936 and netted an F.A. Cup hat-trick for County versus Kidder-minster 3.12.37. He shared digs with Maurice Sullivan at Derby and the Derby team played at Somerton Park as part of his transfer deal. Jack was with the Army during the War, play-ing the occasional Command game. He later ran the Port of Bristol team for many years and recently was still living in the city.

BRITTAN, Charles Healy.

b. Farnham 19.4.1898 d. Newport 29.11.1983
5'6" 10st 7lbs
42-9 (69-21)
Malpas Road Juniors Marshes Hall Npt.
(amateur Aug 1921, pro Jan 1922) Bridgend
Barry Npt. (Aug 1927 to 1928) Bath C. (cs
1928) Npt.

Charlie was a forceful centre-for-ward or winger who had a long ass-ociation with the Club at a first team and reserve level. He begun as an amateur and scored two on his Foot-ball League debut versus Bristol Rovers 21.1.22. He scored one hat-trick for the County, versus Walsall 18.2.28. Later he became a part-time pro and went on the Welsh F.A. tour of Eire in 1927. "As strong as a lion" in the words of one contempor-ary, he was a tough player and a bluffer of defences. Charlie was also a member of the Newport Fire Brig-ade.

BROOK, Gareth.

b. Dewsbury 9.5.64 5'10" 12st 4lbs
14-2 (15-2)
Huddersfield T. (non-contract) Chelsea Barn-sley Ossett Albion Frickley Ath. Npt. (Dec 1987 £6,500+) Scarborough (Mar 1988 £10,000) Blackpool (Nov 1989 £80,000) Notts.C. (loan Sept.1990 Scarborough (loan Oct 1990)

Sheet metal worker signed as a striker by Brian Eastick, reputedly with money raised by the Supporters' Club. Gary did not score many goals, but showed some ability on the ball. County should have paid extra money after he had made a certain number of appearances but Frickley waived this because of the County's parlous financial situation. He was sold exactly three month after he was signed to recoup the cash.

BROOKIN, William J.

b. Tilehurst, Durham 14.6.19
2-0 (4-0)
Npt. (Aug 1946) Chester (1950-51)

Goalkeeper. An R.A.F. Sergeant, Bill was discovered in a Services match at Hereford. He was mainly a reserve and was given a free transfer in the 1947 close season.

BROWN, Gordon.

b. Dundermline 4.2.32 5'8" 10st 6lbs
137-13 (149-14)
Blairhall Colliery (1949) Blackburn Rovers
(Apr 1951) Npt. (July 1955) Gillingham (June
1959 £1,500) Sittingbourne (July 1961)

Old style, nippy winger who played
regularly in the County first team for
four seasons. Gordon spent four
years at Blackburn, but made his
Football League debut for Newport,
later spending two years at Gillingham.

BROWN, Henry.

b. Aberaman 17.3.01   d. Aberaman 17.7.84
5'7" 11st 0lbs
34-3 (38-4)
Aberaman Ath (May 1921) Caerphilly T.
(1922) Aberdare Ath. (Nov 1922) Liverpool
(cs 1924) Southport (June 1925) Aberdare Ath.
(cs 1926) Aderdare Ath. Merthyr T. (June
1928) Charlton Ath. (Apr 1929 £300) Npt.
(Sept 1930) Thames (July 1931 to 1932)

A speedy, forceful outside-right with
an eye for goal. Henry had a long
career in the lower reaches of the
League and in his early days played
for the Welsh League versus Southern League (1922). He was a first
team regular in his one season at
Somerton. Four of his teams have
since left the Football League –
Aberdare, Merthyr, Southport and
County.

BROWN, Jeremy.

b. Cwmbran 13.6.61
2-0 (3-0)
Bristol R. (youth) Npt. (youth, app. June 1978)
Birmingham C. (trial Dec 1979) Yeovil T. (pro
May 1979) Weymouth (Mar 1985) S.Africa
(May 1985) Forest Green Rovers Npt. (non-
contract Mar 1987) Sweden (player/manager
1987) Cwmbran T. (Jan 1990)

Outside-left who had been an associate schoolboy with Bristol Rovers
and joined Newport straight from
school. He was given his Football
League debut after an impressive
friendly display versus Birmingham
C. (marking Tarantini) and later
played 7 reserve games for the Blues.
He struggled to find a first team
place at Somerton and was given a
free transfer, later returning briefly
on a non-contract basis. Jeremy has
since managed a club in Sweden.

BROWN, Robert.

b. Bristol 14.5.49 5'8" 11st 0lbs
8-0 (9-0)
Bristol R. (app., pro June 1967) Npt. (loan
Mar 1970) Yeovil Hereford Utd. Weymouth
Minehead Bath C. (Jan 1979)

Forward who had spell on loan with
the County, without making any great
impact. Later Bobby had a long
career in non-League football in the
West Country.

BROWN, William.

b. Falkirk 5.2.50 5'9" 11st 4lbs
158–50 (183–62)
Burnley (June 1965, pro Feb 1967) Carlisle
Utd. (July 1969) Barrow (loan Sept 1969) Npt.
(July 1970, £1,500) Hereford Utd. (loan Mar
1974) Brentford (Nov 1974, £4,000) Torquay
Utd. (Mar 1975, £5,000) Hele T. Minehead
(Apr 1979 p/manager) Porlock (1984)

Larger than life centre–forward, well
remembered for his goal–scoring
partnership with Roddy Jones. Willie
played in the Scottish Youth international side and won an F.A. Youth
Cup medal with Burnley. The
money was scraped together for his
transfer and he spent four successful
years at Somerton Park in the club's
Fourth Division days. He scored a
hat–trick versus Swansea both in the
League Cup and Welsh Cup in 1972–
73. He was later club steward at
Torquay before becoming a Minehead newsagent.

BRUTON, David E.

b. Uley, Glos. 31.10.52 6'2" 14st 0lbs
85–10 (110–11)
Bristol C. (July 1971) Swansea C. (Aug 1973
– with Bartley for £12,000) Npt. (loan Feb
1977, full–time Oct 1978 £17,500) Gloucester
C. (cs 1981) Forest Green R. Trowbridge

Very solid central defender, who at
first played six games on loan at
Somerton before returning almost two
years later. For a short time the
club's record buy, he was club captain when the side won promotion
and the Welsh Cup, but missed the
vital games through injury. In recent
years Dave has played non–League
soccer for Pontllanfraith, Cwmbran
and Caerleon and is now Manager of
Wootton Rovers. He has also played
cricket for Malpas. He is an execu-
tive of Lee & Turner, whose spon-
sorship helped to keep County alive
in 1987.

BRUTON, Michael.

b. Gloucester 6.5.58 6'0" 12st 8lbs
3–1 (11–1)
Bristol C. (schoolboy) Bristol R. (schoolboy)
Gloucester C. (1978) Npt. (Aug 1979 £2,500)
Gloucester C. (June 1980) Oxford C. (Oct
1980 £1,000+) Forest Green R.

Big centre–forward, brother of Dave.
He could score goals, as shown by
his hat–trick in a friendly versus
Derby, but was more effective at
non–League level. Mick had been
attached to Bristol City and Rovers
as a schoolboy and was released by
County despite scoring 28 Welsh

League goals. In recent years he has played for Merthyr, Cwmbran and Caerleon and is a joiner by trade.

BUCHANAN, John ("Jock").

b. Castlecarry, Edinburgh 3.1.35 5'9" 11st 2lbs
31–7 (35–7)
Edinburgh Waverley Hibernian (pro 1954)
Raith R. Npt. (July 1961 fee)

Centre–forward, one of Bobby Evans' many Scottish signings. Jock was a prolific reserve team scorer at Hibs, where he understudied Lawrie Reilly and Baker.

His best performance was scoring a hat–trick in the 6–1 defeat of Brentford 2.9.61, but he was given a free transfer in the general clearout at the end of the season.

BUCK, Anthony R.

b. Whitwell, Oxon 18.8.44 5'11" 10st 9lbs
49–17 (61–20)
Eastbourne Oxford Utd. (1958) Npt. (Dec 1967 £2,000) Rochdale (Feb 1969 £5,000) Bradford C. (loan Jan 1972) Northampton T. (Jan 1973) Bedford T. (June 1974)

A fair–haired centre–forward, who had been a reserve at Oxford after arriving from Seaford Boys' Club. A skilful goalscorer with a powerful shot, Tony made a big impression on the Somerton crowd after joining at the same time as Tony Jones. He scored 5 goals in the away match at

Bradford P.A. 21.9.68. He was sold because of the club's economic situation in 1969, much to the disappointment of the supporters and these days lives in Northampton.

BUCKLER, Thomas C.

b. ? Cardiff
1–1 (1–1)
Cardiff local football Npt. (Mar 1929)

Very obscure local level player, who scored in his only Football League game versus Luton T. 16.3.29, but never played in the first team again.

BURGESS, John William ("Butcher").

b. Southport early 1908 5'8" 11st 7lbs
103–15 (112–18)
Southport (reserves 1927–28) Burscough Rangers Chester (pro) Tottenham H. (p/exch for Skitt, Aug 1931) Colwyn Bay Utd. (Aug 1932) Kidderminster H. (1933) Npt. (Aug 1933) Barrow (Aug 1936) Rhyl (1937–38)

Very versatile player and a good club man, a regular in the Newport side for three seasons. Billy was the general of the side, a forager with a tremendous shot in both feet who was a perfect partner for Billy Thomas. He played for Southport Schools about 1920, but did not make his Football League debut until he joined County in 1933. He qualified as a masseur before leaving football and returned to his trade in Southport. Billy who joined the R.A.F. in 1940 was a keen golfer.

BURGESS, Michael R.

b. Montreal 17.4.32 6'0" 12st 0lbs
23-7 (26-9)
Bradford C. (amateur) Bradford P.A. (Aug 1952) Leyton O. (July 1953) Npt. (Feb 1956) Bournemouth (June 1957 £1,000) Halifax T. (July 1961) Gillingham (Mar 1963 £250) Aldershot (Nov 1965) Canterbury (Dec 1967)

Despite his Canadian birthplace, Mike was brought up in Bradford. He was not over popular with the Somerton faithful, as he came in part exchange for their hero, Tom Johnston, but he scored a few goals. Later Mike became a half-back, making over 200 more Football League appearances.

BURTON, Alwyn Derek (Ollie).

b. Chepstow 11.11.41 5'11" 10st 12lbs
53-8 (62-11) (Wales 9 1963-72, 5 Under 23 1961-65)

Chepstow junior football Npt. (Dec 1958) Norwich C. (Mar 1961 £12,000) Newcastle Utd. (June 1963 £37,500) retd. 1973

Although he played relatively few games at Somerton, Ollie made a very big impression. A well–built ex–schoolboy cap, normally a wing–half, he was capable of playing centre–forward, as he proved with his League Cup hat–trick at Southampton 26.11.60. It was soon clear that the club would not be able to hang on to him for long and he became a record sale, being later League Cup Winner in 1962 and Fairs Cup Winner in 1969.

His career was later curtailed by injury and he became a brewery rep., settling down in East Anglia. On the way to Ollie's first match at Coventry the team coach was rammed by a lorry, but there were no injuries.

BYRNE, Anthony B.

b. Rathdowney 2.2.46 5'7" 10st 6lbs
80-0 (95-0) (Eire 14 1970-74)
Millwall (amateur 1960, pro Aug 1963) Southampton (Aug 1964) Hereford Utd. (Aug
1974 £18,000) Npt. (Mar 1977) Trowbridge T.
(p/coach June 1979)

Very polished left-back, slightly
built, but quick and enthusiastic.
Tony moved to London when 12 and
joined Millwall straight from school.
He was in and out of the first team
during his long spell at Southampton
missing their promotion season
because of a broken leg. He played
many fine games for County, but
eventually left to go into business in
Hereford and play part-time.

CABRIE, David.

b. Greenock, Port Glasgow 3.6.18 5'10" 11st
3lbs
9-0 (13-0)
St. Mirren (1943) Npt. (May 1946) Barry T.
(1947)

Hardworking Scottish wing-half who
had around eighteen months at Somerton Park before moving into non-
League Football.

CALDER, Robert.

b. ? Glasgow c1909 5'10" 12st 2lbs
14-0 (16-0)
Canadian Football (Montreal) Glasgow
Rangers (Nov 1932) Cardiff C. (Aug 1933)
Bradford C. (Jan 1935) Npt. (Aug 1935)
Barrow (Dec 1937) Milford Utd. (cs 1939)

A right-back who first played in a
Canadian team managed by the Eng-
lish international, Sam Chedgzoy.
His only regular spell in League
football came in one season with
Cardiff City. After his playing
career, Bob became Manager of
Kettering Town.

CAPEL, John Elwyn.

b. Newport 31.3.37
3-0 (3-0)
Npt. (May 1955, pro Dec 1955) Abergavenny
Th. (loan Sept 1956) Npt. (Aug 1957) Abergavenny Th. (Jan 1958)

Welsh Schools international winger
and product of Newport P.T.C. John
played over 50 games for the
reserves without having many first
team opportunities. He was an apprentice motor fitter at the time, but in
more recent times was proprietor of
the "Gaer" Inn before retiring a few
years ago. He was a good all-roun-
der at cricket, playing for Transport
and Centurions and now being Vice
President of Girling's.

CARNEY, James Michael.

b. Bolton 4.12.1891 d. Newport 23.11.80 5'8"
11st 0lbs
118-14 (133-19)
Bolton W. Blackpool Glossop (1910-15)
Bolton W. Stalybridge Celtic (Aug 1921) Npt.
(June 1923 to 1927)

Jimmy was a long serving wing-half
who could also play centre-forward,
scoring a hat-trick verus Merthyr

26.12.25. A regular with two ex-Football League clubs, Glossop and Stalybridge, he was also rarely missing from the County line-up until his career was terminated by a cartilage injury. Settling down in Newport, he was in charge of the "A" team in the mid 1950's and lived to a ripe old age.

CARR, Anthony Gray.

b. Old Hartley, Northumberland 18.5.01   d. Old Hartley 4.2.68 5'10" 11st 10lbs
80-0 (92-0)
Seaton Delaval Villa Npt. (May 1922) Sheffield Wed. (May 1924 £1,200) Seaton Delaval Villa (1925) Preston N.E. (Oct 1926, £500 to cs 1928) South Shields (July 1929 to 1930, the club then changing its name to Gateshead) New Brighton (Oct. 1934 to 1935)

An impressive, agile goalkeeper, who was a Jimmy Hindmarsh discovery. Rarely was Anthony missing from the first team line-up during his two years with County, but the club were forced into selling him for a record fee to Sheffield Wednesday, for whom surprisingly he never appeared in the Football League.

Although he normally had a safe pair of hands, he lost his place with Preston after letting the ball go over his head. He left football, but was persuaded to play for New Brighton when living in Wallasey. He was later the proprietor of a road haulage business in Seaton Delaval. He was also a qualified pilot and played cricket for Co. Durham.

CARR, Darren J.

b. Bristol 4.9.68 6'2" 12st 5lbs
9-0 (10-1)
Bristol R. (YTS Aug 1986) Npt. (loan Oct 1987, later full-time Jan 1988 £3,000) Sheffield Utd. (Mar 1988 £7,000+)

Darren is a very tall central defender, who was originally borrowed by County in an injury crisis, but who had to return to Bristol when they were forced to sign a goalkeeper on loan. He was later bought for a small fee by Brian Eastick, but had to be sold a few weeks later when the club almost folded.

CARR, Edward Miller.

b. Wheatley Hill 3.10.17 5'7" 12st 4lbs
98-48 (109-55)
Wheatley Hill Colliery Arsenal (Feb 1935) Margate Arsenal (cs 1936) war-time with Darlington, Bradford P.A. (1940-44) & Newcastle Utd. (1944-45) Huddersfield T. (Oct. 1945) Npt. (Oct 1946, with Newbold for a fee) Bradford City (Oct 1949 fee) Darlington (Aug 1953)

One of the most popular players to pull on a black and amber shirt. Despite his size Eddie was a prolific goalscorer, as well as being a personality on the pitch. He started with Margate, Arsenal's nursery team and was called up when Ted Drake was injured. He was never on the losing side and scored twice in the League Championship decider. After a knee injury in 1939 he was told that he would never play again, but working as a miner strengthened his leg and he became a prolific war-time goalscorer. For the County he scored hat-tricks versus Sheffield Wed., Walsall and Norwich and he played a prominent part in the F.A. Cup run of 1948-49. His sudden departure after the Cup run upset supporters. Eddie was later trainer and manager at Darlington (1960-64) and Tow Low, as well as being a Newcastle scout.

CARR, Lance Leslie.

b. Johannesburg 18.2.10 5'9" 11st 0lbs
64-14 (128?-29)
Johannesburg Calies Boksburg Liverpool (Aug 1933) Npt. (Oct 1936, with Low for £1,750) South Liverpool (Aug 1937) Npt. (cs 1938) war guest with Swindon T., Aberaman, Bristol C., Aldershot and Middlesbrough Bristol R. (July 1946) Merthyr T.

South African left-winger with slashed back hair, remembered as a member of the 1938-39 promotion side. He scored a hat-trick versus Swindon 27.12.38. Lance was the son of an Irish professional runner and arrived at Liverpool with Nieuwenhuys. He had a fierce shot and scored on his debut versus Exeter C. Lance, who also played baseball for Liverpool, was superstitious and always took the field behind the County Captain.

CARTER, Royston W.

b. Torpoint, Cornwall 19.2.54 6'0" 11st 0lbs
150-21 (197-24)
Falmouth Utd. (c 1964) Hereford Utd. (Apr 1975) Swindon T. (Dec 1977 £22,500) Torquay Utd. (loan Oct 1982) Bristol R. (loan Jan 1983) Torquay Utd. (Feb 1983) Npt (Sept 1983 £10,000) Exeter C. (June 1987)

Well-built player, able to play as striker or central defender. Somewhat ponderous at times, he was nevertheless a popular figure always keen to give of his best. He was known to run the length of the pitch and score. Roy had turned down a move to Somerton Park a year earlier, but finally arrived and gave four years' good service before receiving a free transfer.

CARTER, Timothy D.

b. Bristol 5.10.67 6'2" 13st 8lbs
1-0 (1-0)
Bristol R. (App., pro Oct 1985) Npt. (loan Dec 1987) Sunderland (Dec 1987 £50,000) Carlisle Utd. (loan Mar 1988) Bristol C. (loan Sept 1988)

Promising young goalkeeper, who won three England Youth caps. Tim was signed on loan when Bradshaw was injured, but only played one game and was then recalled immediately to be sold to Sunderland.

CAWSTON, Mervyn W.

b. Diss, Norfolk 4.2.52 6'1" 11st 6lbs
4-0 (4-0)
Norwich C. (App., pro July 1969) Southend Utd. (loan Aug 1974) Leicester C. (loan Aug 1975) Npt. (loan Jan 1976) Gillingham (May 1976) Chicago Stings (1977-78 £8,500) Southend Utd. (Aug 1978 £20,000) Stoke C. (Mar 1984) Chelmsford C. Southend Utd. (Nov 1984 N/C) Woodford T. Barking Maidstone Utd. Brighton (loan Nov 1988) Redbridge Forest

Goalkeeper. An English Schools international, Mervyn was kept out of the Norwich team by the long-serving Kevin Keelan. He had an impressive spell on loan with the County, saving a penalty but unfortunately they were unable to sign him. He is still playing twelve years later.

CHADWICK, Frederick William.

b. Manchester 8.9.13 5'9" 10st 7lbs
40-19 (51-23)
British Dyes, Manchester Wolves (May 1935) Npt. (Sept 1936 fee) Ipswich T. (June 1938) war guest with Clapton O., Norwich C. and Southend Utd. Bristol R. (July 1947 to 1948)

Goalscoring forward who had two seasons at Somerton Park, netting hat-tricks versus Southend and Reading. He then moved on to Ipswich Town in their first Football League season, where he scored a record four goals in an F.A. Cup game versus Street. He had a chequered war-time career, which included 6 goals for Norwich in an 18-0 win versus Brighton and becoming a P.O.W. in Singapore. Fred, it is believed, is still alive.

CHAMBERLAIN, Neville P.

b. Stoke 22.1.60 5'7" 11st 5lbs
45-14 (64-19)
Port Vale (App., Pro Feb 1978) Stoke C. (Sept 1982 £40,000) Npt. (loan Nov 1983) Plymouth A. (loan Mar 1984) Npt. (June 1984) Mansfield T. (loan July 1985, full-time Aug 1985 £7,000) Doncaster R. (Aug 1987) Stafford R. (cs 1988)

Centre-forward or winger, the first coloured player to appear in the County's first team. He is the brother of England international, Mark. Inconsistent, but with real pace, he scored quite a few goals for County.

CHARLTON, Stanley.

b. Little Hulton, Lancs 16.11.1900 d. South
Norwood mid 1971 5'9" 12st 0lbs
32–0 (36–0)
Little Hulton Utd. Oldham Ath. (Aug 1920)
Rochdale (May 1922) Exeter C. (Aug 1923)
Crystal Pal. (May 1928) Npt. (Oct 1932)
Margate T. (Aug. 1933)

A crafty left–back with a sliding
tackle, who exploited the "offside"
game. He played half a dozen games
for Oldham before establishing himself with Rochdale. Stan went on the
1925 tour of Australia and toured
Canada with the F.A. team.
Although allegedly teetotal, he was at
one time a publican near Selhurst
Park. He was the father of the
Arsenal player of the same name.

CHARLTON, William George.

b. Sunderland 10.10.1900 d. Sunderland mid
1981 5'9" 11st 4lbs
89–19 (98–25)
Robert Thompson's F.C. South Shields (cs
1919) West Ham (May 1922) Npt. (Jan 1923 –
fee plus W.F. Edwards) Cardiff C. (June 1925
small fee) Tranmere R. (Mar 1926 to 1930)
Workington (cs 1930)

A talented right winger or centre-
forward, who was an England Schoolboy international. Billy scored
four goals on his first appearance in
the centre versus Watford 20.9.24.
He went on to score over 70 Football
League goals for Tranmere Rovers,
and by the end of 1934 he had scored
over 120 in non–League football for
Workington. Billy was in the Work-

ington side which reached the Fourth
Round of the F.A. Cup in 1933–34
(after defeating the County). He was
the uncle of Jimmy Maidment and
brother of Ted Charlton, a Fulham
and Carlisle Utd. player.

CLARK, Brian David.

b. Bristol 13.1.43 6'1" 13st 8lbs
72–18 (94–20)
Bristol R. (amateur) Bristol C. (1958, pro Mar.
1960) Huddersfield T. (Oct 1966, £2,500 plus
John Quigley) Cardiff C. (Feb 1968 £8,000)
Bournemouth (Oct 1972 £70,000+, including
Ian Gibson) Millwall (Sept 1973 £35,000)
Cardiff C. (May 1975) Npt. (July 1976) retired
1978

A very stylish and popular inside–
forward, a well respected player
remembered for his partnership with
Toshack at Ninian Park. Brian is the
son of Don, who still holds the Bristol City goal scoring record. He
captained Bristol Boys when they
won the English Schools Shield in

1958 and was in Bristol City's 1964–65 promotion side, partnering John Atyeo. He helped Cardiff to win the Welsh Cup for three consecutive seasons and played in numerous European games, scoring against Real Madrid in front of 47,000 spectators. He was in the veteran stage when joining County and his career was ended by a cheek injury, but he coached County reserves and Cardiff City. Brian scored over 200 Football League goals, obtaining his 200th versus Aldershot 18.8.76. In latter years he has Managed Maesteg and AFC Cardiff.

CLARKE, Alfred William.

b. Newport mid 1914 d. Newport 3.8.53
29-7 (34-9) (Wales Amateur 2 1935–38)
Npt. (early 1930's to cs 1934) Lovells Ath. (Aug 1934) Npt. (on loan Jan 1935) Lovells Ath. (to 1946) war guest Npt. and Cardiff C.

Diminutive, terrier type of centre-forward, sharp and with a powerful shot. He was an amateur, employed at Lysaght's and for this reason was able to play for Newport and Lovells, at the same time, when he wanted to. Alfie was the County's best forward in 1934–35 and at other times a regular reserve scorer. He was active in war-time football and played in every Lovells game of 1942–43. He died early of cancer.

CLARKE, William John.

b. Bargoed 26.12.40 5'9" 11st 4lbs
12-0 (16-0)
Bargoed Y.M.C.A. Npt. (amateur, pro May 1959) Merthyr T. (Jan 1962) Weymouth (June 1963 fee) Minehead (June 1974) Weymouth (Nov 1975)

Goalkeeper who was in the Welsh Youth team of 1959.   John was reserve to Len Weare at County. He was signed by Les Graham at Merthyr and this was followed by a much longer spell at Weymouth, where he broke his leg in 1975. He is now Weymouth Trainer, having made 507 first team appearances as a player.

CLARKE, William Vincent.

b. Newport 17.1.11   d. Newport 16.9.70 5'7" 11st 0lbs
46-1 (82-2)
Pontymister Npt. (1929) Charlton Ath. (1932) Npt. (1932) Aldershot (1934) Portsmouth (July 1934) Brighton (May 1935) Aldershot (Aug 1936) Crewe Alex. (Aug 1937) Hereford Utd. Accrington S. (1938–39) Npt. (Nov 1945)

Although no relation to Alfie Clarke, Billy was brought up in the same street. He played for Corporation Road School for three seasons and developed into a strong tackling w-ing–half or centre–half with a long clearance. Being barracked by the Newport crowd in 1933 he moved on, making intermittent Football League appearances for various clubs until the War. He appeared for the County in the last war–time season and afterwards played on in non–League soccer, joining Ebbw Vale in 1950.

CLEMENT, Andrew D.

b. Cardiff 12.11.67 5'8" 11st 0lbs
5-1 (6-1)
Wimbledon (App., pro Oct 1985) Bristol R. (loan Mar 1987) Npt. (loan Dec 1987) Woking (1990) Plymouth A. (Dec 1990)

Andy is a useful full–back and for-mer Welsh Youth international, who arrived on loan during the County's final Football League season. He performed competently, but returned to Plough Lane after a short time.

CLIFFORD, John Charles Thomas ("Jack").

b. Newport 24.9.06 d. Newport 22.6.61 5'8" 11st 0lbs
42-0 (65-0)
Npt. (amateur 1927, later pro) Crystal Palace (Feb 1932) Npt. (Aug 1933 to 1934) Lovells Ath. (1934)

A hard working half–back from Cor-poration Road, Jack spent much of his time at Somerton Park in the reserves. He played 12 Football League games for Crystal Palace before returning for a second spell but only made two further first team appearances. He was the uncle of Joe Clifford, later with the County. He was forced to miss one match after being shot by Len Blakemore on a shooting expedition.

COATES, Walter Albert.

b. Annfield Plain, Co. Durham 5'7" 11st 0lbs
26-5 (29-7)
Army football in Italy Sacriston Utd. Fulham (Aug 1919 to 1920) Leadgate Park (July 1920 to 1921) Leeds Utd. (May 1921) Npt. (July 1925, Fee) Hartlepools Utd. (Aug 1928 to 1929)

Walter was an outside– or inside–right, who played in Leeds United's Division II Championship side. His start with the County was delayed by injury and he only stayed for one season. Two years later he mad a couple of Football League appear-ances for Hartlepools.

COLDRICK, Graham George ("Codgie").

b. Newport 6.11.45 5'11" 12st 0lbs
156-10 (180-10) (Wales Under 23 2 1967-68)
Cardiff C. (App. 1961, pro Nov 1962) Npt. (Mar 1970 £4,000) Merthyr T. (1975) Cwm-bran T.

"Codgie" was a very solid and dep-endable full–back, a Welsh School-boy international who went through

Cardiff City's nursery sides on leaving school. He was prone to knee injuries, however, and was only a City first team regular in 1966–67. He was one of the few County purchases of the time and proved to be a popular and effective skipper. Graham's brother Paul was with the club in the 1980's. He is a former baseball international and now a golf fanatic.

COLES, David A.

b. Wandsworth 15.6.64 6'0" 12st 0lbs
14–0 (14–0)
Birmingham C. (App., pro Apr 1982) Mansfield T. (on loan Mar 1983) Aldershot (Aug 1983) Npt. (on loan Jan 1988) HJK Helsinki Crystal Pal. (1988) Brighton (1988) Aldershot (cs 1990)

A goalkeeper who had an impressive spell on loan during the County's final season in the Football League. David made many good saves, but was not interested in joining Newport full-time because of the situation at the club.

COLLINS, Lyn.

b. Skewen, Glamorgan 30.4.48
16–0 (16–0)
Npt. (amateur 1965, pro June 1966) Llanelli (Aug 1969) Pontardawe

Lyn, a Welsh Schoolboy international from West Wales was signed as a raw amateur at the start of the 1965–66 season. Despite quite a spell here,

he failed to establish himself at League level. Lyn was a part-time pro and an electrician at BP Llandarcy.

COLLINS, Robert L.

b. Winchester 12.8.39 5'10"
1–0 (1–0)
R.A.F. Winchester C. Cardiff C. Npt. (on loan 1962) Swindon T. (Apr 1963) Cardiff C. (Nov 1963)

Goalkeeper, who served with the R.A.F. in Singapore. Bob was spotted by George Swindin of Cardiff C., but was not taken on because they had three pro goalkeepers. He played in goal for County when Clive Rees was unavailable.

COLLINS, Roderick.

b. Dublin 7.8.62 6'1" 12st 8lbs
4–1 (6–1)
Dundalk Mansfield T. (Dec 1985 £17,000) Cambridge Utd. (trial cs 1987) Npt. (trial, then full-time Aug 1987) Cheltenham T. (Sept 1988)

Well-built striker, who was eventually signed full-time after turning down the chance to join Derry County. However, he played so few games because of injury that some supporters never saw him. He was finally signed by Cheltenham on a fee transfer at the start of the 1988–89 season.

COLLINS, William Elvet.

b. Bedwellty 16.10.02 d. Blackwood 23.1.77
5'8" 11st 6lbs
6-1 (6-1) (Wales 1 1931)
Rhymney Cardiff C. (cs 1923) Clapton O.
(May 1927) Lovells Ath. (Sept 1929) Llanelly
(Oct 1929) Npt. (cs 1932 to 1933) Llanelly
Oakdale Welfare (1934-35)

A tricky inside- or outside-right, a
goal maker rather than taker. A
reserve at Ninian Park for four seasons, Elvet moved on to Orient, where
he played in two memorable F.A.
Cup ties versus Aston Villa. After
failing to agree terms, he moved on
to Llanelly, where he won a Welsh
cap when Football League players
were banned from playing. He had
played for the Welsh League in
1925-26. He did not hit form with
County and was unpopular with the
crowd.

COMLEY, Leonard G.

b. Swansea 25.1.22 5'7" 11st 6lbs
76-29 (87-36)
Swansea T. (1939) war guest for Aberaman
Milford Utd. (cs 1948) Npt. (Oct 1948, small
fee) Scunthorpe Utd. (Mar 1951 £850) Llanelly
(cs 1952) Aberystwyth (Dec 1953)

Popular opportunist inside-forward,
who figured in the County's F.A. Cup
run of 1948-49. He was a product
of Swansea schools and youth football and joined the Town around the
beginning of the war. Len would not
re-sign for them in 1948 and chose
County in preference to Millwall or
Reading.
After a brief spell in the North he
returned to South Wales and still
lives in Swansea.

COMPTON, Paul D.

b. Stroud 6.6.63 6'1" 13st 1lb
27-2 (35-4)
Cardiff C. (trial) Trowbridge T. Bournemouth
(Oct 1980 £10,000) Aldershot (Dec 1983)
Torquay Utd. (Feb 1984) Npt. (Dec 1986 loan,
then full-time) Weymouth (cs 1987) Bashley
(Feb 1991)

Big central defender, somewhat slow
on the ground, but useful in the air.
Paul probably did not show the best
of his ability through playing in a
struggling County side, although they
did reach the Welsh Cup Final. He
was later sent off when playing for
Weymouth at Somerton Park. After
being sacked as Weymouth Manager
he moved on to Bashley.

CONNER, John (Jack).

b. Glasgow 27.12.1896 5'8" 11st 8lbs
84–26 (100–31)
Perth Violet Sunderland (May 1912) Belfast
Celtic (May 1914) Distillery Crystal Pal. (July
1919) Npt. (Nov 1922) Bristol C. (Dec 1924)
Millwall (June 1925 to end Jan 1926) Chatham
T. (Mar 1926) Yeovil & Petters (cs 1926)
Southend Utd. (cs 1927) Yeovil & Petters (Jan
1929)

A centre– or inside–forward, who
started as a Scottish junior international. A fast mover, good tackler
and passer of the ball, Jack had
started as a goalkeeper. After a few
pre–war games for Sunderland he
joined Crystal Palace in their Southern League days and later helped
them achieve promotion to Division
II.
He scored regularly in his days with
the County, but after a short stay at
Ashton Gate made no more Football
League appearances. Jack, who bore
an uncanny resemblance to the boxer
Jimmy Wilde, played in all four
home countries.

CONNER, John Cuthbertson Tippet.

b. Kirkmuirhill 26.4.1898 d. Wilshaw 27.5.67
5'10" 11st 7lbs
13–0 (15–0)
Alloa Ath. (1921–22) Glasgow Celtic (1922)
Dykehead (loan 1924–25) Plymouth A. (June
1925) Npt. (May 1926) Torquay Utd. (June
1927)

Scottish half–back, who was transferred to Plymouth after doing well
for Celtic reserves. He made his
Football League debut with the
County and was a regular with Torquay the following season.

COOK, Eric James.

b. c1914 5'10" 12st 7lbs
4–1 (5–1)
Letchworth Tottenham H. Npt. (Aug 1934 to
cs 1935)
Right–back or centre–half, who
failed to make the first team at Spurs
and made little impression at Somerton Park, despite scoring on his
debut versus Crystal Palace 1.12.34.
Eric was something of a free kick
expert.

COOK, Frederick.

b. Aberaman 20.1.1902 5'7" 10st 3lbs
119–8 (139–8) (Wales 8 1925–32)
Albions F.C. Aberdare Ath. (short spell to
May 1923) Npt. (May 1923) Portsmouth (Apr
1926, fee) Southampton (Aug 1933)

Fred was one of the best players
associated with County in their early
years. A dapper, skilful outside–left,
he could draw a man and put over a

pinpoint pass. He scored on his debut versus Exeter 25.8.23 and showed such good form that he was wanted by many clubs, including Liverpool and Wolves. Ultimately he had to be sold to Portsmouth, where he played in every game of their 1926–27 promotion season and was also in their F.A. Cup Final side of 1929. Fred won a number of international caps and went on the 1929 Welsh F.A. tour of Canada.

A cartilage operation ended his career at Fratton Park, and a trial with Southampton proved unsuccessful.

coach with Doncaster Rovers and Bradford P.A., a P.E. teacher and freelance sportswriter. In 1986 Malcolm was appointed to lead Liverpool's youth staff, but later left because of the pressures of commuting.

COOPER, John C. ("Jack") (real surname HOLLOWAY).

b. Sneinton, Notts. c 1889 5'10" 12st 5lbs
81–0 (134–0)
Sutton Town Barnsley (cs 1908) Arsenal (war–time) Npt. (cs 1919) retired 1922

COOK, Malcolm Ian.

b. Glasgow 24.5.43 5'11" 11st 5lbs
30–0 (38–0)
Motherwell Bradford P.A. (July 1963) Npt. (May 1965) Margate (May 1966) Folkestone

A strong tackling wing–half, Malcolm played regularly in his one season with County, but then suffered a knee injury and retired from League football. He was later a

Jack was one of the great characters of County's formative years, having previously found fame in an outstanding Barnsley side. He made his debut as Barnsley goalkeeper versus Clapton Orient 26.12.08 and his final appearance was versus Leeds City 24.4.15. In between he gained an F.A. Cup Winner's medal in 1912, after playing in 12 Cup games and saving a penalty in the semi–final versus Swindon T.

He served in the R.F.A. in World War 1, spending two years in France. Travelling from Nottingham for his matches, he played many fine games for County, missing only 6 in three seasons and added a great deal of colour. On one occasion he accidentally threw the ball into his own net at Bristol Rovers and on another went in to sort out the Millwall crowd, the Den later being closed for a fortnight. Jack reputedly spent his spare time poaching and brought in his wares for the other players. He was also a keen racing man, well known at Nottingham racecourse.

COOPER, STEPHEN B.

b. Birmingham 22.6.64 6'0" 10st 12lbs
39-11 (51-12)
Moor Green Birmingham C. (Nov 1983) Halifax T. (loan Dec 1983) NAC Breda (1 month) Npt. (loan Sept 1984, full-time Jan 1985) Plymouth A. (July 1985 £15,000+ and G. Staniforth) Barnsley (July 1988 £100,000) Tranmere R. (Dec 1990 £100,000)

Well-built centre-forward, an ex Midlands Council roadman who joined Halifax on loan a fortnight after signing for Birmingham.
Steve was something of a raw talent during his days with County and it came as rather a shock when he scored four goals away at Brentford. After three years at Plymouth he joined Barnsley for a large sum, which pleased the County, as they were entitled to a percentage of the fee.

COOPER, Terence.

b. Croesyceiliog 11.3.50 5'9" 11st 0lbs
64-1 (74-3)
Npt. (Juniors, pro July 1968) Notts. Co. (July 1970) Lincoln C. (loan Dec 1971, full-time Aug 1972) Scunthorpe Utd. (Nov 1977) Halifax T. Bradford C. (June 1979 £10,000) Rochdale (Aug 1981)

A very useful right-back or right-half, who joined the groundstaff after having been captain of the Welsh youth side. Terry was voted the most promising player of 1968 and it was something of a surprise when he was given a free transfer two years later. He became a virtual institution in the Lincoln side and was still playing League football ten years later.

COPELAND, Michael.

b. Cardiff 31.12.54 5'9" 11st 0lbs
3-0 (4-0)
Npt. (Junior, pro July 1973) Merthyr T. (1974) Spencer Works. Cwmbran T.

Mike played for County as a young full-back, being voted the Newport Young Sportsman of the Year in 1973. He gave up League football to concentrate on his career, becoming manager of the Leeds Building Society in Cwmbran in 1986. He continued playing soccer, however, with Spencer Works, and later Cwmbran Town.

COSSLETT, Michael P.

b. Barry 17.4.57 6'4" 13st 5lbs
2-0 (2-0)
Reading (trial) Barry T. (c 1974) Q.P.R. (trial
Nov 1977) Carlisle Utd. (trial) Torquay Utd.
(trial) Npt. (Jan 1978 p/exch for D. Murray)
Cheltenham T. (loan Dec 1978) Weymouth
(July 1979) Barry T. (Dec 1979 £1,000)
Aberystwyth

A towering centre-half, who was
given few chances in the County first
team. He was educated at a rugby
playing school in Barry and could
have joined other teams, but preferred not to give up his job as an
electrician with the Vale of Glamorgan Council. He was always a
reserve at Somerton and was given a
free transfer in May 1979. A long
non-League career followed, however, among his teams being Sully,
Ebbw Vale and Aberystwyth (Aug
1987).

COX, William.

b. Govan, Glasgow 5'8" 11st 2lbs
6-2 (6-2)
Clydebank Cardiff C. (Sept 1919) Npt. (loan
Dec 1920) Vale of Leven (Apr 1922)
Workington Nottingham Forest (Mar 1923 to
cs 1924)

Billy was a Scottish centre-forward
or inside-left, who played 20 Southern League games for Cardiff C. and
gained a Welsh Cup Winner's medal
before joining the County. He
played only six first team games
here, but appeared 16 times for the
reserves improving as the season
went on. He later made one Football
League appearance for Nottingham F.

CRADDOCK, Leonard Miller.

b. Newent 21.9.26   d. Ledbury 21.5.60   5'8"
12st 0lbs
7-0 (7-0)
Hereford Utd. (war-time) Chelsea (amateur)
Npt. (May 1946) Hereford Utd. (on loan 1947)
Aston Villa (Sept 1948 £5,000 to 1950)

An enthusiastic fair-haired centre-
forward, who played for Aston Villa
in their Division I days. He played
just seven Division II matches for the
County, including the 0-13 defeat at
Newcastle, but later established himself as a top class performer before
meeting a sad end. He was stricken
by a serious illness at the height of
his ability and became a permanent
invalid, dying in his early thirties.

CRAVEN, Joseph Gerrard.

b. Preston 28.12.03   d. Chorley mid-1972
5'11" 12st 7lbs
28-0 (29-0)
St. Augustine's Stockport Co. (1923) Preston
N.E. (Oct 1925) Swansea T. (June 1931) Port
Vale (June 1934) Npt. (June 1935) Accrington
S. (June 1936 to 1938)

A big, strong defender, good with his
head and capable to being constructive. The son of a former Nelson
player, Joe began in Preston local
football and did not establish himself
in League soccer until his mid
twenties. He won a Welsh Cup
Winner's medal with Swansea and
was Port Vale captain before becoming one of Louis Page's first signings.
After leaving Newport he was ever-
present in Accrington's side the following season.

CRISP, George Henry.

b. Pontypool 30.6.11 d. Penrhiwceiber 27.3.82
5'8" 11st 0lbs
10-1 (12-3)
Llanelly Coventry C. (1933) Bristol R. (July 1935) Npt. (June 1936) Colchester Utd. (cs 1937) Nottingham Forest (1938 to 1945) wartime for Notts. Co., Aberaman & Lovells Ath. Merthyr T.

George was a winger who was around for a long time in football without really making the grade at League level. He was in the Bristol Rovers' side when Joe Payne scored his ten goals for Luton and in the Colchester team which won the Southern League Championship. After the war he was in the Merthyr team which lost the 1947 Welsh Cup Final.

CUNNINGHAM, Joel.

b. Lochie, Dundee c 1905 6'0" 11st 4lbs
2-0 (2-0)
Logie Aberdeen (1923) Npt. (cs 1925) Q.P.R. (June 1926) Walsall (May 1932) York C. (Aug 1934) Dartford (July 1935) Folkestone T.

Joey was a good, but somewhat adventurous goalkeeper, who loved to swing from the crossbar and make sliding tackles on opposing forwards. He never really established himself until moving to Q.P.R., where he played over 160 games. He was later an ever present for Walsall in 1932-33 and York C. in 1934-35. In 1936 Joey was a member of the Dartford side which put Cardiff City out of the F.A. Cup.

CUNNINGHAM, Joseph Bernard.

b.Cwmbran 20.4.05
3-0 (3-0)
Npt. (1932)

A local player who made three appearances for the club at right-half when it regained its Football League status in 1932-33. Bernard later worked for Fords in Dagenham and recently still lived in Benfleet.

DARRELL, Michael A.

b. Bilston, Staffs 14.1.47 5'8" 11st 7lbs
8-0 (8-0)
Birmingham C. (App., pro Jan 1965) Npt. (loan Oct 1970) Gillingham (loan Dec 1970) Peterborough Utd. (May 1971 to 1973)

Forward who had a month on loan with the County. Although he had five years with Birmingham, Mickey only made eleven Football League appearances for them and failed to find the net for County.

DAVIES, Albert Llewellyn.

b. Pontypridd 11.3.33
1-0 (2-0)
Merthyr T. Npt. (May 1951 to Jan 1953) Merthyr T.

A Wales Youth "cap", who joined the County Colts. Albert was an amateur who played one Football League game at outside-right, at the age of eighteen.

DAVIES, Edward.

b. South Wales
3–1 (3–1)
Npt. (Sept 1946 to May 1947)

Forward from local Welsh football, who had a very brief spell at Somerton Park just after the War. He was with the R.A.F. at the time and stationed at Hereford.

DAVIES, Grant.

b. Barrow 13.10.59 5'10" 11st 4lbs
147–1 (193–1)
Preston N.E. (App., pro Oct 1977) Npt. (trial July 1978, full–time Aug 1978) Exeter C. (loan Feb 1983) Risca Utd. Cwmbran T. (1985)

There was nothing fancy about Grant's play, but he formed an effective central defence with Keith Oakes. A Wales Youth international, he made no Football League appearances for Preston, but became a regular at Somerton. He played in their promotion and Welsh Cup winning sides and was voted "Player of the Year" in 1982. He was prevented from joining Yeovil T. in 1983 when he entered the Police force. In recent years Grant has played for Cwmbran and the Welsh Police.

DAVIES, John Howard.

b. Machynlleth mid 1916 5'10" 12st 0lbs
36–0 (39–0)
Merthyr T. (amateur 1934) Npt. (July 1934 to 1936)

Powerfully built half–back. He joined Merthyr T. as an amateur for the last two months of the 1933–34 season, then moved to County as a professional. John attracted the scouts of other clubs, but went no further in League football.

DAVIES, Peter.

b. Merthyr Tydfil 1.7.42
1–0 (1–0) (Wales amateur 2 1964–66)
Merthyr T. Npt. (May 1964) Merthyr T. (loan Sept 1964) Retford T. Merthyr T.

Welsh amateur international centre–forward, who, despite some obvious ability, only made one appearance in the County first team.

DAVIES, Vincent.

b. Aberaman 2.7.06 d. Aberaman mid 1980
5'9" 12st 3lbs
23–7 (31–8)
Aberdare Ath. (amateur, pro Nov 1926) Merthyr T. (Aug 1927) Llanelly Npt. (May 1930) Accrington S. (1931)

Vince started as a promising reserve in Aberdare's Welsh League side. He was fast, with excellent ball control and could shoot with judgment and direction. Unfortunately, his only full season with the County saw them voted out of the Football League and he played no first team games for Accrington.

DAVIS, John Arthur R. (Jack).

b. Plymouth 1899
34-20 (39-21)
R.N. Barracks Devonport   R.N. Barracks
Plymouth   Plymouth A. (reserves) Torquay
Utd. c.1921 Exeter C. (1922) Npt. (July 1925)
Plymouth A. (Sept 1926 fee to Apr 1928)

An ex-Royal Navy man, who proved a useful goalscorer at lower League level. Jack played over 60 games for Exeter before being signed by County. He became the only Newport player to score a hat-trick on his debut, achieving the feat against Brighton 29.8.25 and the following month scored one versus Q.P.R. Jack made little impression on his return to Plymouth, although he played three first team games in place of Jack Cock in November 1927.

DAVIS, Samuel George.

b. Plymouth c 1895 5'9" 12st 0lbs
13-0 (15-0)
Oreston Rovers (1910) Gillingham Plymouth
A. (pro Nov 1913) war-time for Clapton O.
Npt. (June 1920) Torquay Utd. (cs 1921)

A defender, who was a reserve for Southern League Gillingham and Plymouth before World War 1, during which he rose from Private to Captain and played for an Army XI. Sam had a season with the County before moving to Torquay, then a non-League side.

DEACY, Michael.

b. Cardiff 29.11.43 6'3" 13st 0lbs
46-2 (50-2)
Npt. (amateur Aug 1966, pro Jan 1968) Barry
T. (July 1970) Retired Feb 1971.

Mike was a strapping centre-half, who was mainly a reserve during his time at Somerton Park. He still managed to make 50 first team appearances, however, the first two as an amateur.

DELANEY, James Christopher.

b. London 22.7.45
1-0 (1-0)
Swansea T. (Welsh League) Npt. (cs 1969)
Ammanford T. (1972) Afan Lido (1979)

Well-built, amateur centre-forward, who was signed on trial. He only played in the first game of the season and was substituted, as he seemed out of his depth in League football. Jim had played for the British Universities XI and was a P.E. teacher. He was later player-coach at Ammanford and a Welsh F.A. coach.

DEPEAR, Ernest Roland.

b. Spalding 10.12.23 6'2" 13st 11lbs
16-0 (17-0)
Boston Utd. Leeds Utd. (May 1948) Npt
(June 1949, part exchange for H. Williams)
Shrewsbury T. (July 1950) Bangor C. (June
1952 to 1955 p/manager)

Half-back, who had a been Royal Marine commando. Roley joined in exchange for Harold Williams, which did nothing for his popularity with the crowd, especially as he was somewhat ponderous. Later he became Shrewsbury captain on their entry into the Football League and Bangor City player–manager.

DERRETT, Steven C.

b. Cardiff 16.10.47 5'10" 13st 4lbs
61–0 (71–0) (Wales 4 1969–71, Under 23 3 1970–71)
Cardiff C. (App 1963, pro Oct 1965) Carlisle Utd. (Apr 1972 £6,000) Aldershot (loan Oct 1973) Rotherham Utd. (Dec 1973) Npt. (June 1976) Barry T. (Oct 1978) Bridgend T. (Mar 1979)

Steve was a full–back or sweeper, capped by Wales at most levels. He was rarely a regular at his clubs, however, despite his ability. At Rotherham he helped United win promotion into Division III and was later brought to Somerton Park by Jimmy Scoular. He did a competent job before dropping down into non-League football. Nowadays Steve lives in St. Meltons.

DERRICK, Albert Edward.

b. Newport 8.9.08 d. Newport 5.6.75 5'8" 11st 0lbs
125–45 (175–74)
Npt. (amateur Mar 1935, pro Oct 1935) wartime for Aberaman, Crewe Alex. Chester & Wrexham Swindon T. (Jan 1946) Ebbw Vale (1947)

A persistent centre–forward and earlier outside–right, whose virile methods brought him many goals.

He joined the club after serving in the Army for 7 years, including 5 on the North West frontier. Albert scored many reserve goals and was soon doing the same in the first team, managing 4 in the Welsh Cup–tie versus Swansea 15.3.37. He was the only local to play regularly in the 1938–39 promotion side. An Army reservist, he was called up in 1939. He was selected to play for the British Army XI, but was on the high seas at the time. Albert was playing local level football for Girling's in his fifties.

DERRICK, Edward Albert.

b. Newport 6.8.39 5'10" 11st 0lbs
28–9 (34–9)
Npt (Sept 1960) Merthyr T. (1961) Cambridge C. (June 1961) Hereford U.(Feb 1964 £1,000) Npt. (July 1969) Worcester C. (July 1970) Barry T.(July 1971) Merthyr T.(July 1972)

The son of Albert (he is also known by that name), he had a brief stay with County in 1960–61, but left after refusing part–time terms.

Despite having an operation, which left one leg 2 inches shorter than the other, he became a prolific scorer in the Southern League, with 43 League and Cup goals in 1968–69. Albert returned to Somerton not long after scoring a goal which put County out of the Welsh Cup. After a successful early run the goals dried up to due cartilage problems and he was given a free transfer. He later coached Standard Telephones and still lives in Newport.

DEVLIN, William.

b. Hebburn–on–Tyne c 1893 5'7" 11st 0lbs
57–21 (86–31)
Wallsend Stockport Co. (cs 1911–12) Cardiff C. (Sept 1912) Npt. (Nov 1919) Exeter C. (June 1922 to May 1923)

A successful goal–scoring forward, who had been at Ninian Park in Cardiff's Southern League days. Billy played in the County's last Southern League season and their two in the Football League. He broke his nose at Easter 1920 and was out for 15 weeks with a knee injury in 1921. A wonderful shot, he was the only County player to register an F.A. Cup hat–trick against Football League opponents (versus Wrexham 21.12.21).

DEWSBURY, John.

b. Swansea 16.2.32 5'6" 10st 9lbs
2–0 (2–0)
Swansea T. (June 1950) Npt. (July 1955) Milford Utd. (1956)

John was a Swansea born wing–half, who joined the Vetch Field ground–staff. He played 20 reserve team games in his season here, but only appeared twice in the Football League. He still lives in Swansea.

DILLON, Andrew.

b. Salford 20.1.69 5'11" 11st 0lbs
15–0 (26–0)
Npt. (YTS 1985, pro July 1987) Merthyr T. (c Mar 1988) Bridgend T. (1989)

A young goalkeeper who, despite his limitations, played some gallant games in a twice relegated Newport side. He played in the Welsh Cup Final versus Merthyr and later joined the Martyrs, but was recalled by County to play when needed, as they had no other goalkeeper. Andrew was re–signed after the club had entered the Vauxhall Conference.

DIMMICK, Edmund (Ted).

b. Blaina late 1896 5'7" 11st 0lbs
84–0 (97–0)
Blaina Albertillery (1919) Lambton Star, Co. Durham Npt. (cs 1922) Albertillery (1925) Chesterfield (cs 1926 to 1927)

An ex–Royal Navy man, Ted proved a very consistent left–back during his time at Somerton Park. He made only three Football League appearances during a later spell at Chesterfield. His achievements included playing for the Welsh League in Ireland.

DIXON, Cecil Hubert.

b. Trowbridge 28.3.35 5'7" 10st 10lbs
107–15 (121–18)
Trowbridge T. Cardiff C. (July 1954) Npt
(July 1957 £2,000) Northampton T. (Aug 1961
£1,000 to May 1962) Latrobe (Brisbane) St.
Just (Melbourne c 1966)

A fair–haired outside–right, an unmistakeable figure as he ran down
the right wing. He could beat a man
and put over a good centre. Cecil
was developed by Harry Haddon at
Trowbridge and became a reserve at
Cardiff in their First Division days.
He later emigrated to Australia, but
makes the odd visit home.

DOBSON, Harry.

b. Newcastle c 1894 5'7" 10st 6lbs
66–8 (118–20)
North Shields Coventry C. (1913) Npt (July
1919) Southend Utd. (Feb 1922, fee, to 1925)

An inside–forward, "Dobbie" was the
artiste of the side which saw the
County into the Football League,
though he was no mean goalscorer.
In 1914 he had played in a 10–1
defeat of County and later Hearts
tried to sign him. During his time at
Somerton Park he travelled down
from Coventry to play. A much
bigger offer from Cardiff had been
turned down when he was allowed to
join Southend, where he played regularly for three years. He was
selected for the Southern League
Welsh clubs versus England in 1919–
20 and for the Welsh League two
years later.

DOCHERTY, Thomas.

b. Penshaw, Co. Durham 15.4.24 5'9"
107–1 (121–2)
Sunderland (amateur war–time) Murton Colliery Welfare (1945) Lincoln C. (July 1947)
Norwich C. (June 1950 £1,500) Reading (July
1953) Npt. (June 1955) Kings Lynn (cs 1958)
retired 1966

Tommy was originally a speedy
winger, but later converted to a wing
–half. A persistent player, with a
skilled left foot he was renowned for
his pinpoint passes. He had a long
career in the lower Divisions and
now lives near Cambridge.

DONALDSON, James D.

b. South Shields 11.6.27
36–1 (46–2)
South Shields (pro 1947–48) Chesterfield (Sept 1949) Npt. (Aug 1951) Kidderminster H. (July 1953)

Constructive wing–half. Jimmy was a regular first teamer in his first season, but was later mainly a reserve and freed in 1953.

DOWLER, Michael J.

b. Caldicot 12.10.57 5'8" 11st 0lbs
19–0 (21–0)
Hereford Utd. (App. c June 1974) Npt. (non-contract Oct 1975, pro June 1976) Wichita Wings (Nov 1980)

Short, but quite useful goalkeeper, a former Welsh Schools and Youth international who began his football with Caerwent. He was mainly a reserve to Plumley, and was released when Kendall was signed. Later Mike spent some years playing for Wichita in the American Indoor League, but suffered a serious hamstring injury in 1986. He is the brother–in–law of Mark Williams.

DOWMAN, Steven J.

b. Manor Park, N.London 5.4.58 5'11" 12st 4lbs
9–1 (11–1)
West Ham, Chelsea, Fulham (trials) Colchester Utd. (App. pro Aug 1976) Wrexham (July 1980 £75,000) Charlton A. (loan Aug 1983, Jan 1984 £15,000) Npt. (July 1985) Cambridge Utd. (Oct 1985 to cs 1987)

Experienced, hefty central defender, who was running a carpet firm in Colchester when arriving at Somerton Park. After three months he was allowed to join Cambridge on a free transfer. Became manager of Brightlingsea Utd. from 1987–88.

DOWNES, Walter J.

b. Hammersmith, London 9.6.61 5'10" 10st 11lbs
4–2 (4–2)
Wimbledon (App., pro Jan 1979) Npt. (loan Dec 1987) Sheffield Utd. (Feb 1988)

Versatile player, nephew of boxer Terry Downes.
Wally was with Wimbledon during their phenomenal rise and played over 300 games for them, but was out for nine months when he broke an ankle. He played well during his loan spell and agreed to extend it, but had to be sent back when goalkeeper Coles was signed.

DREYER, Frederick.

b. Woodburn nr. Durham 19.3.08 12st 7lbs
1–0 (2–0)
St. Patrick's. Army amateur games for Portsmouth, Fulham & Southampton Gateshead (pro 1931–32) Npt. (July 1932 to cs 1933)

Half–back, who learned his football in the Army, with the Southern Command. Fred did not appear in Gateshead's Football League side and played only once for County, being the captain of the Colts and kept out of the first team by Willie Summers. In his Army days he appeared as an amateur for several Football League clubs.

DRINNAN, James McKay.

b. Harthill, Lanark 28.5.06 d. ?England 1936
5'7" 11st 0lbs
42-11 (49-13)
Larkhall Thistle Bristol C. (1923) Aberaman Ath. (cs 1924) Merthyr T. (1924-25) Npt. (cs 1925) Brentford (June 1927) Luton T. (July 1929) Burnley (June 1930 to 1931)

A clever, hard working inside-forward, who came South to start his career with Bristol. Jimmy played for Merthyr in their Third Division days and was a fairly consistent goalscorer.

DUGGAN, Henry Anthony. (Harry)

b. Dublin 8.6.03 d. Leeds Sept 1968 5'7" 10st 3lbs
88-13 (112?-21) (N.Ireland 8 1930-36, Eire 5 1927-38)

Richmond Utd. (Dublin) Leeds Utd. (May 1925) Npt. (Oct 1936 £1,500 to 1940)

Harry was a fine outside-right, always remembered as the Captain of the County's promotion side. A fast and tricky winger, he was a worrier of defences. He scored 49 goals for Richmond in 1924-25 and was signed up by Leeds. After starting in their reserves established himself in the first team and was Captain of their 1932 promotion side. ARP duties prevented him playing at times in 1939 and in March 1940 he returned to Leeds, where he worked for a glass merchant.

DUNCAN, Thomas Montgomery.

b. Shores Inn, Portsoy nr. Banff 15.7.36
1-0 (1-0)
Airdrieonians (Aug 1952) Npt. (loan Mar 1958)

Scottish inside-forward, who had a short spell on loan with the County during his National Service.

EDMUNDS, Redvern E.

b. Newport 10.1.43
4-0 (4-0)
Portsmouth (juniors 1958, pro June 1960) Npt. (July 1961) Merthyr T. (Feb 1962) Abergavenny Th. (1962) Latrobe (Brisbane) Hakoah (Sydney) (c 1966)

A prolific scorer for St. Andrew's School, who represented Newport

Boys at Soccer, Cricket and Baseball and was a Welsh Schoolboy international. He made his debut for Portsmouth at 17, then broke his leg and joined Newport part-time. Redvern, who later emigrated to Australia, is the nephew of Trevor Ford.

EDWARDS, David S.

b. Bargoed c 1919
2-0 (2-0)
Deri Npt. (pro Sept 1937) Gloucester C. (1938) Ipswich T. (June 1939) Swindon T. (May 1946)

Dai was signed from local Bargoed football, but only made the first team on a couple of occasions at outside-left. After a season with Gloucester he joined Ipswich in their early Football League days. He made three appearances for Swindon after the war.

EDWARDS, Ernest Arthur.

b. Stourbridge early 1892 5'9" 11st 0lbs
113-0 (155-0)
Old Hill Unity W.B.A. (1913) Birmingham (1914-15) Tipton Excelsior (war guest) Merthyr T. Npt. (Oct 1919) Southend Utd. (cs 1923) Dudley T. (1927 to 1932)

Ernie was one of the County's strongest assets in their early days. A very consistent half-back, he was also a useful centre-forward. After three reserve games he played in

W.B.A.'s first team until breaking a leg versus Newcastle in January 1914. He travelled from Birmingham for Newport's matches and became Captain for his final season. After leaving Somerton Park he played on to the veteran stage.

EDWARDS, Leslie.

b. Nuneaton 1912 5'10" 11st 10lbs
41-1 (45-1)
Leicester C. (1930) Folkestone T. (1932) Crystal Palace (June 1933) Npt. (May 1936 to 1938)

Right-half, who played a few games for Leicester before becoming a reserve at Crystal Palace, although he did play 24 Football League games in three seasons. Les became the County Captain in November 1936 and only missed two games, but just made a couple of appearances the following season.

EDWARDS, William Francis ("Fluffy").

b. Aston, Birmingham mid 1896 d. Hereford
4.6.52 5'7" 10st 12lbs
79–12 (86–12)
Shrewsbury T. Brentford Watford (1914)
Llanelly (1914) Fulham (1919) Npt. (Aug
1920) West Ham (Jan 1923, in part exchange
for Billy Charlton, to 1926) Hereford Utd.
(1926)

Billy really established himself after
World War I. Normally a right sided
player, he filled all five forward
positions for County and proved
himself a keen and forceful player.
He never made himself a regular at
West Ham and eventually moved on
to Hereford, where he was their
leading scorer and later a Director.
Billy, who was the licensee of the
"Commercial Hotel" in Hereford, was
in the Hereford bowls team which
won the English Bowling Association's Triples Championship in 1952.

EGAN, Christopher A.

b. Limerick 6.8.53 5'9" 11st 0lbs
5–0 (7–0)
Fairview Rangers Cork C. (£200) Sligo B.
Derby Co. (Oct 1973 £9,000) Npt. (Aug to Oct
1976) abroad Eastwood T. Arnold

An Irish Youth cap, converted from
left–back to winger by Fairview. He
was sold for £200, so that the team
could have a TV and billiard table.
Brian Clough signed him for Derby,
then he had an exceedingly short

spell at Newport, leaving because of
his wife's illness. Chris is a painter
and decorator by trade.

ELLIOTT, David.

b. Tantobie, Co. Durham 10.2.45 5'8" 12st 3lbs
21–0 (27–0)
Gateshead (c 1960) Sunderland (App. 1961,
pro Feb 1962) Newcastle Utd. (Dec 1966
£10,000) Southend Utd. (Jan 1971) Npt (Apr
1975) Bangor C. (1976) Npt. (Oct 1978)

Sturdy defender, who had played in
promotion sides with Sunderland and
Newcastle.   Dave   was   County
Player–Manager until sacked in February 1976, but returned two years
later as injury cover. He had coaching or managerial posts with Cardiff
City, Caernarfon and Bangor and has
also run his own sports shop.

ELLIS, Brinley R.

b. ? Pontypridd 1917
2–0 (2–0)
local Pontypool football Npt. (c 1936) Gloucester C.

Bryn joined County as an amateur in
the late 1930's. He was an "A" team
find, regarded as having potential, but
made just one appearance at left–
back in 1937 and one at outside–left
in 1938.

ELSEY, Karl W.

b. Swansea 20.11.58 5'10" 12st 6lbs
114–13 (164–16)
Pembroke B. (1978) Swansea C. (late 1978)
Pembroke B. Q.P.R. (pro Jan 1979) Npt. (trial
July 1980, full–time Aug 1980) Cardiff C.
(Sept 1983 p/exchange) Gillingham (June
1985) Reading (1988) Maidstone Utd. (July
1989). Gillingham (cs 1991)

The son of an old Swansea professional, Karl has proved himself to be
a versatile player of ability, though
with a tendency to be inconsistent.
He left school at 15 to become a
chrome plater and did not play for
two years, preferring fishing as a
hobby. He went to London for a
trial and signed professionally after
one Combination game, moving from
the Welsh League to Division I in
four months. At Somerton he was
capable of scoring goals or playing as
a tough tackling defender. He later
joined Cardiff in a multi–player
exchange and played for Maidstone
in their inaugural Football League
season.

ELWELL, Thomas Dennis Oakly.

b. Wolverhampton 20.9.01 d. Newport 11.2.74
5'8" 11st 7lbs
4–0 (4–0)
Somerton Park Juniors Orb Utd. Npt. (amateur 1923, pro 1925) Lovells Ath. (c Apr
1928)

Dennis was a local half–back, who
made the County first team on only a

few occasions, but then had a long
career in the colours of Lovells Athletic, playing on until the mid 1930's.

EMANUEL, W. John ("Ivor").

b. Treherbert 5.4.48 5'8" 12st 0lbs
79–4 (87–4) (Wales 2 1973, Amateur 2 1970–
71)
Blaenrhondda Swansea T. (amateur 1964)
Ferndale (c 1966) Bristol C. (May 1971)
Swindon T. (loan Nov 1975) Gillingham (loan
Feb 1976) Npt. (June 1976) Barry T. (July
1978) Ton Pentre Maesteg Park

John was a very skilful midfield
player, who made a late start in
League football when he played in
Bristol City's Division II promotion
side. He came to the County as a
free transfer, after turning down a
move to St. Louis All Stars and it
was a blow when he decided to can-
cel his contract two years later. He
has remained involved in non-
League football since leaving Somerton Park and was recently the Manager of Maesteg Park. John, who
was nicknamed after the well–known
Welsh singer, is a painter and decorator by trade.

EMERY, Herbert James.

b. Bristol 18.2.08 5'11" 12st 0lbs
77–0 (89–0)
Ely Utd. Cardiff Corries Clapton Orient (trial
1928, later pro) Rotherham Utd. (May 1929)
Clapton O. (May 1931) Npt. (June 1933 to
1935)

A very safe and cool goalkeeper,
rarely beaten by long shots. Bert

learnt his football at Lansdowne Road School and although he played no first team games during his first spell at Orient he later returned to take over from the legendary Arthur Wood. He played in the first floodlit game in the South – at the White City 4.1.33. In two seasons for the County he missed only 7 Football League games.

EMMANUEL, David Leonard.

b. Treboreth 3.9.17 5'10" 12st 0lbs
33–7 (36–7)
Swansea T. (cs 1936) Npt. (May 1947) Bristol R. (1948) Kidderminster H. (cs 1948) Llanelli (1950 to 1953)

Full–back or wing–half, a Welsh Schools international who played for Swansea in the 1930's along with his brother Tom. Len became the only Swansea Town player to appear before and after the War. He was something of a penalty expert and converted six in his short spell here. He is the father of Gary.

EMMANUEL J. Gareth.

b. Swansea 1.2.54 5'9" 11st 0lbs
12–0 (16–0) (Wales Under 23 1 1975)
Birmingham C. (App., pro July 1971) Bristol R. (Dec 1978 £50,000) Swindon T. (July 1981 p/exchange) Npt. (July 1984) Forest Green R. (May 1985) Bristol C. (trial Aug 1985) Swansea C. (Aug 1985) Merthyr T. (July 1988) Ton Pentre (Dec 1988) Llanelli (1990, p/manager)

Cultured half–back, who could have played a leading role at Somerton Park but for injury. He arrived after Swindon Town had told him to take a pay cut or move on, but his debut was delayed until the end of the season because of a bad back injury and he was given a free transfer. Gary took some stick from the Ashton Gate crowd for being an ex–Rover and moved on to Swansea.

EVANS, Emrys Brian.

b. Tonypandy 16.9.30
18–4 (19–6)
Gilfach Tottenham H. (amateur) Npt. (Aug 1952) Llanelly (Mar 1954) Abergavenny Th.

Inside–forward whose first team chances were limited even though he scored a hat–trick on his home debut versus Torquay 24.1.53. Although that was over thirty years ago, Emrys has remained involved in non–League soccer, managing Merthyr T., Barry T., Ton Pentre and Brecon. Now living in Merthyr he still scouts for Merthyr Tydfil and Leicester City.

EVANS, Hubert, W.R.

b. Swansea 10.8.22
14–1 (15–1) (U.S.A. International)
Swansea T. (1940) war guest for Southport Lovells Ath. (1948) Npt. (Apr 1951) St. Andrews, Toronto (1952) Llanelly (1953)

Hubert joined Swansea as a promising wing–half in 1940 and played quite a few war–time games, though no Football League games afterwards. After a short spell at Somerton he left for Canada in the Summer of 1952, but returned the following year.

EVANS, John Henry (Jack).

b. Grangetown, Cardiff 19.1.03   d. Cardiff c. Jan 1989 5'10" 12st 0lbs
4-0 (5-0)

Riverside Albion (war-time guest) Cardiff C. (1919) Barry (1921) Cadoxton Npt. (1923) joined Merchant Navy Feb. 1924, making guest appearances for Leghorn (1924), Gibraltar (1925) and Boca Juniors (1926) British Cellophane (Sept 1936 to 1938)

A centre-half, who started his soccer career at Cardiff High School, progressing to Cardiff C. reserves and Barry. He had a trial for the Welsh Amateur side and was signed up by Jimmy Hindmarsh, who had earlier been shown the door by Jack's disapproving mother. He was a promising player, making around 30 reserve appearances, but left to concentrate on his engineering career, becoming Chief Engineer of a 10,000 ton vessel. After his seagoing adventures, which included being ice-bound on one occasion, Jack helped to build British Cellophane's Bridgewater Power Station. In the 1960's he designed and superintended a fleet of dredgers, later moving back to Whitchurch, Cardiff, where he died recently.

EVANS, Paul.

b. Brentwood 14.9.64
9-2 (15-4)
Cardiff C (Sept 1982) Ferndale   Barry T. Brecon Corries Npt. (reserves 1987, non-contract Aug 1987) Barry T. (cs 1988)

Paul is a big, burly striker, whose career has been mainly restricted to the Welsh League. He has ability and scored two memorable goals in the League Cup match at Ninian Park, but was ignored by Brian Eastick, who claimed he was badly unfit. He moved back into non-League football, soon rejoining Barry, for whom he scored 43 goals in 1988-89. He turned down the chance of joining Newport A.F.C.

EVANS, Robert.

b. St. Anthony, Glasgow 16.7.27 5'8" 12st 0lbs
31-0 (36-0) (Scotland 48 1949-60)
Thornliebank Methodist   St. Anthony's Glasgow Celtic (Sept 1944) war-time for Motherwell and Aberaman Ath. Chelsea (May 1960 £12,500) Npt. (p/manager June 1961) Morton (coach July 1962) Third Lanark (cs 1963 coach, then p/manager) Raith Rovers (cs 1965) retired 1967

Famous red–haired Scottish international Captain, voted Scottish Player of the Year in 1953. He started as an inside–forward, but became a brave and skilful half–back. Bobby spent 16 years with Celtic, winning Scottish League, Cup and League Cup medals. He had an unfortunate spell as player manager at Somerton Park. Although the team played good football, they did not get results and he was sacked on 21.3.62. Bobby later ran a Glasgow news–agent's and is now living in East Kilbride.

FEARNLEY, Harrison L. (Harry).

b. Morley, Leeds 27.5.23 5'8" 10st 6lbs
103–0 (116–0)
Bradford P.A. (amateur) Leeds Utd. (Nov 1941) Halifax T. (Jan 1949) Npt. (July 1949) Selby T. (1953) Rochdale (July 1955)

Useful goalkeeper, who was a Commando during the War and represented the R.N. XI versus an Army XI. He had played against Newport in the F.A. Cup, when with Leeds. Harry played fairly regularly for County and in his spare time shared a window–cleaning round with Cliff Birch. He turned down part–time terms in 1953–54 and left.

FERGUSON, Alexander.

b. Lochore, Scotland 4.8.04 6'1" 13st 7lbs
41–0 (127–0)

Vale of Clyde Wigan Borough (Nov 1924) Gillingham (June 1925) Swansea T. (Feb 1927) Bury (1936) Npt. (June 1938) war guest for Lovells Ath. and Bristol C. Bristol C. (May 1946) Swindon T. (Sept 1947)

Well known goalkeeper, a Junior international, whose brother Albert played for Dumbarton and James for Notts Co. and Brentford. Alex had huge hands, wonderful positional sense and one of the longest kicks in football. He was well into the veteran stage when joining County, but, quite apart from missing just one game in the promotion season, was still playing regularly at the end of the War. His last Football League appearance was with Swindon at the age of 43.

FERGUSON, Robert Burnett.

b. Dudley, Northumberland 8.1.38 5'9" 11st 9lbs
71–2 (82–2)

Newcastle Utd. (juniors, pro May 1955) Derby Co. (Oct 1962) Cardiff C. (Dec 1965 £4,000) Barry T. (Jan 1969 p/manager) Npt. (July 1969 £250) Hereford Utd. (June 1971 p/coach)

Competent, rugged full-back, who began in the same boys' team as Bobby Charlton. He was a P.E. instructor with the Commandos and played for the Army team. Bobby had two years down the pit and lost four fingers when run over by a coal tub, the injury requiring plastic surgery. He rarely had a first team game at Newcastle, but played regularly at Derby and Cardiff, where he replaced Peter Rodrigues. He became the youngest Manager in the League with County, but was sacked after 2 points in 19 games and a disastrous 1-6 F.A.Cup defeat at Barnet. He had a long career on the Ipswich staff. Bobby was appointed Manager to replace Bobby Robson in 1982, but became the first Ipswich Manager to be sacked in May 1987. After a spell as the Birmingham City coach, he became a member of the Colchester United staff in March 1991.

FINLAY, Allan Jackson.

b. Edinburgh 9.1.39 5'8" 10st 7lbs
20-1 (25-1)
Heart of Midlothian   Barry T.   Npt. (July 1961)

One of the Scots recruited by Bobby Evans. An inside-left, who had been a Scottish Schools and Youth "cap" and guested for Barry T. whilst in the Forces. Allan was given a free transfer when Bobby left.

FLANDERS, Fred.

b. Derby 1.1.1894   d. Birmingham late 1967
5'8" 12st 0lbs
15-0 (85+-7+)
Sheldon Utd. (1910) Derby Co. (1911) Npt. (cs 1913 to 1919) Mansfield T. (1919) Npt (cs 1921) Hartlepools Utd. (cs 1922) Nuneaton (1923)

A talented youngster, who captained both the Derby Boys' side which won the English Schools' Championship and the English Schools' team which played Wales in 1908. After a season with Sheldon Utd. reserves he joined Derby at 17. A vigorous, powerful full-back, Fred reputedly possessed the highest kick in the Southern League. He played intermittently for the County from the second year of their existence to their Football League days.

FLETCHER, Harry W.

b. Willenhall, Staffs 5'6" 10st 12lbs
1-1 (1-1)
Ellesmere Port Southport Chester Willenhall Birmingham (cs 1920) Npt. (cs 1922) Barry

Harry was a reserve, who had previously played for Birmingham's second team. He only made one first team appearance for County, at centre-half versus Bristol R. 7.9.22 and scored. He played over 20 reserve team games, but drifted into non-League soccer.

FOOTE, Ernest.

b. ?Ebbw Vale
1–0 (1–0)
Ebbw Vale Npt. (c 1937) Gloucester C.

A hard–working centre–half, who was only given one chance for the County in the Football League.

FORD, Trevor.

b. Swansea 1.10.23 5'11" 13st 4lbs
8–3 (9–3) (Wales 38 1947–57, 1 War–time 1946)
Tawe Utd. Swansea T. (1942–43, pro Dec 1944) war guest for Clapton O. Aston Villa (Dec 1947 £10,000 plus Tommy Dodds) Sunderland (Oct 1950 £29,500) Cardiff C. (Nov 1953 £30,000) P.S.V. Eindhoven (1957) Npt. (June 1960 £1,000) Romford (Mar 1961 to cs 1961)

Fiery, physical centre–forward, probably the greatest that Wales has produced. The son of a Swansea referee, Trevor started as left–back and was a Schoolboy international at cricket and soccer. After being passed over by Arsenal and Cardiff C. he joined the Royal Artillery and guested for Swansea and Clapton O., scoring 41 goals in 1945–46. Then followed a legendary career as an international personality, which saw him the costliest player in the country. A 3 year ban, related to under the counter payments resulted in him playing in Holland, but he returned for a short spell with the County, where an Achilles tendon injury prevented him from playing regularly. Trevor has since worked in the car sales business.

FORWARD, Frederick John.

b. Croydon 8.9.1899   d. Bournemouth mid 1977 5'8" 11st 0lbs
101–11 (114–12)
Croydon Brighton Railway Crystal Palace (amateur, pro Sept 1921) Npt. (June 1924) Portsmouth (Feb 1927, fee) Hull C. (July 1932) Bath C. (trial Aug 1933) Margate (Oct 1933)

A talented and versatile forward, who enjoyed a long and successful career. After three years with Palace reserves he came to Somerton Park and immediately became a first team regular. Fred was snapped up by Southampton and played in their 1929 F.A. Cup winning side, as well as scoring in the final game of their promotion season. He also appeared in Pompey's record 9–1 win versus Notts Co. along with Fred Cook and Ted Smith. Later he was in the Hull team which won the Division III (North) Championship.

FOX, William Victor.

b. Middlesbrough 8.1.1898 d. Withington, Manchester 17.2.1949 5'9" 11st 9lbs
37-0 (41-0)
Tees-side Juniors South Bank Juniors wartime for South Bank, East End and Bradford P.A. Middlesbrough (c. 1918) Wolverhampton W. (Oct 1924) Npt (Aug 1930) Exeter C. (Sept 1931) Manchester Central (Nov 1931) Nantwich (Aug 1932)

Victor, who had been a prominent schoolboy footballer, was a spoiling full-back, who first impressed with Bradford Park Avenue and then had long spells with Middlesbrough and Wolves. He was a regular in the County side which lost Football League status, in 1931. He was equally well-known as Worcestershire's opening batsman from 1923 to 1932. The son of a well-known Northern cricket pro, Victor scored 1,000 runs in a season three times and was pro to Abertillery C.C. during his time with County.

FRASER, Gordon.

b. Elgin 27.11.43 5'8" 10st 12lbs
11-2 (14-2)
Rothes Forres Mech. Cardiff C. (Jan 1961) Millwall (Sept 1963) Elgin C. (June 1964) Barry T. (June 1965) Npt. (Aug 1966 £500) Weymouth (June 1967)

Forward who never really made the grade at Football League level. Although Scottish, Gordon came up through Cardiff's reserve teams. He played on in non-League football after a short spell with County, but was advised to give up the game because of an ankle injury in 1968.

FREESTONE, Roger.

b. Caerleon 19.8.68 6'2" 13st 3lbs
13-0 (16-0) (Wales under 21 1 1990)
Npt. (YTS, pro Mar 1986) Chelsea (Mar 1987 £90,000+) Npt. (loan Mar 1987) Swansea C. (loan Aug 1989) Hereford Utd. (loan Mar 1990) Swansea C.(loan Sep 1991)

A magnificently built goalkeeper, with a safe pair of hands. He was a youngster with potential when with the County, although in a struggling side. Roger trained at Watford in 1986 and the following year moved to Chelsea in a life-saving deal for County. He was supposed to stay at Somerton Park on loan until the end of the season, but was soon recalled to Stamford Bridge, where he played in Division I.

FROWEN, John.

b. Treharris 11.10.31 5'11" 11st 9lbs
67-0 (77-0)
Tredomen Nelson Cardiff C. (May 1951) Bristol C. (Aug 1958) Npt. (Mar 1963) Merthyr T. (Jan 1966 p/coach)

Competent full-back or centre-half, who had a long career, but was often a reserve, especially in Cardiff's First Division days. Although in his thirties when joining County, John had three years here before being released to join Merthyr. He is now in business in South Wales being a Director of Pipe Line and Metal Coatings Ltd.

FRY, Keith Frederick.

b. Cardiff 11.4.41 5'8" 10st 3lbs
58–2 (65–2)
Npt. (amateur, pro Oct 1958) Notts Co. (Feb 1962) Merthyr T. (cs 1964) Chesterfield (trial Jan 1966) Merthyr T. Latrobe (Brisbane) Hakoah (Sydney)(1966) Merthyr Bridgend T. (Oct 1971)

Outside–right, who had been a Welsh Schools international and joined County's groundstaff from Cardiff local football. Keith had some ability, but was often in the reserves. He had a spell with Notts Co. and played in their Centenary game (the first such achievement by a Football League team). He later emigrated to Australia.

GARDNER, Fred Charles.

b. Bell Green, Coventry 4.6.22 d. Coventry 12.1.79 5'10" 11st 6lbs
4–2 (4–2)
Birmingham C. (1940) war guest for Northampton T., Coventry C. and Notts Co. Coventry C. (Sept 1946) Npt (May 1949) Rugby T. (Aug 1950) Lockheed Leamington

Inside–forward, who was better known as a cricketer. Although scoring twice on his debut for County (versus Millwall 24.9.49) he proved disappointing and went into non–League football, being later trainer-coach to Lockheed Leamington. Fred was a defensive opener at cricket, with a highest score of 215. In 1953 he scored a century versus the Australians, the first Warwickshire player to do so and he was an umpire from 1962 to 1965.

GARDNER, James.

b. London 5'6" 11st 7lbs
13–12 (13–12)
Walton (Felixstowe) Ipswich T. (?cs 1921) Yeovil T. (cs 1922) Bristol R. (cs 1925) Clapton O. (cs 1926) Lovells Ath. (Sept 1929 to 1933) Npt. (loan Feb 1933) Lovells Ath. (cs 1933) Basle (Switzerland)

Jimmy, a snap scorer and terrier in attack, started with Ipswich in their amateur days and went on to sign professional for Yeovil. He was the top Orient reserve scorer in 1927–28 and leading marksman in the Welsh League in 1931–32, having scored 60 during the previous season for Lovells. He scored almost a goal a game in his short stay at Somerton, during which the Supporters' Club paid part of his wages. He played for the Welsh League versus the Irish Free State League in 1930–31 and later had a period in Switzerland.

GARDNER, James Robert ("Rufus").

b. West Hartlepools 5.3.05 d. Watford mid 1977 5'10" 11st 0lbs
3–0 (3–0)
Shotton Hartlepools Utd. (cs 1926, amateur) Middlesbrough (June 1927) Charlton Ath. (1929) Aldershot (1929 to 1931) Belfast Celtic (1931–32) Npt. (July 1932 to 1933) ?Lancaster T.

A red–haired half–back, who was around a long time without making any impact at Football League level. He played around 100 games for Aldershot in their non–League days and appeared in their record 11–1 win versus Kingstonians. He was sacked by them for getting drunk at a New Year's party and being outstandingly incompetent on the pitch at Folkestone the next day (the team let in 7), but was later allowed to stay until the end of the season. He was only selected for three first team games with the County.

GAUGHAN, William Bernard

b. Devonport 20.1.1892 d. Cardiff 25.1.1956
5'7" 10st 5lbs
94–7 (149–14)
Cardiff C. (1912–13) Manchester C. (1913–14)
Npt. (cs 1919 to cs 1924)

Billy scored on his Cardiff City debut, a friendly versus Treharris in March 1912 and was good enough to play ten times for Manchester City's first team. He then joined the Army, becoming a lieutenant in the Welsh Regiment and serving in France and Salonika. An impressive left winger with great speed, Billy's reluctance to head the ball led to the rumour that he had a metal plate in his head. He was a fully qualified accountant.

GIBBINS, Roger Graeme.

b. Enfield 6.9.55 5'10" 11st 12lbs
79–9 (106–14)
Tottenham H. (app., pro May 1971) Oxford Utd. (Aug 1975) Norwich C. (June 1976) New England Teamen (Mar 1978 £60,000) Cambridge Utd. (Sept 1979) Cardiff C. (Aug 1982) Swansea C. (mid 1985–86, p/exchange) Npt. (Aug 1986) Torquay Utd. (Mar 1988) Npt. (Jan 1989 £10,000) Cardiff C. (Mar 1989, non–contract)

A very useful, competitive and versatile player. The son of the old Spurs player Eddie Gibbins, Roger was an England Schoolboy international and played for Spurs in the F.A. Youth Cup Final. Before coming to Somerton Park he had joined Swansea in exchange for Chris Marustik. He did a good job for County, playing in every League game of the 1986–87 season, and was made player–coach at the end of the season. He left for Torquay when the club sold off their first team squad and helped them to reach the end of season play–offs. He rejoined County just before they were wound up, then surprisingly re-established himself in the Cardiff City Football League side, where be became captain.

GILES, David C.

b. Cardiff 21.9.56 5'7" 10st 5lbs
28–1 (46–3) (Wales 12 1980–83, Under–21 4 1977–83)
Cardiff C. (app., pro Sept 1974) Wrexham (Dec 1978 £30,000) Swansea C. (Nov 1979 £70,000) Orient (loan Nov 1981) Crystal Palace (Mar 1982 p/exchange) Birmingham C. (loan 1984) Npt. (loan Oct 1984, full-time Nov 1984) Cardiff C. (1985, at first on trial) Barry T. Merthyr T. Npt. (Jan 1989 £1,000+) Sully (Mar 1989) Merthyr T. AFC Cardiff Cardiff Civil Service p/coach 1990–91.

Versatile, livewire player who can play anywhere from forward to full-back. He is the only player to play and score for all four Welsh Football

League clubs. David was in the Swansea City side promoted to Division I and they turned down a £450,000 bid for him. He was moving home to Cardiff when he joined County, where he made little impact, but he later made a come-back with the City. He rejoined the County just before they were wound up. David is the elder brother of Paul.

GILES, Paul A.

b. Cardiff 21.2.61 5'7" 10st 4lbs
28-2 (38-4) (Wales under-21 3 1982)
Cardiff C. (Juniors 1977, pro June 1979) Exeter C. (at first on loan Mar 1982) Excelsior (Holland) Plymouth A. (non-contract) SVV (Holland) Npt. (non-contract Dec 1984) Merthyr T. (Nov 1985) Npt. (Mar 1987, pro May 1987) Merthyr T. (1987)

Like his brother David, Paul is a player of definite ability, capable of beating a man on the touchline, but is prone to inconsistency. Although he did play some good games during his second spell at Somerton, he was given a free transfer because his style did not fit in with Eastick's ideas and rejoined Merthyr.

GILL, Kenneth J.

b. Swindon 5.11.55
12-1 (22-3)
Swindon T. Devizes Frome Forest Green Rovers Npt. (Sept 1985 non-contract) Swindon Ath. (cs 1989)

Versatile player, who operated on the wing for County and had the ability to beat a man. He joined as a non-contract player, as he had a good job, being a quantity surveyor and a Director of Longs Building Co. (Bath). Eventually Kenny left, as football was just a hobby.

GILLIGAN, James M.

b. Hammersmith 24.1.64 6'2" 13st 2lbs
4-1 (5-1)
Watford (App., pro Aug 1981) Lincoln C. (loan Oct 1983) Grimsby T. (June 1985 £120,000) Npt. (loan Feb 1987) Swindon T. (Mar 1987) Lincoln C. (Mar 1987 £12,000) Cardiff C. (cs 1987 £17,500) Portsmouth (Oct 1989 £215,000) Swansea C. (Aug 1990 £175,000)

Big, strong striker, who partnered Luther Blissett at Watford. Although he was an England Youth player, he had little chance to show his ability during his short loan spell at Somerton Park. Jimmy was with Lincoln when they were relegated from the Football League and moved on to Ninian Park, where he became something of a folk hero, scoring many goals including one on his debut versus Leyton Orient. Cardiff turned down a Bradford City offer of £330,000 in 1989, but 6 months later Ashurst accepted a lower fee to strengthen his struggling side. He has since returned to South Wales.

GITTINS, James.

b. West Bromwich 8.10.1900 d. West Bromwich 8.11.75 5'7" 10st 7lbs
256-65 (309-83)

Npt. (Jan 1920) Shrewsbury T. (July 1933) Brierley Hill Alliance (July 1934)

Although born in the Midlands, Jimmy was very much a club product. "General Gittins" was a cunning attacker, a hoodwinker of defences. An elegant player with an "educated" right foot, he could score goals from thirty yards and once scored 6 in a reserve game. He had a tremendously long career with County, captaining the side at times, and was part-timer being a supervisor at Braithwaite's.

GLIDDEN, Sydney.

b. Cox-Lodge 30.1.08 5'9" 11st 4lbs
4-2 (6-2)
Cox-lodge Sunderland West End W.B.A. (Nov 1925) Halifax T. (June 1928) Worcester C. (Nov 1928) Doncaster R. (trial Aug 1929) York C. (trial Sept 1929) Peterborough (Jan 1930) Npt. (July 1930) Loughborough Corries (Aug 1931) Larne (Aug 1932) Wigan Ath. (Aug 1933) Blyth Spartans (Oct 1933)

Forward, brother of the famous Tommy of W.B.A. and Gilbert (Sun-

derland, Port Vale and Reading). Syd was a bright boy and useful player, but preferred the bright lights to football. He ended up having more clubs than Arnold Palmer. He had a string of non-league clubs, finally Colwyn Bay Utd. (player-manager July 1936) and then Hereford Utd., long before their Football League days.

GODDARD, Howard J.

b. Over Wallop, Hants 10.5.57 5'8" 10st 6lbs
97-40 (117-46)
AFC Bournemouth (App. Aug 1972, pro July 1974) Swindon T. (June 1976) Npt. (Aug 1977) Blackpool (loan Sept 1981) Bournemouth (Dec 1981) Aldershot (loan Aug 1982) Finland Andover Sliema Wanderers (Malta)(c 1984) OSS20 (1985) Vivihlem

Very talented striker, who made his Football League debut at 15. He had a great shot, a good head and speed, but his potential was marred by a broken leg at Portmouth, which forced him to miss the second half of Newport's promotion season and resulted in his release. Howard, who was voted the Player of the Year in 1977–78, afterwards scored on his debut for Bournemouth, whom he helped to promotion, and Aldershot. He then played abroad and has played in Holland since 1985.

GODFREY, Brian Cameron.

b. Flint 1.5.40 5'9" 11st 11lbs
117–14 (133–16) (Wales 3 1964–65, Under–23 1 1962)

Flint Alexandra (1955) Everton (amateur, pro May 1958) Scunthorpe Utd. (June 1960) Preston N.E. (Oct 1963 £8,000) Aston Villa (Sept 1967) Bristol R. (May 1971 p/exchange) Npt. (June 1973 £10,000) Portland Timbers (on loan 1975) Bath C. (1976 p/manager)

A stocky half–back with a powerful kick. He made only one Football League appearance for Everton, but was reserve to Preston's F.A. Cup Final team of 1964 and captained Aston Villa versus Spurs in the 1971 Football League Cup Final. Brian became the County's record buy and missed few games over three seasons. He scored a hat–trick versus Workington and made his 500th Football League appearance versus Bradford City in 1975. He was noted for his strong free kicks, though the ball was apt to end up in Cromwell Road. He became player–manager of Bath City, who narrowly missed election to the Football League and managed Exeter City when they beat Leicester C. and Newcastle in the F.A. Cup. He took over at Weymouth in 1984 and is now Manager of Gloucester City.

GORDON, Peter John.

b. Northampton 21.5.32 5'9" 11st 8lbs
8–1 (9–1)
Norwich C. (Dec 1949) Watford (July 1958) Exeter C. (July 1960) Npt. (July 1962, with Sullivan for £1,000) Poole T. (July 1963)

Right–sided forward or half–back, who graduated from Northampton local football and played over 100 Football League games for Norwich, where he laid on goals for Ralph Hunt. Peter later became coach at Harlepools, Southend and Northampton. He left football in the early 1970's and has, in recent years, resided in Ipswich, where he works for insurance brokers.

GRAHAM, Harry.

b. Belfast c 1902 5'7" 10st 7lbs
6–1 (6–1)
Pill Utd. Npt. (c 1921) Lovells Ath. (c 1923)

Very good left winger with an effective centre. He was an amateur, who played a few Football League games in 1922 and around 50 reserve games over 2 seasons. He played in the 1923–24 Welsh Amateur Cup Final and was still playing for Lovells in the late 1920's.

GRAHAM, Leslie.

b. Flixton, Manchester 14.5.24 5'8" 10st 6lbs
160–56 (179–62)
Blackburn R. (Apr 1947) Npt. (Feb 1953 £2,500) Watford (June 1955 fee) Npt. (Sept 1957 £1,250) Cambridge C. (July 1959) Merthyr T. (1959–60 p/manager)

Talented inside–forward, who had two spells with County in the 1950's and was later Manager. Les was a skilful ball player, who could score many goals. He got his chance in football due to a Major in India, who was impressed with his displays and asked Blackburn to send out amateur forms. He had played over 100 games for Rovers in Division I and II when joining County with Wharton. After two years with Watford Les returned to Somerton Park, dropping back to wing–half. He also had spells as Coach and Manager with Merthyr and Cwmbran, as well as scouting for Spurs.

GRANT, Alec F.

b. Camerton Peasedown, Somerset 11.8.16 6'0" 12st 11lbs
20–0 (25–0)
Bury Aldershot (cs 1938) Leicester C. wartime games for Aldershot, Nottingham Forest, Derby C. and Mansfield T. Derby C. (Nov 1946) Npt. (Nov 1948) Leeds Utd. (Aug 1949) York C. (Mar 1950) Worksop (July 1950) Corby T. (July 1953)

Talented goalkeeper, who played a prominent part in the 1948–49 F.A. Cup run. Alec had already had a long career and was studying for a P.E. Diploma at Loughborough College, allegedly reading poetry and Classical books on away trips and at half–time. His contract was cancelled in August 1949, when he failed to obtain a Newport teaching post and he became reserve to Searson at Leeds.

GRANVILLE, Norman Trevor.

b. Newport 25.11.19 5'7" 10st 6lbs
1–0 (24–4)
Raith R. (1944–45) Cliftonville (1945) Npt. (1945) Exeter C. (Oct 1946) Gillingham (1949) Gloucester C. (1951) Llanelly (1953) Nelson Chepstow T.

A local forward, whose football career was marred by the War, during which he spent five years in the Royal Navy. He mainly performed in the war–time League (South) for County, then left for Exeter with Billy Owen. He achieved the unusual feat of playing in all four home counties inside 3 seasons. Trevor is still living in Newport.

GREEN, Philip ("Peeny")

b. Cardiff 30.10.57 5'11" 12st 12lbs
11-2 (18-2)
Cardiff Corries trials with Exeter C., Cardiff C. & Blackburn R. Barry T. Merthyr T. Bridgend T. Barry T. Npt. (Mar 1984, non-contract) Barry T. Tung Sing (Hong Kong) Qatar Ton Pentre Npt. (Mar 1987, non-contract) Tung Sing Ton Pentre Parlinini (Cyprus) Merthyr T. (Sept 1987) Newport AFC (Mar 1991 £3,500)

A high–scoring forward of some ability, who made a late start in League football with Newport County. He was signed on a three month trial, but left because of the pressures of the family business. After a fair amount of globe–trotting he settled down with the Merthyr Vauxhall Conference side, scoring almost a hundred goals for them. Phil, who now works for the "Western Mail, was the first player to be bought by Newport AFC.

GREEN, Roger.

b. Cardiff 20.9.44
1-0 (2-0)
Cardiff C. (Welsh League 1964–65) Barry T. Npt. (amateur Aug 1971, pro Jan 1972) Cardiff Corries (1973)

Defender, who failed to establish himself in the County first team and spent most of his career in Welsh non–League football.

GREEN, Thomas Foster ("Tucker").

b. Easington 24.8.07 d. Easington late 1972 5'9" 10st 0lbs
57-17 (65-24)

Easington Colliery ex–Schoolboys Easington Rovers (1930) Easington Colliery (1931) Npt. (cs 1932) Easington Colliery (1936)

A versatile forward, who had been scoring 50 goals a season in the Wearside League before arriving at Somerton Park. Tommy scored on his debut versus Coventry C. 17.9.32 and spent four seasons with Newport before returning home.

GRIFFIN, James Henry.

b. Newport late 1898 d. Newport 27.5.74 5'9" 11st 9lbs
76-0 (127-0)
Oak Villa Npt. (cs 1919) Stockport Co. (May 1923) Ebbw Vale

Local product, a determined left-back with a fearless tackle and a sure kick under pressure. Jimmy gave good service to the County and, after a short time in the North, returned to South Wales, appearing in the Welsh Cup Final. He was a pigeon fancier and lived close to Somerton Park.

GRIFFITHS, Arthur A.

b. Tonypandy 5'7" 10st 7lbs
1-0 (3-1)
Torquay Utd. (c 1932) Npt. (July 1933) Barry (July 1934) Glentoran Rochdale (Aug 1938) Stoke C. (Nov 1938)

Arthur was a forward, who had a few Football League clubs, but was mainly a reserve. After playing in Ireland he had a short spell with Rochdale. He moved on to Stoke, where he made 4 Division 1 appearances before War intervened.

GRIFFITHS, Kenneth George.

b. Cardiff 11.11.25 d. London 17.2.85 5'8" 10st 0lbs
14-6 (19-7)
Cardiff C. (Aug 1939 to Apr 1943, then post-war) Royal Navy, assisting Torquay Utd. & Plymouth A. Metters (Sydney) Swansea T. Torquay Utd. (Jan 1948) Distillery (Sept 1949) Npt. (Sept 1949) Barry T. (Nov 1950) Bridgewater

The Welsh Schoolboy captain, Kenny was an inside-forward who could lay on chances for his centre-forward. He became Cardiff's youngest professional at 13 and played in Australia whilst serving in the Royal Navy. Before arriving a Somerton Park he had a brief stay in Ireland, but left because of accommodation difficulties. He was a well-known baseballer with Splott U.S. and Wales. In later life Kenny was a Wholesaler, with two shops. He was travelling home from the Bahamas, when he collapsed and died on leaving the plane.

GRIFFITHS, Wyn Rhys.

b. Blaengwynfi 17.10.19 6'0" 12st 6lbs
3-0 (3-0)
Gwynfi Cardiff C. (1941) war-time with Derby Co. Arsenal & Worcester C. Npt. (Nov 1946) Cardiff C. (amateur 1947) Npt. (1951) Lovells Ath.

Brilliant amateur goalkeeper, whose best years were confined, unfortunately, to the war. He played numerous war-time games for Cardiff and appeared in the Arsenal versus Dynamo game, though he was kicked in the head after 15 minutes and replaced at half-time. Wyn also represented the Welsh Services. His three Football League appearances for the County came in an injury crisis, when he had been out of the game for a few seasons and was practising as a vet in Blaengwynfi. Wyn played polo for ten years, now breeds and races horses and has watched almost 50 Derbys, including every one since 1944. He has broadcast regularly on Welsh language radio and television and had his life story filmed for TV.

GROVES, George
(real name LUCAS)("Pitt").

b. Wolverhampton 8.10.1894 d. Newport 1963
5'8" 11st 6lbs
100-4 (192+-12+)
Oak Villa Lysaght's Amateurs Npt. (cs 1912)
Llanelly (cs 1913) Abertillery Llanelly Npt.
(cs 1914 to 1924, inc. war-time) Taunton (5
years) Watchett (2 years) Newport Excelsiors
(Sept 1931) retired c. 1933

Despite the different surname (caused
by his mother's second marriage),
George was the father of Billy Lucas
and also brother of the famous
Wolves' captain Albert Groves, who
played for the earlier Newport F.C.

George was a versatile and consistent
player, at home in the half-back line
or the attack. He was very much a
club product, beginning as an amateur in their first ever season. Not
long after receiving a benefit in 1923
he dropped into non-League football,
which included a five year stint at
Taunton. He appeared in the 1914
Welsh Cup Final and played for the
Welsh League in 1923-24. George
was also a Powderhall sprinter. In
later life he was steward of the
Maesglas Working Men's Club.

GUSCOTT, Raymond M.

b. Newport 18.11.57 5'9" 11st 0lbs
12-1 (20-1)
Clifton Ath. (1971) Bristol R. (App. 1973, pro
Nov 1975) Northampton T. (trial c July 1977)
Minehead (Sept 1977) Torquay Utd. (trial Sept
1977) Npt. (trial Oct 1977, pro Dec 1977)
Minehead (loan, then full-time Sept 1978)
Barry T. (Jan 1982) Caerleon (1982) Cinder-
ford (cs 1984) Ellwood

A Welsh Schools international forward educated at St. Julian's, Ray
was expecting to play for the
County's Welsh League side when
signed, but was pitched into the
Football League. He struggled
somewhat and was given a free
transfer in September, 1978, playing
on for many years in non-League
football.

GWYTHER, Bertie Perseus.

b. Merthyr 22.8.06 d. Cardiff 29.10.81
1-0 (1-0)
Cardiff Corries Roath Villa made Football
League appearance for Npt. (1925-26) and
Merthyr T. (1926-27) was also with Cardiff C.
in 1933

An amateur footballer good enough
to play in the Football League. Educated at Monkton House in Cardiff,
he became articled to this brother and
then founded his own firm. He also
played baseball for Penylan.

GWYTHER, David.

b. Birmingham 6.12.48 5'10" 13st 4lbs
85-29 (147-41) (Wales Under-23 2 1972)
Swansea T. (1966, pro Jan 1967) Halifax T.
(Aug 1973 £12,000) Rotherham Utd. (Feb
1976) Npt. (Dec 1979 £40,000) Crewe A.
(loan Jan 1982) Gloucester C. (cs 1983) Port
Talbot (July 1984) Npt. (Mar 1985, non-
contract) Briton Ferry Port Talbot

Useful goalscoring forward, popular
with the crowd for his endeavour and
humour. Dave had enjoyed eleven
seasons of regular League Football
when becoming County's record signing and had gone on the Welsh
F.A.'s tour of New Zealand in 1971.
He played in the County's promotion
game and Welsh Cup Final win and
scored the club's first goal in Europe.
Later he re-signed on a non-contact
basis in a crisis. He is now working
in the family painting and decorating
business.

HACKETT, Ernest.

b. Royston, Herts. c 1908 5'9" 12st 0lbs
4-0 (4-0)
Frickley Colliery Wolverhampton W. (Oct.
1930) Coventry C. (cs 1931) Npt. (July 1932)
Frickley Colliery (Aug 1934)

A goalkeeper, who never succeeded
in establishing himself as a regular
despite having three Football League
clubs.

HADDON, Henry Llewellyn (Harry).

b. Cardiff 8.4.23 5'6" 11st 5lbs
10-1 (10-1)
Cardiff C. (1944) Bangor C. Npt. (Jan 1947)
Bristol R. (Nov 1948) Trowbridge T. (Aug
1949, later p/manager)

Forward, who played for Cardiff
reserves whilst in the Royal Navy.
Although his first team opportunities
were limited at Somerton Park, Harry
made almost 50 Welsh League appearances. He became one of the most
popular Trowbridge players, and later
manager. He was the first Welshman
to gain a full F.A. coaching award.
From 1960, Harry was a teacher in
Bradford-On-Avon until his recent
retirement.

HAINES, Donald Noah.

b. Llanwonno 23.9.25 5'8" 11st 0lbs
78-1 (90-1)
Bournemouth (pro Oct 1948) Yeovil T. (cs
1949) Npt. (Dec 1950 £250) Abergavenny Th.
(1954)

Solid and reliable full-back, remembered for his partnership with Len Staples. Don spent three years at Somerton Park before dropping down into non-League football. He is the younger brother of Mervyn.

HAINES, Mervyn John.

b. Llanwonno 2.5.23 5'4" 10st 4lbs
14-2 (14-2)
Swansea T. Bournemouth Hereford Utd. (1948-49) Yeovil T. (cs 1949) Npt. (May 1950) Gloucester C. (cs 1952) Llanelli Bargoed Utd.

Little winger, who played fairly regularly during his first few months with County, but then dropped into the reserves. Later Mervyn did a tour of Welsh League sides, ending up with Abercynon and Tynte.

HALE, Alfred.

b. Waterford 28.8.39 5'6" 10st 6lbs
34-21 (38-24) (Eire 13 1962-72 & Amateur)
St. Joseph's Juniors Waterford Aston Villa (June 1960 £4,500) Doncaster R. (July 1962) Npt. (July 1965 for L.Sheffield) Waterford (July 1966 £3,000) St. Patrick's Ath. (1975)

Fair-haired centre-forward, whose goal-scoring exploits lit up the 1965-66 season. He came to the mainland from Ireland, like his brother Dixie, who played for Swansea and Barrow. After a few first team games for Aston Villa. Alfie played over 100 for Doncaster and scored 4 goals in their record 10-0 win versus Darlington. He almost joined Oldham, but came instead to Somerton, where injury delayed his start. He later returned home and could not be tempted back. Alfie became player-manager of Waterford and played versus Manchester United in the European Cup.

HALL, George W.E.

b. Worksop late 1912 5'9" 11st 7lbs
28-0 (31-0)
Worksop T. Sheffield Utd. (c 1932) Coventry C. (cs 1935) Npt. (cs 1936) Bristol C. (May 1937)

Non-stop, spoiling half-back, an exponent of the third back game. George made himself a first team player at Newport, although he made no Football League appearances at Coventry and only one subsequently in two seasons at Ashton Gate.

HAMER, Kevin.

b. Merthyr 2.2.69 5'11" 11st 2lbs
15-1 (22-1)
Watford (YTS 1985) Npt (YTS July 1985, later pro) Merthyr T. (Sept 1988) Abergavenny Th.

Solid central defender, who joined as a YTS trainee and became Captain of the youth and reserve teams. Kevin played rugby for Merthyr Schools and obtained Welsh Schoolboy soccer caps. He was injured in the 1987-88 season. He returned at the end of the season, but left early in the County's first Vauxhall Conference season, as he was unable to obtain a first team place.

HAMILTON, Ian.

b. Bristol 12.9.40 5'9" 11st 0lbs
11-2 (13-2)
Bristol R. (1956, pro Jan 1958) Exeter C. (loan
Nov 1967) Npt. (July 1968 to May 1970)

Forward who had a long career with
Bristol Rovers, but underwent knee
and cartilage operations and never
found his form at Somerton Park.
He never made a first team appearance during his second season and
was given a free transfer. Ian is a
qualified toolmaker.

HAMMILL, John (Jack).

b. Irvine, nr Kilmarnock 8.1.24 5'11" 12st 0lbs
12-0 (12-0)
Arbroath   Npt. (loan Mar 1947) Llanelly
(1948)

Scottish wing-half, who had a brief
spell with County just after the War.
At the time he was serving with the
R.A.F. in Barry and his debut was
delayed by technicalities.

HAMPTON, Joseph Harry
("Happy Harry").

b. Wellington 21.4.1885 d. Rhyl 15.3.63 5'8"
10st 10lbs
14-2 (16-4) (England 4 1913-14)
Shifnal Juniors Wellington T. Aston Villa
(April 1904) war guest with Fulham, Reading
and Stoke Birmingham (Feb 1920) Npt. (Sept
1922 to cs 1923) Wellington T. (Jan 1924)

A very famous centre-forward, who
joined the County at the end of his
career. He was a dashing, fearless
player, although he was quiet and
sensible off the pitch. Harry was a
splendid track athlete from 100 yards
to a mile and would use his acceler-
ation to charge unsuspecting goalkeepers into the net. He scored a
remarkable number of goals in the
Birmingham League in 1903-04 and
was signed by Villa, where he scored
215 League goals, which is still their
record. He won F.A. Cup Winner's
medals in 1905 (scoring in every
round) and 1912, a League Championship medal in 1910 and a Division II medal with Birmingham in
1921, after being badly gassed in the
War. Harry had a short spell as
Preston coach in 1925 and afterwards
lived for many years in Rhyl, where
he had catering interests.

HANCOCK, Michael.

b. Cardiff 17.2.54 5'10" 11st 0lbs
51-2 (67-2) (Wales Amateur 3 1972-73)

Cardiff College of Education Npt. (amateur 1972, pro Aug 1973) Barry T. (July 1976) Bridgend T. (Mar 1981) Aberaman

Stylish, athletic looking defender, who began as a Schoolboy international. He was spotted by Graham Reynolds and spent three years at Somerton Park having made his debut versus Crewe as a Schoolboy. Somewhat injury prone, he had cartilage trouble, a broken jaw and fractured skull. He was a baseballer for Grange Catholics.

HARPER, Robert.

b. Glasgow 6.6.20 d. Scotland 1980 5'5" 9st 8lbs
114–12 (129–16)
Partick Th. Ayr Utd. (1944) Huddersfield T. (1945) Npt. (Oct 1946) Southend Utd. (June 1950 fee) Linfield (c 1952)

Fast left winger, a bundle of tricks who was a regular for the County in the immediate post–war period. Bobby played in the 1948–49 F.A. Cup run. Later he played for Linfield. He used to make the Stran-raer–Larne ferry crossing and was one of the few survivors when the "Princess Elizabeth" sank in 1953.

HARPER, Thomas.

b. Marsden late 1903 5'8" 10st 7lbs
23–5 (26–5)
South Shields (c 1926–27) Npt (July 1927) Whitburn (June 1929) Accrington S. (Nov 1929) Marsden Whitburn Villa

A North–Easterner, whose only Football League appearances were at Newport. He played on the right wing and managed to find the net on a few occasions, but picked up an early injury in 1928–29.

HARRIS, Brian.

b. Bebington 16.5.35 5'9" 11st 10lbs
85–0 (97–2)
Lever Bros., Port Sunlight Everton (amateur, pro Jan 1954) Cardiff C. (Oct 1966 £15,000) Npt (July 1971) Chepstow

Supremely stylish wing–half, who began as a direct winger and went on to become one of the best uncapped players of his day. Brian spent over ten years with Everton, playing in their 1962–63 Championship side, as well as the 1966 F.A. Cup Final team. After a successful spell at Ninian Park, with numerous European games, he became a Newport player, then Assistant Manager in February 1972 and Manager in January 1974. Later he resigned because he was disillusioned He went to manage a Chepstow pub, afterwards having spells as Cardiff coach and Ipswich coach.

HARRIS, Derek Henry ("Harry").

b. Magor 2.11.33 5'11" 12st 0lbs
174–58 (191–69)
Npt. ("A" side 1949) Chepstow T. (1951) Undy Utd. Npt. (pro Sept 1954) Portsmouth (July 1958 £10,000) Npt. (loan Oct 1970) retired 1971

Harry began as a 16 year old in County's "A" side, his career being interrupted through National Service in the West Indies with the Royal Welch Fusiliers. He signed professional in 1954. A goal–scoring inside–left, he scored a hat–trick at Millwall 12.11.55 and was selected to represent the Division III (South) in 1957–58. He was sold to Portsmouth, where he was converted to wing–half and went on to play almost 400 Football League games. In 1961–62 he appeared in their

Division III Championship side. He rejoined County on loan during their dark days of 1971 and at the end of the season retired. Harry returned to run a shop in Magor.

HARRIS, George Alfred.

b. Lambeth 10.6.40 5'7" 11st 7lbs
31–8 (34–9)
Tottenham H. Fulham Woking Chelsea (loan) Npt. (July 1961) Watford (Apr 1962 £2,000) Reading (July 1966 £3,500) Cambridge Utd. (Oct 1969, with Colin Meldrum for £4,000)

George was a forward who played in the County's ill–fated 1961–62 season. Having played for South London Schoolboys and twice for London, he guested for Chelsea while with Woking. He displayed reasonably good form at Somerton Park and scored a hat–trick versus Bristol City 16.10.61, but he was allowed to leave and later beat Reading's record score for a winger. Afterwards George became Cambridge United's record signing, scoring a hat–trick on his debut and playing in their first Football League game. He later joined Maidenhead United and became Manager.

HARRIS, Peter.

b. Neath 9.8.53 5'7" 11st 0lbs
20-1 (36-1)
Npt. (App. Oct 1968, pro Aug 1971) Bridgend T. Briton Ferry (1974)

Peter was a nippy midfielder, who often came on as a substitute. He began with the youth side and showed some ability, but eventually moved down into non–League football.

HARVEY, John H. (Jack).

b. Lanchester 6.4.15 5'9" 11st 0lbs
2-0 (2-0)
Manchester C. Bradford P.A. (May 1936) Bristol C. Npt. (cs 1938 to April 1939)

A forward who was never more than a reserve at any of his clubs. He was one of the few players to be freed at the end of County's promotion season.

HAWKINS, Dennis Ronald.

b. Swansea 22.10.47 5'9" 11st 6lbs
9-1 (12-1) (Wales Under-23 6 1967-70)
Leeds Utd. (App. Oct 1964) Shrewsbury T. (Oct. 1968 £10,000+) Chester (loan Sept 1970) Workington (loan Mar 1972) Npt. (May 1972)

Shrewsbury T. Telford Utd. (July 1973) Nuneaton Borough (1975)

Dennis was a Welsh Schoolboy international, whose brother Peter was also a professional. He was a strong, fast, hard shooting player, who joined Leeds straight from school. His good early season form for Newport soon deserted him and he decided to move on.

HAYCOX, John H. (Jack).

b. Cheltenham 1910 5'10" 11st 2lbs
13-4 (19-9)
Cheltenham Npt. (c Jan 1934, pro June 1934) Bristol C. (May 1936) Torquay Utd. (Feb 1938) Northampton T. (Nov 1938, for R. Allen, to June 1939)

A high scoring forward, Jack could use both feet equally well. He scored over thirty goals for the reserves during his time at Somerton Park. He underwent a cartilage operation in 1935 and left the club the following year. He continued to find the net at Third Division level, however, and managed to score hat–tricks for Torquay and Northampton in the same season.

HAYES, Michael.

b. Newport 11.9.54 5'11" 12st 0lbs
4-0 (5-0)
Dairy Utd. (Newport and District Lge.) Npt. (cs 1972 amateur)

A well built defensive player, Mike joined the club soon after leaving

Duffryn High School. A non-contract player and reserve, he made a few first team appearances. He was employed at the time as a toolmaker at Standard Telephones.

HAYWARD, Douglas Stanworth.

b. St. George's, Wellington 23.8.20 5'9" 12st 0lbs
259-11 (292-14)
Huddersfield T. (1936-39) war guest with Barry T., Bristol C. and Bury Bristol R. (Sept 1946) Npt. (Nov 1946) Bath C. (July 1956) Frome T. (p/manager June 1958 to June 1966)

Dougie, who was born in the same village as Sir Gordon Richards, was a regular fixture in County's post-war team. After R.A.F. service and a few months at Eastville, he joined County and scored four on his Welsh League debut. Originally a forward he became a left-back and did not leave for ten years. He was a penalty expert. Later Dougie was

player-manager with Frome until injury forced him to retire at 45, and was the unpaid Manager at Weston, where he also played for the cricket club. Dougie was not, as often claimed, a relation of professionals Eric and Basil, lives in Weston.

HAYWARD, William A.

b. Blaina 5'10" 11st 5lbs
4-0 (5-0)
Blaina West Side Npt. (at first on trial, Aug 1924) Clapton O. (1926) Tottenham H. (at first on trial, Aug 1927) Clapton O. (cs 1931 to 1932)

A left half who never seemed to rise above reserve team status, only making 14 Football League appearances in eight seasons.

HELSBY, Thomas.

b. Runcorn 1904 d. Runcorn mid 1961 5'9" 12st 0lbs
10-0 (11-0)
Rhyl Ath. Wigan Borough (cs 1925) Runcorn (1927) Cardiff C. (Apr 1928) Bradford C. (May 1931) Swindon T. (June 1933) Port Vale Hull C. (May 1934) Npt. (June 1935 to 1936)

A well-built half-back, who was capable and reliable. He played in the Football League for the long defunct Wigan Borough side, then won a Welsh Cup Winner's medal with Cardiff C. in 1930. During his pell with Bradford City Tom was told he would never play again because of heart trouble, but was still in the game five years later.

HERRITY, Alan M.

b. Newport 24.10.41 5'10" 10st 10lbs
28-0 (32-0)
Npt. (Dec 1958) Yeovil T. (July 1962)

Alan is the younger brother of Bill. He was a full-back, who played for Newport Boys in 1956 and the Welsh Schoolboys in 1957. He became a pro in 1958. Eventually Alan moved onto Yeovil, where he spent around nine seasons and played over 600 games. He is now employed at the Spencer Works.

HERRITY, William Raymond.

b. Newport 2.9.38 5'8" 10st 7lbs
62-12 (70-17)
Npt. (Juniors 1954, pro May 1957) Worcester C. (June 1963) Bath C. Merthyr T. (1964) Lovells Ath. Barry T. (Oct 1968)

Skilful inside-forward, who played for Newport Schoolboys and the Welsh Youth side. He was very much a local product, arriving at Somerton Park as an amateur. Although he spent a considerable time at the club, his career was badly interrupted by National Service. In his schooldays, Billy was an all-round athlete, excelling at all sports.

HICKIE, William.

b. Larkhall, Lanarks. 9.12.02 d. Lancaster 27.4.57 5'7" 11st 7lbs
24-2 (27-2)
Aberdare Ath. (1924-25) Aberaman (late 1925) Aberdeen (1929) Npt. (July 1930)

Fulham (July 1931) Aldershot (cs 1932) Guildford C. (Aug 1933) Retired May 1936

Popular and much travelled full-back, who played in England, Scotland and Wales. He was a strong tackler, quick to recover. He played in most of the games of the ill-fated 1930-31 season, after which he was released.

HICKMAN, John Edward Arthur W.

b. Golds Hill, West Brom. Mar 1915 d. Birmingham Aug 1985 5'11" 12st 0lbs
71-21 (97-27)
W.B.A. amateurs W.B.A. traders W.B.A. (Nov 1930) Npt. (June 1936 to 1946)

A polished, stylish player. Arthur was a neat dribbler with a good physique, who could score goals. An English Schools "cap", he was only ever a reserve at West Brom., but gradually established himself in the County first team. The War virtually finished his career. He was in the A.R.P. at the start of the War and returned home to the Midlands in November 1939. Although retained in 1947, he never appeared in the League again.

HIGGINS, Andrew Kincade.

b. Gartsherrie 29.4.09 d. Newport 9.11.66 5'8" 11st 0lbs
42-12 (57-17)
Gartsherrie Ath. Stoneyburn Juniors (2 months) Cowdenbeath (1929) Millwall (July 1931) Exeter C. (May 1932 fee) Npt. (June

1933) Notts Co. (Sept 1934) Lille (June 1935) Racing Club d'Arras (p/coach June 1936 to Nov 1938) Npt. (1939 to 1940)

Auburn haired wing–half or inside–forward, who was a regular in his first spell at Newport, but started being barracked and sought a transfer to Notts Co. Afterwards he spent over two years in France until the political situation deteriorated. Andy had a short time with County just before the War, afterwards becoming Assistant Trainer and in later life a regular supporter. The brother–in–law of Albert Wardell, he became an electrician at Stewarts and Lloyds. He was a gentleman on and off the pitch.

HILES, William Robert.

b. Cardiff 28.11.01 d. Newport 24.7.78 5'5"
10st 5lbs
28-4 (31-4)
Lovells Ath. Npt. (cs 1924) Swansea T. (May 1927) Merthyr T. (May 1928) Lovells Ath. (Aug 1928 to the late 1930's)

A diminutive winger, who was a Welsh Junior international. Billy moved to Newport in 1920 to work at the Docks, playing local football and baseball for the Docks. He was later a professional for Lovells Athletic and the County, going on the 1927 Welsh F.A. tour of Ireland. After a fairly short time at Swansea, Billy made a quick return to Lovells, where he worked for 34 years. In the late 1930's he was as good as ever and represented the Welsh

League in Belgium. He was also a capable cricketer.

HILL, John Thomas (Jack).

b. Monkwearmouth c. 1908 5'8" 11st 0lbs
2-0 (2-0)
Jarrow Npt. (July 1928) Darlington (June 1929) West Stanley (Sept 1931) Spennymoor Utd. (mid 1930's)

A young and dashing forward, who was Jarrow's star marksman in 1926–27. During his spell with County Jack was a regular goalscorer for the reserves. After leaving Somerton Park he spent two seasons with Darlington (where he scored 14 goals in 22 Football League appearances) before returning into non–League football.

HILL, Leonard Winston.

b. Caerleon 14.4.42 5'8" 10st 6lbs
360-65 (421-74)
Caerleon Lovells Ath. Npt. (Nov 1962) Swansea T. (July 1970 £4,950) Npt. (Mar 1972 £2,500) Barry T. Minehead

Skilful inside–forward or wing–half, who had been a Wales Youth international. Len became a part–time professional with Lovells Athletic and then spent the rest of his career with the County, apart from an un-successful spell at Swansea. He was part of the furniture at Somerton Park for ten years, playing in some mem-orable games. He was a very keen Glamorgan cricketer. Len, who was later Manager of Cinderford is now a local building contractor.

HILLIER, Ernest John Guy ("Joe").

b. Bridgend 10.4.07 d. Fareham 9.1.79 5'11" 11st 8lbs
22–0 (24–0)
Swansea T. (trial 1926) Bridgend Cardiff C. (Aug 1927) Middlesbrough (Jan 1930) Npt. (June 1936 to cs 1937)

A tall and agile goalkeeper with a good reach, understudy to Farquharson at Ninian Park. He was involved in a multi–player deal with Middlesbrough, along with Jennings and Warren. Joe played fairly regularly in his only season at Somerton and later became a butcher and hotelier at Eastleigh. His son played for Chester and Southampton in the 1950's.

HILLMAN, Alfred George.

b. Newport mid 1892
16–0 (19–0)
Abertillery Npt. (cs 1920 to 1921) Chepstow Standard Institute (Aug 1921)

George was a centre–half from Jeddo Street, who played a fair number of games during the County's first ever Football League season. He was an especially good header of the ball. He also played baseball for Holy Cross Old Boys.

HINSHELWOOD, Walter Alexander A.

b. Battersea 27.10.29 5'6" 10st 13lbs
3–0 (3–0)
Fulham (Oct 1946) Chelsea (Jan 1951 p/exchange) Fulham (May 1951) Reading (Dec 1952) Bristol C. (Feb 1956 £15,000) Millwall (June 1960 (£1,100) Canada (Summer 1961) Npt. (trial Nov 1961) Dartford Canterbury C. (Feb 1962) Sittingbourne (Jan 1963)

A speedy forward, who had a long career in League football at various levels. Wally began as a junior at Fulham, where his progress was affected by Army service. He was something of a veteran by the time he had a short trial at Somerton, after which he was not retained. He is better known today as the father of Martin and Paul.

HINTON, Ivor Francis.

b. Barry early 1897 d. early 1936 5'7" 11st 7lbs

84–0 (88–0)
Barry (c. 1921) Npt. (July 1926) Barry (1929)

Full–back or winger, who gave good service during his three seasons at Somerton Park (being an ever–present in 1972–28) and was a fixture with Barry before and afterwards. He died at an early age.

HODGE, Eric.

b. Edmonton, London 1.6.28 d. 1963 5'10" 12st 8lbs
7–0 (9–0)
Tottenham H. (pro. Sept 1948) Npt. (Aug 1949 to 1950) Bury T.

Fair–haired, spectacular goalkeeper, who had been Spurs' fourth choice. He impressed in the County's 1949 pre–season trial, but finished with the club in January 1950.   Later Eric refereed in the Edmonton and Enfield areas. He died in his 30's.

HODGE, James Oswald.

b. Perth 23.10.26 5'10" 11st 0lbs
1–0 (2–0)
?Plymouth (1945) York C. (amateur) Npt. (Aug 1946 to 1948)

Young full–back, whose only Football League appearance was in a 0–13 defeat at Newcastle, before a crowd of over 50,000. Jimmy played regularly for the reserves the following season.

HODSON, Simeon Paul.

b. Lincoln 5.3.66 5'9" 10st 2lbs
34–1 (42–1)
Notts Co. (App., pro Mar 1984) Charlton Ath. (Mar 1985) Lincoln C. (Jan 1986) Npt. (July 1987) W.B.A. (Mar 1988 £5,000)

Very tough and resolute defender. He had been with Lincoln C. when they were relegated from the Football League and virtually suffered the same fate with the County. Simeon was their most consistent player in their disastrous season and was allowed to leave for the ridiculously low fee of £5,000 in order to take him off the wagebill.

HOLLAND, John (Jack).

b. Preston 3.4.01 5'8" 11st 0lbs
10–2 (10–2)
Preston N.E. (1919) Swansea T. (June 1922) Wrexham (cs 1925) Crewe A. (mid 1925–26) Npt. (cs 1926) Clapton O. (cs 1927) Carlisle Utd. (July 1929) Barrow (July 1930) Darvel Blackpool (May 1932)

An inside–right, who began in Preston's Central League side of 1919–20. Afterwards Jack continued his somewhat chequered career into the 1930's. He scored on his County debut versus Plymouth 28.8.26.

HOLLYMAN, Kenneth Charles.

b. Cardiff 18.11.22 5'7" 10st 10lbs
231–4 (259–5)
Cardiff Corries Cardiff C. (1938) Npt. (Nov 1953) Ton Pentre (p/manager 1961–62) Trelai (c.1964)

Very popular and perky right–back or right–half, who gave many years of excellent service to Cardiff and Newport. Ken helped to take City from Division III (South) to Division I. He was very game and loved his upfield sorties, and scored a long–range goal in the cup–tie at Spurs. He was well–known for his defensive partnership with Alf Sherwood. He was also a leading baseball player. Ken is still living in his native Cardiff.

HOLTHAM, Dean M.

b. Pontypridd 30.9.63 5'8" 10st 5lbs
4–0 (9–1)
Swansea C. Cardiff C. Weymouth Yeovil Bath C. Npt. (Sept 1987) Bridgend T. Ynysybwl (p/manager Sept 1988) Barry T. (1 app 1989–90) Bridgend

Fairly versatile player, who was signed on a non–contract basis during an injury crisis. He could not always get time off work to play. Later Dean was appointed player–manager of Ynysybwl.

HOOPER, Wynne.

b. Seven Sisters nr. Neath 5.6.52 5'9" 10st 12lbs
165–22 (211–28)
Npt. (schoolboy Jan 1966, app. Apr 1968) Swindon T. (Dec 1976) Aldershot (July 1977) Bridgend (June 1979) Merthyr T.

Capped for the Welsh Youth side, Wynne was a winger or midfielder who made his Football League debut at 16. An awkward looking player he endured a fair share of barracking from the Somerton Park crowd, but by the time he left he had become the longest serving player at the club. His achievements included a hat–trick versus Rochdale 5.4.75. He carried on in non–League soccer and also became the Swansea City pools promoter in the late 1970's.

HOPKINS, Anthony.

b. Cwmbran 17.2.71
2–0 (6–0)
Coed Eva Npt. (1987) Chelsea Bristol C. (YTS 1988) Panteg IFK Euddevalla (Apr 1990) Panteg Merthyr T. Ebbw Vale (Sept 1990)

Anthony was one of a number of young players given their debuts in the County's troubled season of 1987–88. He had the ability to beat a man on the touchline, but became one of the many players to leave the club. He recently appeared for a side in Southern Sweden.

HUDSON, Colin Arthur Richard ("Rocky").

b. Undy 5.10.35 5'6" 11st 0lbs
112-23 (129-29)
Undy Juniors Chepstow T. Npt. (amateur Apr 1951, pro Apr 1954) Cardiff C. (June 1957 p/exchange) Brighton (June 1961) Npt. (June 1962 £2,000) Worcester C. (July 1963) Barry T. Bath C. (1964)

A red haired right winger, well-known for his ability to hare down the touchline after the ball. He could also score plenty of goals and netted four versus Bournemouth 7.3.57. Colin was in the R.A.F. when making his Football League debut for the County. He was mainly a reserve for Cardiff and Brighton, but laid on the goal which took City into Division I. After a season back with the County he went into non-League football, later appearing for Cwmbran. Colin also played as a wicket-keeper in local cricket.

HUGH, Arthur Ronald.

b. Rogerstone 5.8.09 5'11" 10st 7lbs
57-0 (85-0) (Wales 2 1930, Amateur 2 1930)
Rogerstone Newport Y.M.C.A. Thursdays Lovells Ath. (c 1928) Npt. (Aug 1929, pro Oct 1932) Lovells Ath. (c Jan 1933) Npt. (reserves cs 1935)

A local amateur centre-forward, who became a full-back in an emergency. Ron was a shrewd, lanky, long-legged tackler. As an unknown he scored a hat-trick in a pre-season trial for the County. Many teams tried to sign him, but he preferred to stay in South Wales and he was later capped whilst on the County's books. He owned Hugh's Horticultural House, which advertised in the club programme for many years, and is still living in the area.

HUGHES, Glyn.

b. Coedpoeth nr. Wrexham 29.11.31 5'8" 11st 0lbs
4-0 (4-0)
Sheffield Wednesday (1950) Wrexham (Aug 1952) Npt. (July 1955) Caernarvon (July 1956)

Right winger, whose games at Somerton were mainly restricted to the reserves, although he was a regular first teamer at Wrexham. He was last heard of employed as a steel-worker in Wrexham.

HUGHES, Iorwerth (Iorrie).

b. Llandulas 26.5.25 5'11" 11st 6lbs

106–0 (113–0) (Wales 4 1951, Amateur 2 1949)
Llandudno Luton T. (amateur, pro Apr 1949) Cardiff C. (Aug 1951 £15,000) Worcester C. (1952) Npt (Aug 1953) Hastings Utd. (Aug 1959)

An agile goalkeeper, "capped" as an amateur and professional, who had played in Division II for Luton T. Iorrie was also in Cardiff's promotion side, having been bought when Phil Joslin was injured. He spent five seasons at Somerton Park, but in later years was often kept out of the first team by Len Weare. Iorrie now lives in Luton.

HUNT, Ralph Arthur Robert.

b. Portsmouth 14.8.33 d. Grantham 17.12.64 5'10" 11st 7lbs
83–37 (100–48)
Gloucester C. (1949) Portsmouth (pro Aug 1950) Bournemouth (Feb 1954) Norwich C. (July 1955) Derby C. (Aug 1958) Grimsby T. (Aug 1959) Swindon T. (July 1961 p/exchange) Port Vale (Dec 1961 £3,500) Npt. (July 1962 £2,500) Chesterfield (July 1964)

Prolific goalscorer, who started with the England Youth XI. Ralph was often top scorer for his teams, with almost 200 Football League goals in his career. His uncle Douglas, and brother Dennis, were also footballers. He was an effective striker for County, scoring in almost every other game and obtaining 3 hat–tricks, but was eventually allowed to leave and tragically died following a car crash on the way home from a Chesterfield game.

HYDES, Arthur J.E.

b. Barnsley 24.11.10 5'9" 11st 5lbs
27–13 (42–21)
Ardsley Utd. Barnsley (amateur c. 1928) Southport (trial May 1929) Ardsley Ath. Leeds Utd. (May 1930) Npt. (May 1938) war guest for Barnsley, Bradford C., Nottm. Forrest and York C. Exeter C. (Feb 1946)

A wiry inside– or centre–forward, always associated with the 1938–39 promotion side. He was a good dribbler and distributor of the ball and had an effective shot. After being signed by Leeds he scored 16 goals in his first three reserve games. Later Arthur scored a hat–trick away from home to knock Newcastle out of the F.A. Cup, but was affected by injury at Leeds.

JAMES, Leighton.

b. Llwchwyr nr. Swansea 16.2.53 5'9" 12st 6lbs
21–2 (36–3) (Wales 54 1972–83, Under–23 7 1972–75)
Burnley (App. Feb 1970) Derby Co. (Oct 1975 £140,000) Q.P.R. (Oct 1977 £180,000) Burnley (Sept 1978 £165,000) Swansea C. (May 1980 £130,000) Sunderland (Jan 1983) Bury (Aug 1984) Npt. (July 1985, small fee) Burnley (Aug 1986 to cs 1989)

An outstanding, livewire outside–left, capable of both creating and scoring goals. Leighton was a member of the Welsh team for over ten years and amongst other achievements in his distinguished career he helped Swansea win promotion to Division I. He joined Newport as a player–coach, but was somewhat troubled by injury and decided to leave at the end of the season, after being overlooked for the Manager's job. He returned to Burnley, playing the odd game and becoming their youth team coach. Leighton is now the Bradford City coach.

JAMES, Walter George.

b. Swansea 15.6.24 5'11" 12st 4lbs
13–5 (15–8)
Tawe Utd. Swansea T. (war–time and later) Npt. (June 1950 £1,500) Milford Utd. (1952–53)

A Welsh Schools international from Swansea. George normally played full–back, but also appeared at centre–forward for County after some good performances in the reserves. He requested a move and his contract was cancelled in February 1952.

JAMES, Wilfred Bernard.

b. Cross Keys 19.2.07 5'9" 11st 10lbs
20–9 (22–9) (Wales 2 1931–32)
Ynysddu Crusaders Npt. (Oct 1925 to cs 1927) Thorne Colliery Notts Co. (trial Oct 1928) West Ham (May 1930 £250) Charlton A. (Feb 1932 £1,000+) Workington (?cs 1933)

Wilf was an amateur in the Monmouthshire League when signed on by County. In his second season he played fairly regularly at centre–forward or inside–right. He moved North to Doncaster to seek work and later played at a higher level. He was apparently well–known for his bowler hat, which he even wore in the showers.

JARMAN, Harold J.

b. Bristol 4.5.39 5'8" 10st 4lbs
34–8 (45–11)
Clifton Villa W.B.A. (trial 1955) Victoria Athletic (c 1955) Bristol R. (Aug 1959) Npt. (May 1973) New York Cosmos Mangotsfield Utd.

Very skilful, ball–juggling winger and penalty expert. Harold was in the twilight of his career when he arrived from Bristol R., for whom he had made well over 400 appearances. For 14 years he was a Gloucestershire cricketer. Since retiring as a player he has three times been employed and sacked by Rovers in various coaching and managerial posts. He was also Assistant Manager at Blackburn and recently Manager of Bath C. He is now running a carpentry business, and coaches the Bristol University X1.

JENKINS, David J.

b. Bristol 2.9.46 5'9" 11st 6lbs
6-1 (6-1)
Arsenal (trial c Aug 1962, later app.) Tottenham H. (Oct 1968 £55,000 plus J. Robertson) Brentford (July 1972) Hereford Utd. (Mar 1973) Npt. (loan Mar 1974) Shrewsbury T. (Aug 1974) S.Africa Workington (Oct 1975)

Courageous and intelligent striker, who never quite made it at the top level, although he played for Arsenal in the 1968 League Cup Final. David scored the goal which brought Hereford promotion in their first season in the Football League, but only had a short period at Somerton Park.

JENKINS, Edward Jonathon.

b. Cardiff 16.7.09 5'11" 12st 0lbs
34-0 (37-0)
Cardiff East Cardiff C. (amateur 1929, pro cs 1930) Bristol C. (cs 1934) Npt (July 1935)

Tall full-back or wing-half, who had been a schoolboy international. He played over 80 Third Division games for Cardiff and was a regular first teamer in his one season with County. Afterwards Eddie concentrated on the family milk business and became President of the Cardiff Chamber of Trade. In the War he spent four years on H.M.S. "Teviot" and ran the ship's football team. For over 30 years a member of the Cardiff bowls team, he wrote the history of the club and has also written a book on Splott. He is still living in Cardiff.

JENKINS, S. Harold.

b.?Newport
3-1 (3-1)
Risca Npt. (cs 1924) Ebbw Vale (to cs 1930)

Local amateur. Harold appeared in the 1924 trial games and made three first team appearances at outside-right a short time afterwards, scoring against Southend. He was still playing for Ebbw Vale six years later. He was also a Minor Counties cricketer.

JOHN, Emlyn James.

b. Tonypandy mid 1907 5'11" 10st 7lbs
55-1 (66-1)
Mid-Rhondda (pro 1926) Cardiff C. (Apr 1928) Npt. (Aug 1932 to 1934) Barry

A schoolboy international. Emlyn was a talented half-back with a skilful left foot. After four years as a Cardiff City reserve he became a regular at Somerton Park, before drifting into non-League soccer.

JOHN, William Ronald ("Roy").

b. Briton Ferry 29.1.11 d. Port Talbot 12.7.73
5'11" 11st 10lbs

10-0 (11-0) (Wales 14 1931-39, Wartime 1 1939)

Briton Ferry Swansea T. (amateur, then pro May 1928) Walsall (1929) Stoke C. (Apr 1932) Preston N.E. (June 1934 fee) Sheffield Utd. (Dec 1934) Manchester Utd. (June 1936) Npt. (Mar 1937 fee) Swansea T. (July 1937) officially retired Nov 1939, but played war-time games for Swansea T., Blackburn R., Burnley and Bolton W.

Roy began as a Briton Ferry school-boy centre-forward and was the Walsall reserve left-back, before becoming goalkeeper in an emerge-ncy. He had uncanny anticipation and was seldom caught out of posit-ion. He could have had more caps and was made Captain for his last Welsh international. His Swansea pub was blitzed early in the War and he later went on Tommy Walker's tour of India. He spent his last 16 years with British Steel. He was the Briton Ferry wicket-keeper and a sound batsman.

JOHNSON, George Henry.

b. Darnall, Sheffield late 1903 5'6" 11st 0lbs
38-8 (40-8)
Swansea T. Southend Utd. (cs 1923) Npt. (cs 1926) Coventry C. (cs 1927) Torquay Utd. (1927-28)

Speedy right winger, good at cutting in and scoring surprise goals, though less reliable at trapping the ball. He began in Sheffield junior football and played over 60 games for Southend before joining the County.

JOHNSON, Jeffery D.

b. Cardiff 26.11.53 5'8" 11st 12lbs
34-2 (40-2) (Wales Under-23 2 1976)
Clifton Ath. Manchester C. (Nov 1970) Swansea C. (loan July 1972) Crystal Pal. (loan Dec 1973, full-time Jan 1974 £12,000) Sheffield Wed. (July 1976) Npt. (July 1981 £60,000) Gillingham (loan Sept 1982, full-time Nov 1982 £9,000) Barrow Port Vale (July 1985)

Welsh schools and youth "cap", a wing-half who had played in an F.A. Cup semi-final for Crystal Palace. Jeff was signed by Ashurst at Sheff-ield Wednesday, where be became Player of the Year in 1979-80. He was the County's second highest signing, but like Waddle was a major disappointment. He soon moved on to Gillingham, where the fee was decided by a Tribunal.

JOHNSTON, George.

b. Glasgow 21.3.47 5'7" 10st 5lbs
2-0 (3-0)
Cardiff C. (May 1964) Arsenal (Mar 1967 £30,000) Birmingham C. (May 1969 £22,000) Walsall (loan Sept 1970) Fulham (Nov 1970 £6,000) Hereford Utd. (Aug 1972 loan, then full-time £2,000) Npt. (July 1973) Caerau (Ely)(1974)

Forward, who joined Cardiff C. from Scottish junior football as a teenager and scored in seven consecutive European matches. Later George played in Fulham's promotion side of 1970-71. He had a short stay at Somerton Park, his contract being cancelled in November 1973.

JOHNSTON, Thomas Bourhill.

b. Loanhead, Midlothian 18.6.27 5'10" 11st 7lbs
63–46 (68–53)
Loanhead Mayflower Peebles Rovers Falkirk (trial) Third Lanark (trial) Kilmarnock (1949) Darlington (Apr 1951) Oldham Ath. (Mar 1952) Norwich C. (June 1952 £500) Npt. (Oct 1954 £1,800) Leyton O. (Feb 1956 £4,000 & M. Burgess) Blackburn R. (Mar 1958 £15,000) Leyton O. (Feb 1959 £7,500) Gillingham (Sept 1961 £3,000) Folkestone (July 1962)

One of the best centre–forwards ever to play for Newport County. Tommy worked in the pits as a youngster and suffered a withered arm, as a result of which he always wore a bandage. He was signed by Norman Low at Norwich and in one famous game scored twice to put Arsenal out of the F.A. Cup. After accumulating an impressive goal tally at Somerton Park and establishing himself as a firm favourite, he was reluctantly sold by County in 1956 and proceeded to set Orient goalscoring records which still stand today.

During 1957–58 he was the top Football League goalscorer, helping Blackburn Rovers to Division I. Later Tommy emigrated to Australia, where he worked for Lysaght's and coached their football side. He has now moved to Sanctuary Point, N.S.W. since retiring recently.

JONES, Anthony Peter.

b. Birmingham 12.11.37 6'0" 11st 6lbs
53–9 (60–10)
Birmingham C. (amateur) Oxford Utd. (pro 1959) Npt. (Dec 1967) Cheltenham T. (June 1969) Merthyr T. (Mar 1970) Witney T. (p/–manager)

Tony was a tall, long–striding wing–half or inside–forward, who gave many good performances for County. He played in Oxford United's first Football League side and was an ever–present for them in three seasons. He joined the County around the same time as Tony Buck and the two helped to strengthen the side considerably.

JONES, Brinley H.

b. Llandrindod Wells 8.2.48 5'7" 9st 11lbs
13–0 (13–0) (Wales Under–23 1 1971)
Cardiff C. (App., pro Feb 1966) Npt. (loan Feb 1969) Bristol Rovers (May 1969) Yeovil T. (June 1975)

Wales Schoolboy "cap", an inside–forward who never made the grade at Cardiff, despite playing versus Moscow Dynamo. Bryn had a spell on loan at Somerton Park, but was unwilling to stay and moved on to Eastville.

JONES, Brinley R.

b. Swansea 20.5.31 d. Swansea 14.11.90 5'6"
10st 7lbs
71-11 (82-12)
Swansea T. (Sept 1951) Npt. (June 1958 £2,600) Bournemouth (Feb 1960 £5,000) Northampton T. (Oct 1963) Watford (Nov 1963) Chelmsford (Oct 1966) Folkestone T. (p/manager)

Aggressive, popular wing-half capable of scoring goals (he netted a hat-trick versus Reading 24.8.57). The elder brother of the famous Cliff and son of Ivor, Bryn played in the same Swansea boys' team as Len Allchurch, Mel Charles and Terry Medwin. He spent 15 years in League soccer and his departure in 1960 was regretted by the Somerton crowd. After a kidney illness forced his retirement, he was a sports teacher at Holloway Boy's Comprehensive from 1971 to 1989.

JONES, David Albert Brynmawr (Dai).

b. Ton Pentre 31.3.41 5'8" 11st 4lbs
124-36 (149-42)
Gwynfi Ton Pentre Millwall (Mar 1964) Npt. (July 1965) Mansfield T. (Dec 1967 £1,500) Npt. (Nov 1971) Bath C. (loan Nov 1973) Spencer Works

Centre-forward, not the most stylish of players, but a trier who scored plenty of goals. He began as a Welsh Youth international before helping Millwall to promotion. He soon established himself at Somerton and scored a hat-trick versus Chesterfield 26.9.66, but asked for a transfer when Buck was signed. Later Dai played a prominent part in Mansfield's sixth Round F.A. Cup run before obtaining a transfer back to Newport to look after his sick father. He has since had managerial jobs with Spencer Works, noticeably when they played Swansea C. in the Welsh Cup.

JONES, David Gwilym.

b. Ynysddu 10.6.14 5'10" 12st 0lbs
15-1 (15-1)

Ynysddu Npt. (1930) Northfleet (c 1931) Cardiff C. (Aug 1934) Npt. (June 1935) Wigan Ath. (July 1936) Manchester Utd. (1937) Swindon T. (cs 1938) Cheltenham (1946-47)

Left-half or outside-left, brother of Bill. After a few years with Spurs' nursery at Northfleet he made his Football League debut with Cardiff. He never really established himself in football and after the War concentrated on his career. He settled in Swindon, where he still lives.

JONES, David Richard.

b. Onllwyn nr. Neath 18.1.46 5'10" 12st 0lbs
3–0 (3–0)
Derby Co. (July 1965) Burton Albion Npt. (May 1968) Rugby T. (June 1969) A.P. Leamington (cs 1973) Atherstone

David spent three years with Derby County, but was released because they had too many goalkeepers. He was taken on three months' trial, but was later given a free transfer by County and went into non–League football.

JONES , "Ted Whiskey" (real name Edwin Ambrey SPICKETT–JONES).

b. Newport 3.7.1892 d. Newport 4.2.78 5'11" 11st 0lbs
8–0 (38–1)
Oak Villa Npt. (1912–13 & war–time) Lysaghts Excelsior Npt. (cs 1919) Caerphilly (1921)

Robust and popular half–back or full–back, who was associated with the club in their early Southern League and Football League days. He obtained his nickname as a small boy by pinching a bottle of Whiskey and proceeding to drink it. At the time of his death Ted was mine host of the "Bridge Inn", Usk.

JONES, Glyn A.

b. Newport 29.3.59 6'0" 13st 11lbs
3–0 (4–0)
Bristol R. (app., pro 1975) Shrewsbury T. (cs 1980) Gloucester C. Yeovil T. Newport Y.M.C.A. Npt. (Sept 1983 non–contract) Albion Rovers of Newport

Glyn first joined the County after suffering from pneumonia and not playing League football for four years. He was educated at Dyffryn School and employed at Risca Leisure Centre. Glyn was never more than a reserve as a player, but has been better known in recent years for running the County's youth side.

JONES, Linden.

b. New Tredegar 5.3.61 5'6" 10st 8lbs
141–6 (181–12) (Wales Under–21 3 1982)
Bargoed Y.M.C.A. Cardiff C. (app., pro Feb 1979) Npt. (Sept 1983 p/exchange) Reading (July 1987 £33,000)

Gutsy, tough–tackling full–back, very popular on the terraces. He led by example and was always in the thick of the action. Linden was the penalty taker and could also score the odd goal from long range. He picked up the occasional bad injury because of his no–nonsense approach. He was eventually sold to Reading because the club was in dire need of the money.

JONES, Peter.

b. Caerphilly 22.9.57
54–1 (72–3)
Pontllanfraith Merthyr T. (1977) Npt. (non-contract Aug 1985, full–time Sept 1985) Merthyr T. (Jan 1987)

Left–back and elder brother of Linden. Peter was a late starter in League Football, joining the County at 27. He had been an S.A. Brain Trophy winner with Merthyr in 1980–81. He has pace and tackling ability and can score the occasional long distance goal, but was allowed to leave after losing his form. He rejoined Merthyr, who ironically beat County in the Welsh Cup Final.

JONES, Ralph.

b. Maesteg 19.5.21 5'10" 11st 8lbs
19–0 (21–0)
Leicester C. (1944) Npt. (May 1946) Bristol R. (Dec 1947) Bath C. (1952) Trowbridge T. (1955–58)

Half–back, who had once played rugby for Caerau. Ralph joined

County in the immediate post–war era, making 17 appearances in Division II. He joined Bristol R. on a free transfer, but was injured in March 1948 and out of the first team for two years. His career was later terminated by a knee injury. During his time with Bath he sang as a baritone with the Glyndebourne Opera Company. He afterwards worked as a manufacturer's agent in South Wales and now lives in Bridgend.

JONES, Richard.

b. Usk 26.4.69 5'11" 11st 1lbs
31–1 (46–1)
Npt. (App. 1986, pro 1987) Hereford Utd. (Sept 1988)

Versatile, hard–tackling player. Wimbledon were to sign him for a substantial fee in August 1987, but the deal fell through and he was not allowed to play for a lengthy period because of the legal wrangle. Richard refused to play for County in the 1988–89 season because of their financial position and decided to try his luck with Hereford, being voted "Player of the year" for 1988–89.

JONES, Roderick.

b. Rhiwderin 14.6.46 5'11" 12st 0lbs
271–65 (323–71) (Wales amateur 2 1971)
Alcan Lovells Ath. (cs 1968) Npt. (Aug 1969, part–time pro cs 1971) Barry T. (Dec 1978) Npt. (Welsh League 1983) Forest Green Rovers (1986) Spencer Works (1987)

One of the most popular of post–war players at Somerton Park. Roddy is well remembered for his striking partnership with Willie Brown, but he also played in defence. Subtlety was never his strong point, but nobody could every doubt his commitment or enthusiasm. He came to Somerton Park as an amateur on the demise of Lovells and was only ever a part–timer, being employed as a maintenance fitter for Alcan after a short time at sea with P&O. Roddy returned as player–coach to County reserves in 1983 and still lives locally.

JONES, Samuel E.

b. Newport d. England
2–0 (11–4) (Wales amateur 3 1933–34)
Npt. (1931) Lovells Ath. (1933) Bristol R. (1934–35) Epsom T. (1935) Lovells Ath.

Sam was a forward who was good enough to play for the Welsh amateur side. A reserve at Somerton Park, he joined the County in their Southern League season and played in two away Football League games the following year. He lived next door to the Wardells in Nash Road and died after moving to live with his daughter in the South of England.

JONES, Trevor R.B.

b. Cefn Coed c 1913 5'8" 11st 5lbs
11–0 (11–0)
Cefn Coed Barry Walsall (cs 1935) Npt. (loan Mar 1936)

Useful right–back and stopper, who spent a short time at Somerton Park. He made only five Football League appearances for Walsall.

JONES, Vaughan.

b. Tonyrefail 2.9.59 5'8" 11st 11lbs
67–4 (88–4) (Wales Under 21 2 1979–81)
Bristol R. (App. 1976, pro Sept 1977) Npt. (cs 1982) Cardiff C. (July 1984) Bristol R. (Dec 1985)

Whole–hearted full–back, who attended a rugby playing school, but was spotted by Rovers playing for his village team. Vaughan made his Football League debut at the age of 17. He played many excellent games for County, but was released when Linden Jones was signed – a move which upset some supporters. He had a short spell at Ninian Park before becoming Rovers' Captain and displaying his usual consistency.

JONES, Vincent Wellfield.

b. Carmarthen mid 1900 5'9" 11st 7lbs
33-1 (36-1)
Cardiff C. (trial, 1922-23) Merthyr T. (1923)
Ebbw Vale (cs 1924) Millwall (Aug 1927)
Luton T. (Aug 1931) Norwich C. (Sept 1932)
Npt. (Sept 1933) Cardiff C. (1934)

An excellent attacking half-back with
a powerful shot, hard to beat and
popular with the Somerton crowd.
Vince was invited to tour Canada
with the Welsh F.A., but prevented
by injury. He suffered from appendicitis during his time with Luton.

JONES, William.

b. Ynysddu 26.11.10 5'8" 11st 2lbs
6-0 (26-0)
Pontlottyn Ynysddu Crusaders Npt. (amateur
c 1927) Notts Co. (1930) Npt. (?loan 1931,
full-time 1933) Barry (1934-39 & 1946-47)

Elder brother of David. Bill was a
versatile and adaptable half-back,
who came to prominence in school
football. After a long spell at Barry
he became Ipswich T. scout (1947)
and Manager of Barry T. (1951).
After managing Worcester C. he
served Cardiff City in various capac-
ities until becoming Manager (1958-
62). Bill was noted as a strict disc-
iplinarian. He was later with Abergavenny Th., but finished with football
in 1969. He is still living in Barry.

JORDAN, George.

b. Methil, Fifeshire 1904 5'8" 11st 0lbs
32-0 (37-0)
Rosslyn Connah's Quay Bury (June 1929)
Yeovil & Petters Utd. Bradford C. (May
1932) Npt. (July 1933) Rochdale (July 1934)
Prescot Cables (Aug 1935) Shirley T. (July
1936)

Long-legged half-back, who won a
Welsh Cup Winner's medal with
Connah's Quay in 1929. George was
the strong man of the County team,
which went to pieces when he was
out injured. He later drifted back
into non-League football.

JOY, Harold Cuthbert.

b. Ebbw Vale 8.1.21
Pontllanfraith Cardiff C. (1940) Norwich C.
(Feb 1947) Ipswich T. (Dec 1947) Npt. (Jan
1948) Llanelli (1948) Treharris Chippenham
T. & other non-League, retiring 1954

Local centre-forward who played a
few Football League games, but is
possibly better known as a scout
today. As Spurs' scout he discovered
Mark Kendall and was later with the
County and Cardiff.

KEAR, Michael P.

b. Coleford 27.5.43 5'9" 10st 4lbs
6-0 (9-0)
Cinderford T. Npt. (Apr 1963, pro Aug 1963)
Nottm. Forest (Dec 1963 £7,000) Middlesbrough (Sept 1967 £25,000) Barnsley (loan
Aug 1970) Bercham (Belgium)(1971) Cheltenham (Jan 1977)

Winger, who first played as an amateur in County's Welsh League side. It came as something of a surprise when, after a mere six Football League games, he was sold for a large fee. After four years as a Forest reserve, he went to Ayresome Park for an even large fee and later had a long period playing in Belgium.

KEENAN, William George.

b. Llanelli 29.12.18
4–1 (4–1)
Llanelli Clyde Glasgow Celtic Derry City Hereford Utd. (1945–46) Everton Leicester C. Npt. (June 1946) Llanelli Pembroke (1948)

Outside–left, who had a brief spell at Somerton Park just after the War. His contract was cancelled in February 1947.

KELLOW, Anthony.

b. Falmouth 1.5.52 5'10" 12st 7lbs
17–8 (24–9)
Falmouth T. Exeter C. (July 1976 £3,000 plus a later £10,000) Blackpool (Nov 1978 £125,000) Exeter C. (Mar 1980 £70,000) Plymouth A. (Nov 1983 £5,000) Swansea C. (1 month non–contract) Npt. (Nov 1984 non–contract) Exeter C. (July 1985 non–contract)

Prolific scorer and something of a character on the pitch. Tony joined Exeter after leaving his job as an electrician at Falmouth Docks. He joined Blackpool for a large fee, but had a poor spell there. He helped out on a non–contract basis as Som-erton Park, giving useful experience to the side and scoring some good goals. He left because of his pub in Exeter (the "Clifton Inn") and was later licensee of the Exeter City Social Club.

KELSO, James.

b. Cardross nr. Dumbarton 8.12.10 d. Newport 13.3.87 5'8" 11st 4lbs
119–1 (133–1)
Helensburgh Dumbarton (c 1929) Bradford P.A. (cs 1933) Port Vale (July 1934) Npt. (June 1935) Cardiff C. (July 1938 £1,050) war games for Bristol C., Cardiff C., Liverpool, Swindon T., Swansea T. & Bath C. Ebbw Vale (as amateur 1946–48)

A fast full–back, good with both feet and hard to beat. Jimmy was the County Captain, but was unfortunately sold just prior to the promotion season. He played little war–time football because of the R.A.F. He was a Powderhall sprinter and scratch golfer. Settled in Newport. Jimmy spent 25 years at Alcan and was an usher at the Civic Centre courts. At one time he scouted for Blackpool.

KELSON, Henry James (Harry) "Kelly".

b. Bath late 1889 d. Ystrad Mynach 24.6.66 5'5" 11st 0lbs
11–1 (52–1)
Bristol C. res (pre-war) Npt. (cs 1919) Mardy (c Apr 1921)

Harry was a gritty player, the handyman of the County side. He was normally a wing–half, but played outside–left on occasions. For 9 years he had performed in Bristol junior football, but he did not appear in the Football League for Bristol. In World War 1 he spent 12 months in the R.A.S.C., mainly in France. Something of a comic by nature he was a well–known figure in County's post–war team. He later left for the delights of Mardy.

KENDALL, Mark.

b. Blackwood 20.9.58 6'0" 13st 9lbs
272–0 (347–0) (Wales Under–21 1 1978)
Tottenham H. (App., pro July 1976) Chesterfield (loan Dec 1979) Npt. (loan Sept 1980, full–time Oct 1980 for £45,000) Wolverhampton W. (loan Dec 1986, full–time Jan 1987 for £25,000) Swansea C. (cs 1990)

Mark was a very popular goalkeeper with the Somerton crowd, somewhat unorthodox in his methods and excellent at blocking the ball with his legs. A Welsh Schools and Youth

international, he was recommended to Spurs by Harold Joy. He was the County's record buy when arriving at the club and missed only 7 Football League matches in five seasons. It was a sad day and a blow to attendances when he was allowed to go to Wolves because of the critical financial situation. After spending most of last season in Swansea's reserves, he won a Welsh Cup winners medal.

KENT, Kevin J.

b. Stoke 19.3.65 5'10" 11st 0lbs
23–1 (42–2)
W.B.A. (App., pro Dec 1982) Npt. (June 1984) Mansfield T. (July 1985, at first on three months trial) Port Vale (Mar 1991)

A skilful forward who showed promise with County. He was a regular in W.B.A.'s Central League Championship side of 1982–83, but had few first team chances (made his debut versus Everton in 1984). Kevin was given a free transfer by County when taking too long to decide about a contract. He has since established himself in League football and scored 4 for Mansfield versus Port Vale in 1987.

KING, Gerald H.

b. Radnor 9.4.47 5'10" 12st 0lbs
49–9 (62–12)
Cardiff C. (Juniors, pro June 1964) Torquay Utd. (June 1965) Luton T. (June 1966) Npt. (trial July 1967, full–time later) Ton Pentre Barry T. Bridgend

Left–winger, who played fairly regularly for County and scored a few goals. A Welsh Schoolboy international, he made his League debut at 17 in August 1964. Gerald was retained in 1969, but retired from League football to run his coal business. He is now drayman for Ansell's Brewery and coaches Marshfield. His son Jamie played for the club in the Vauxhall Conference.

KING, Simon A.

b. Ebbw Vale 19.7.64 5'9" 10st 6lbs
1–0 (1–0)
Cwmbran T. Npt. (App. 1984) Cwmbran T. (Nov 1985)

Young full–back, who was given just one outing in the County first team. The rest of the career has been confined to non–League soccer, where he still operates with Cwmbran.

KITSON, George.

b. Newport 16.5.11 5'8" 11st 3lbs
6–0 (26–0)
Npt. (amateur 1925, pro 1933) Barrow (cs 1935) Kidderminster H. (1937) Bangor C. Tunbridge Wells Rangers

A local wing–half or full–back, who began with Corporation Road School. George came from local football and never really established himself in the County first team, but later played 48 Football League games for Barrow. From 1946 he was the Assistant Trainer for over twenty years and after that for a long time a matchday

steward at Somerton Park. George, who in 1931 achieved the rare feat of playing for the reserves and first team on the same day, is now residing in a local nursing home.

KNOWLES, Frank.

b. Hyde, Manchester 5'11" 12st 0lbs
16–0 (17–0)
Skelmersdale Utd. Manchester Utd. (c 1912 to 1915) Hartlepools Utd. (cs 1919) Manchester C. (1919) Stalybridge Celtic (cs 1920) Ashington (cs 1921) Stockport Co. Npt. (cs 1923) Q.P.R. (Feb 1924 to 1925)

A very experienced centre–half, who had just over six months with County. Before World War 1, Frank played fairly regularly for Manchester United and his later career included a season in Division III (North) with former League team Ashington.

LATCHFORD, Robert D.

b. Birmingham 18.1.51 6'0" 13st 8lbs
20–5 (22–5) (England 12 1978–79, Under–23 6 1974)
Birmingham C. (App., pro Aug 1968) Everton (Feb 1974 £350,000) Swansea C. (July 1981 £125,000) NAC Breda (1983) Coventry C. (July 1984) Lincoln C. (Aug 1985) Npt. (loan Jan 1986, later full–time) Malta Merthyr T. (Oct 1986)

A strong, bustling international striker, a familiar and popular figure at the top level. Bob scored over 200 Football League goals and was involved in the record British transfer deal of the time. He scored a hat–trick in Swansea's first Division I game versus Leeds and played in their 12–0 win over Sliema Wanderers. By the time he joined County he was well over the top, but, despite his lack of speed, played some useful games and helped out until the end of the season. He later missed Merthyr's Welsh Cup Final win against County because of injury. Bob, whose brothers Dave and Peter were League goalkeepers, is now an Alvechurch director.

LAWRANCE, Raymond Stanley

b. Gainsborough 18.9.11 d. Castleton 7.1.87
6'2" 13st 6lbs
38–0 (55?–1)
Gainsborough Trinity Hull C. (1933) Npt. (May 1936) war-time games for Swindon T. and Lovells Ath. Haarlem

A massive, reliable, long–striding half back, who was clever at mastering the ball in the air. Ray captained his school at soccer, cricket and swimming. He played seven games in the County's promotion side and

was in the Fire Service during the War. He then became coach to Haarlem, who won the Dutch Championship in 1946–47. Ray was appointed County's trainer–coach in 1948 and became their acting Manager in 1950. Afterwards he was Manager of Abergavenny Thursdays.

LAWSON, Hector Stewart Ramsay.

b. Shettleston, Glasgow 21.5.1896 5'8" 11st 7lbs
57–1 (63–1)
Shettleston F.C. Glasgow Rangers (Aug 1916) Liverpool (Jan 1924) Aberdeen (cs 1926) Brighton (June 1928) Npt. (Aug 1929) Shamrock Rovers (Aug 1931)

Constructive Scottish half–back or winger, who played fairly regularly during his spell with County. Hector began with Rangers, but made few first team appearances because of the famous Alan Morton. He was retained as coach to the County reserves in 1930, but still played 29 first team games before heading for Ireland.

LAWSON, Thomas.

b. Boldon Colliery, Co. Durham c 1906 d. 1936 5'8" 11st 0lbs
11–0 (11–0)
Newcastle Utd. (Reserves) Scotswood Boldon Colliery Fulham (May 1927) West Ham (May 1931) Aldershot (June 1932) Npt. (Aug 1934 to 1935)

Wing-half, who had been a regular with Aldershot for two seasons and played in their first Football League game versus Southend Utd. At Somerton Park he was often forced to play in the Centre. He was somewhat unpopular with the Somerton crowd, who considered him a bit too dainty. Tommy died not long after leaving the club.

LAYTON, John H.

b. Hereford 29.6.51 6'0" 13st 2lbs
1-0 (1-0)
Gloucester C. Kidderminster H. Hereford Utd. (Sept 1974) Gloucester C. Trowbridge T. (p/manager) Npt. (Jan 1984) Hereford Utd. (1984) Worcester C. (1984 non-contract)

Well-built central defender, who had played over 200 games for Hereford. In his last game, in 1980, he was sent off in a 0-5 defeat versus Newport. He later joined County as injury cover, when Oakes was out injured. After giving a poor performance he was not retained.

LEAMON, Frederick W.

b. Jersey 11.5.19 d. London 27.8.81 5'8" 11st 9lbs
4-3 (20-15)
Bath C. Npt. (Jan 1946) Bristol R. (Nov 1946) Brighton (July 1949) Chippenham T. (Oct 1950)

Goalscoring centre-forward, who had a year with the County. Although born in the Channel Islands he spent a long time living in Chepstow. A

bowls international, he played over 20 times for Wales. Fred was later a security man for a BBC TV unit and died of a heart attack at St. Paul's when the Prince of Wales' wedding was taking place.

LEE, James Alfred.

b. Rotherham early 1892 5'9" 12st 8lbs
4-0 (4-0)
Rotherham County Grimsby T. (Sept 1912) West Ham (Aug 1919) Npt. (July 1922 to 1923)

A very experienced full-back or half-back, a clean kicker of the ball. Alf was normally a reserve at West Ham, but played in their first Football League game versus Lincoln C. in 1919. He was one of the 24 Hammers released in the 1922 close season and never established himself in the Newport side, although he made around 30 reserve appearances.

LEE, Terrence W.G.

b. Stepney 20.9.52 5'11" 11st 0lbs
1-0 (2-0)
Tottenham H. (schoolboy 1967, App., pro May 1970) Cardiff C. (loan c Aug 1974) Gillingham (loan Feb 1975) Torquay Utd. (July 1975) Npt. (trial Nov. 1978, full-time Dec 1978) Minehead (Apr 1979)

A goalkeeper who made one first team appearance for Spurs when Pat Jennings was playing for Ireland. Terry made over 100 appearances for Torquay, but was freed after damaging a cartilage. He was signed after some impressive reserve team displays, but was released once Dowler regained fitness. He is a qualified chef.

LEES, Terence.

b. Stoke 30.6.52
25–0 (31–1)
Stoke C. (App., 1971) Cape Town City (c 1974) Crewe A. (loan Mar 1975) San Jose Earthquakes Port Vale (Aug 1975 £3,000) Sparta, Rotterdam (1975 £30,000) Roda (1977) Birmingham C. (July 1979 £60,000) Npt. (Aug 1981) Holland Morning Star (Hong Kong)(Aug 1982) Blackpool Stafford R. Scunthorpe Utd. (Sept 1984)

An experienced full–back, who had been signed by Birmingham for £60,000 and was a regular member of their side until they bought Colin Todd. Terry was signed by County as a free transfer on a three year contract, but failed to show any dominant form and was released at the end of his first year.

LENNOX, Wilson ("Billy").

b. Holytown, Lanarks 27.5.01   d. Plumstead 4.2.76 5'8" 12st 0lbs
22–0 (24–0)
Ashfield (Glasgow) Mid–Annandale (c 1926) Charlton Ath. (July 1927) Thames (June 1931) Npt. (July 1932) Accrington S. (cs 1933)

A clever player, normally a centre–forward, but converted to a wing–half by County. He scored 41 goals in 71 appearances for Charlton and appeared in their division III Championship side. Billy became the only Charlton player to score five goals away from home, versus Exeter City in 1929. He played in Thames' final Football League game before joining the County and breaking his nose in his first match, versus Swindon Town. The next season he moved to Accrington, appearing in their record 8–0 win versus New Brighton, along with Jimmy Maidment. He became a coach in Holland in July 1934 and later returned to live in Woolwich, working for A.E.I. until his retirement.

LESTER, Leslie James ("Danny").

b. Cardiff 17.11.23 5'8"   d. Cardiff May 1991 10st 7lbs
2–0 (2–0)
Cardiff Corries   Cardiff C. (1940) Torquay Utd. (Aug 1948) Npt. (Sept 1950 £1,000)

"Danny" was a wing–half, who joined Cardiff City at 16 in the war period. He played over 20 reserve games during his one season at Somerton Park, but had few first team opportunities. He also played baseball for Splott. In his later days he lived in Whitchurch, Cardiff.

LEVER, Arthur Richard ("Buller").

b. Cardiff 25.3.20 5'11" 12st 7lbs
72–0 (81–1) (Wales 1 1953)
Machine Products (war–time) Cardiff Corries Cardiff C. (1943) Leicester C. (Sept 1950 £10,000) Npt. (July 1954) retired 1957

Talented full–back, a speedy player and a hard hitter of a dead ball. A product of Cardiff local football, Arthur was an ever present in City's promotion side and played in 111 consecutive first team games for them. At the end of this career he wanted to return to South Wales and joined County. Despite his Achilles tendon problems, he spent three years with the Club. He could later be heard doing commentaries on BBC radio. A former baseball player and market gardener, he is still living in Cardiff and enjoying his golf and gardening hobbies.

LEWIS, Dudley Reginald.

b. Kensington 1909 5'11" 12st 0lbs
10-0 (10-0)
Q.P.R. Bristol R. (1932) Exeter C. (cs 1934) Bath C. Npt (cs 1935 to 1936) Milford U.

A thrustful wing–half, who first came to prominence with Bristol R. Dudley suffered from cartilage trouble during his spell at Somerton Park.

LEWIS, Idris S.

b. Tonypandy 26.8.15 5'6" 10st 5lbs
27-4 (29-4)
Swansea T. (1935) Sheffield Wed. (c 1938) war-time games for Coventry C., Cardiff C. & Swansea T. Bristol R. (July 1946) Npt. (Nov 1946, small fee) Haverfordwest (cs 1948)

A winger first spotted by Glyn Evans at Swansea. Idris later played 18 games for Sheffield Wednesday, before being replaced by Toseland. He left Bristol because of accommodation difficulties and played regularly during County's Division II season.

LEWIS, John (Jack "Ginger").

b. Newport ?early 1902 5'7" 10st 10lbs
26-0 (27-0) (Wales 1 1926)
Somerton Park Juniors Npt. (c 1921, amateur, later pro) Cardiff C. (Jan 1924) Tranmere R. (Mar 1926 to Apr 1934)

"Ginger", a talented wing–half, was very much a local product and made over 60 reserve appearances before reaching the County first team. He failed to make the Cardiff Division I side, but became a fixture in the Tranmere team, making over 260 Football League appearances. He was heard of many years ago working as a steeplejack in London.

LEWIS, John.

b. Tredegar 15.10.55 5'9" 11st 3lbs
154-9 (202-11) (Wales Under-21 1 1983)
Aberbargoed Buds Pontllanfraith Cardiff C. (Aug 1978) Npt. (Sept 1983) Swansea C. (Oct

1987) Abergavenny Th. (Feb 1989, later player-coach) Newport AFC (trial July 1990)

A midfield player of ability, who joined the County in the multi-player exchange of 1983. John was a late entrant into professional soccer, being a pay clerk at Llanwern. John played regularly at Somerton for four seasons, being eventually made player-manager by the Administrator in February 1987. He was sacked as Manager the following season when County were bottom and refused to remain as a player. He helped Swansea C. to win promotion, but was forced to retire from League football through injury at the end of the season. He turned down the chance to join Newport AFC, but his Abergavenny side have became Welsh League Champions.

LEWIS, Norman.

b. Snedshill, Shropshire 28.5.27
15-0 (15-0)
Shrewsbury T. (1948, pro Aug 1950) Gravesend & North Fleet (1952) Npt. (June 1954) Gravesend & N (cs 1955)

Full-back, who had played over 60 games for Shrewsbury in their early Football League days. Norman was in the County reserves for much of his only season here and drifted back into non-League soccer.

LEWIS, Wilfred (Billy).

b. Cardiff 4.7.23 5'8" 11st 2lbs
49-11 (52-12)
Cardiff C. (war-time) war guest for Distillery and Bradford C. Npt. (Oct 1947 £4,500) Lovells Ath. (Sept 1950)

A Welsh Schools international, who joined the County from Cardiff C. after playing seven games in their promotion season. Towards the end of his stay he dropped into the reserves and moved on to Rexville. Lewis, who comes from Grangetown, Cardiff, was also a baseball player.

LILYGREEN, Christopher.

b. Bettws, Newport 9.6.65 5'8" 8st 4lbs
18-4 (39-5)
Newport Y.M.C.A. Npt. (Sept 1982, youth, then non-contract) Yeovil T. (loan Oct 1984, full-time cs 1985) Forest Green Rovers Bath C. Mangotsfield Ebbw Vale (Sept 1988) Newport A.F.C. (June 1989)

A lightly built forward, who was signed by County on a non-contract basis as he was too old to become an apprentice. Although he showed promising form at first, he was later given a free transfer. Chris eventually became one of the first players signed by the newly formed Newport A.F.C. He was their leading scorer in their first season in exile and has been one of their most consistent players. He is now employed as a postman. Chris, who has already scored 50 goals for A.F.C., was voted "Player of the Year" for 1990/91.

LITHERLAND, Edgar Harold.

b. Carlisle 28.10.11 d. Carlisle mid 1971 5'9"
12st 7lbs
1-0 (1-0)
Everton (reserves c 1934) Npt. (July 1934 to
cs 1935)

Harold was a dashing centre-forward, who started in Army football and played in two representative games before becoming the Central League understudy to "Dixie" Dean. He made only one Football League appearance for the County, but scored 32 reserve team goals.

LOVE, Alastair.

b. Edinburgh 9.5.55 5'7" 10st 0lbs
41-2 (47-3)
Melbourne Th. Rangers (Schoolboy 1968)
W.B.A. (Mar 1973) Southend Utd. (May 1974
fee) Npt. (July 1975) Partick Th. (cs 1976)
Ayr Utd. (1980) Falkirk (1982)

Quite skilful Scottish inside-forward, who came to Newport with Dave Elliott, but was given a free transfer after Dave was sacked. He had a long career in Scottish football until he retired through injury in 1984.

LOVEMAN, Robert Keith.

b. Greenock 30.9.21
20-0 (21-0)
Baillieston Juniors Npt. (Mar 1948) Arbroath
(mid 1948-49) Aldershot (trial Aug 1950)

Scottish goalkeeper, who had less than a year with the club. Bobby later returned to England for an unsuccessful trial with Aldershot.

LOW, Norman Harvey.

b. Newcastle Upon Tyne 23.3.14 6'1" 12st 7lbs
115-0 (208-0)
Rosehill Villa   Newcastle Utd. (amateur)
Liverpool (Oct 1933) Npt. (Nov 1936 £2,000)
war guest for Bristol C., Liverpool, Everton,
Swindon T. & Lovells Ath. Norwich C. (Oct
1946 fee, Manager from 1950)

Norman achieved local immortality by captaining County's only side to reach Division II. He was a solid, impressive centre-half, especially good in the air. His father and uncle had also been well-known footballers and two brothers-in-law were boxing champions. He understudied Tiny Bradshaw at Liverpool before becoming County's record pre-war signing. After leaving the club he became Manager of Norwich City (May 1950 to April 1955), Workington (Jan 1956) and Port Vale (Feb 1957 to Oct 1962), as well as Liverpool's Chief Scout (1965-67). In the 1960's he coached Cleveland Stokers. Norman has now been living in Canada for some considerable time, but recently visited Newport.

LOWE, Edward.

b. Newport late 1901.
3-0 (3-0)
Npt. (1918) Marshes Hall Caerphilly Npt. (c
1921)

Ted was a young amateur goalkeeper, who played in the reserves, along with his brother. He had played in war-time football and made a few

Football League appearances in place of Anthony Carr.

LOWES, Thomas.

b. Walker, Newcastle c 1897 5'8" 11st 0lbs
109–35 (125–41)
Wallsend Park Villa Newcastle Utd. (Sept 1910 £25) Coventry C. (guest c 1914, full-time July 1919 £50) Nuneaton Caerphilly (Aug 1920) Npt. (July 1922) Yeovil (1926 p/coach and later Manager)

An able inside–left or winger with good ball control. An educated man on and off the pitch, he started as an understudy to Newcastle's pre–1914 stars. Tommy was a regular first teamer for the County, scoring plenty of goals. After managing Yeovil he had spells running Barrow and Wals-all, and after World War II he was a scout for Arsenal and Norwich. He was one of soccer's shrewdest brains, discovering such players as Bert Williams, Johnny Hancocks and John Barnwell.

LOWNDES, Stephen R.

b. Newport 17.6.60. 5'7" 11st 0lbs
200–39 (258–47) (Wales 8 1983–86, Under-21 4 1979–81)
Cwmbran T. Npt. (schoolboy 1974, pro Sept 1977) Millwall (Aug 1983 £55,000) Barnsley (Aug 1986 £40,000) Hereford Utd. (c Oct 1990 £10,000) Wrexham

An elusive touchline player, whose obvious talents were not always appreciated by the Somerton crowd. His deceptive pace was good enough to win him a number of Welsh caps. Steve, who was brought up in Cwmbran, signed as an associate schoolboy at 14 and became top scorer for the reserves in 1977–78. He broke John Rowland's record of consecutive County appearances at Carl Zeiss Jena. In 1983 he refused terms and joined Millwall, the fee being decided by a Tribunal. In 1984 he was out for a long time with an achilles tendon injury.

LOWRY, Sydney H.

b. Hay–on–Wye 5'11" 12st 0lbs.
14–2 (15–2)
Hereford T. Merthyr T. Swansea T. (Mar 1933) Swindon T. (June 1935) Npt. (June 1936 to 1937) war–time for Swansea T.

Syd was a goal scoring inside–forward, who had been in the Army before playing professional football. He had played League soccer fairly regularly for three years prior to his arrival at Somerton Park. In his Swansea days he was apparently fined for threatening a tram conductor with a pistol whilst inebriated!

LUCAS, William Henry.

b. Newport 15.1.18 5'6" 11st 3lbs
94–6 (110–13) (Wales 4 1949–50, War–time 8 1942–46)
Npt (1933) Brookside Ath. Treharris Wolverhampton W. (1935, pro 1936) Swindon T. (1937) war guest for Mansfield T., Lovells Ath., Chesterfield, Hull City, Chester, Blackburn R & Aldershot Swansea T (Mar 1948 £11,000) Npt (Dec 1953 small fee as player–manager, then Manager at regular intervals).

Billy could well be called "Mr. Newport County". His father George Groves, played in the County's first season and as a teenager Billy made a brief appearance in the reserves. He was educated at Corporation Road School, where he won four Schoolboy caps, and was then recommended to Wolves by his uncle, Albert Groves, their former Captain. He became a very skilful inside–forward

or wing–half, but his career was to some extent marred by the War. He helped Swansea to win promotion in 1948–49 and was later released to become County's player–manager, which he combined with pub management. He resigned in 1961, but returned for another five year stint as Manager in 1962, before leaving for a short stay at Swansea. He had another four years in charge from 1970 and another brief time in temporary control in 1975. He held other posts with the club until its demise and now lives in retirement in Ponthir.

LUMLEY, Sydney

b. Lanchester early 1910
14–2 (16–5)
Eshwinning Sunderland District Omnibus Co. (1930–31) Newcastle Utd. (trial June 1931) S.D.O.C. Sunderland (Sept 1931) Hartlepools Utd. (1931) Npt. (July 1932) Barrow S.D.O.C. (c 1936)

An inside–forward, who had scored 18 goals for Hartlepools in 25 games in 1931–32. He never managed to capture the same consistency elsewhere, despite scoring a Welsh Cup hat–trick for County at Bristol City 1/2/33, and played mainly in North Eastern non–League football for his works side. He was dogged by injury during his time at Somerton Park.

LUNN, William John.

b. Lurgan, N.Ireland 8.5.23. 5'9" 10st 11lbs
6–1 (9–2)
Shanklin Distillery(1940) Glenavon Hereford Utd.(1945–46) W.B.A. (Jan 1946) Bournemouth (Feb.1948) Npt.(July 1950) Yeovil T.(June 1952) retired c 1955

An inside–forward, who had two Northern Irish caps as a schoolboy and one as a junior amateur. Billy was engaged in the linen industry before turning pro. He was Yeovil's leading scorer in 1952–53 and 1953–54, but mainly played in the reserves at Somerton Park, scoring 49 goals in 56 Welsh League games. His brother Harry played for Swindon Town and figured in their record 0–9 defeat versus Torquay. Billy is still living in Bournemouth.

LYNCH, Terence J.

b. Newport 17.5.52 6'1" 14st 0lbs
56–0 (60–0)
Newport (Juniors, pro Nov 1969) Bath C. (July 1972) Barry T. (Aug 1973) Cwmbran T.

(1974) Pill Y.M.C.A. Npt. (loan Mar 1978) Caerleon

Terry was a very well–built goalkeeper, a former Youth international who was developed by the club. For a short time he established himself as the County's first choice custodian and later returned as cover during an injury crisis. He left professional football and decided to pound the beat with the Gwent Constabulary.

LYTHGOE, John (Jack).

b. Dixon Fold, Little Hulton 3.4.1892 d. Little Hulton 5.6.69 5'7" 11st 0lbs
35–5 (37–5)
Walkden Central (1912–13) Bury (Nov 1913) Army, with games for Bolton W. & Nottm. Forest Nottm. Forest (July 1919 £1,000) Npt. (cs 1921) Manchester C. (1922) Norwich C. (June 1922) Eccles Utd. (Nov 1923) Crewe A. (cs 1924) Margate T. (Aug 1925)

Jack was a powerful inside–left and a useful goalgetter. He only missed eight games for Bury in 1914–15 and then served in the Machine Gun Corps and Tank Corps during World War 1. He later played fairly regularly for Nottm. Forest and Newport, but by then he was reaching the end of his career.

MABBUTT, Raymond William.

b. Aylesbury 13.3.36 5'6" 11st 0lbs
39–4 (51–5)
Aylesbury Yorkshire Amateurs Oxford C. Bristol R. (amateur 1955, pro Aug 1956) Npt. (Sept 1969, at first on trial) Trowbridge (June 1971) Bath C. (1972) Clevedon (1975)

Ray was a dapper little player, who became an institution during his time at Eastville. He played well over 400 games for Rovers and turned out in every outfield position except centre-half. He was well in the veteran stage when joining County, but still retained a fair amount of ability and enthusiasm. He suffered a back injury in early 1970–71 and retired from League soccer at the end of the season, although he still turned out for more than half a dozen non-League clubs afterwards. He later became a successful insurance broker and is the father of Kevin and Gary, the latter the captain of 'Spurs 1991 F.A. Cup team.

MACEY, John Robert Thornbury.

b. Bristol 13.11.47 5'9" 11st 6lbs
194–0 (220–0)
Abbotians Bristol C. (App. 1963, pro May 1965) Shrewsbury T. (loan 1967) Grimsby T. (July 1968) Npt. (June 1970) Minehead (July 1976) Bridgend T. (cs 1979) Barry T. (Feb 1980) Npt. (Aug 1982 non-contract) Forest Green R. (cs 1986)

English Schoolboy "cap", a competent and consistent goalkeeper, although he did play outfield once for Grimsby. John left there after breaking a wrist and was taken on a two months' trial at Somerton Park, but eventually stayed for six years. A keen cricketer, John has long had his own sports shops and been involved in local sport. He was signed as injury cover in 1982 and became

reserve team Manager. He continued playing non-League football, but suffered a collapsed lung. He had played rugby for Bristol Tech. before taking up soccer.

MAIDMENT, James Henry C. ("Jake").

b. Sunderland 28.9.01 d. Rushcliffe, Notts. early 1977 5'10" 12st 0lbs
219–3 (241–4)
James Thompson's F.C. of Sunderland Southend Utd. (cs 1923) Npt. (June 1924) Lincoln C. (May 1930) Notts. Co. (May 1931) Accrington S. (July 1933)

A very fine and consistent goalkeeper, who had a long career and only missed ten Football League games in five seasons. At one time Jimmy took penalties for County. He saw off the challenge of various reserve keepers at Somerton Park. His younger brother Tom was a well-known player and Billy Charlton was his uncle.

Utd. (loan Feb 1984) Swansea C. (July 1984) Npt. (July 1985) Cardiff C. (Mar 1987) Hereford Utd. (Sept 1988) Sweden Cheltenham T. (Nov 1989) Darlington (?Mar 1990)

Coloured forward, who had showed early promise, including scoring the winner in a 1–0 result at Anfield. He could be something of a comedian at times, always likely to fall on his backside while performing a bicycle kick, but always tried his best when others had given up, and scored quite a few goals. Steve's Darlington, became 1990–91 Division IV champions.

MANN, Adrian G.

b. Northampton 12.7.67 5'7" 9st 4lbs
17–0 (19–1)
Northampton T. (YTS 1983, pro May 1985) Southampton (loan 1985) Torquay Utd. (loan Mar 1987) Bath C. (loan 1987) Altrincham (loan 1987) Npt. (Nov 1987) Wycombe W. (Mar 1988 £1,000) Aylesbury (cs 1988) Fisher Ath.

Busy little midfield player, who helped Northampton to win promotion from Division IV. He became the youngest player to turn out for the Cobblers at 16 years of age. Adrian had a brief stay a County, but was then sold to prune the wage bill.

MARDENBOROUGH, Stephen A.

b. Selly Oak, Birmingham 11.9.64 5'8" 11st 9lbs
50–10 (82–14)
Coventry C. (App., pro Aug 1982) Wolverhampton W. (Sept 1983) Cambridge

MARSH, Frederick J.

b. Dudley, mid 1914 5'11" 12st 0lbs
6–0 (7–0)
Dudley T. Npt. (Sept 1936)

Amateur goalkeeper with a remarkable reach. Fred was recommended to Major Buckley of Wolves when Hillier was injured in the first game of the 1936–37 season. He let in seven in his last appearance for the club, at Millwall.

MARTIN, Tudor James ("Ted").

b. Caerau 20.4.04 d. Newport 6.9.79 5'9" 11st 8lbs
29–34 (32–37)
Caerau Bridgend W.B.A. (Oct 1926) Npt. (July 1929) Wolverhampton W. (May 1930 £1,500 plus C.Pearce) Swansea T. (July 1932) West Ham (June 1936) Southend Utd. (Feb 1937 to 1940)

Tudor game up his mining job to enter football with Bridgend and W.B.A. He had a cartilage operation in 1929 and was recommended to Manager Jimmy Hindmarsh by Sammy Richardson. He proved a prolific goalscorer with a fierce shot and still holds the seasonal scoring record for Newport, one which cannot be broken. Later Tudor scored a hat-trick on his West Ham debut, but then became the first Hammer to be sent off for 25 years and was transferred. He played against Ipswich in their first Football League game. After the War he worked for Stewart's & Lloyd's for many years and was Vice President of Newport Defence Snooker League.

MARTINEZ, Eguene.

b. Chelmsford 6.7.57 5'8" 10st 10lbs
18-1 (27-3)
Harrogate R.I. Bradford C. (non-contract, pro July 1977) Rochdale (July 1980) Npt. (Aug 1983 on trial, full-time Nov 1983) Northampton T. (loan Feb 1984)

Winger or midfielder of Spanish parentage, who paid his own expenses to join County on trial. He was eventually given a full contract, but was no more than adequate and went to Northampton on loan, leaving League football at the end of the season.

MATSON, Francis Robert (Frank).

b. Reading 21.11.05 5'10" 11st 0lbs
1-1 (1-1)
Cardiff Corries Reading Cardiff C. (amateur Dec 1926, pro Feb 1927) Npt. (Aug 1930) Southampton (?1930 to 1932)

Frank made his Cardiff City debut in Division 1 as an amateur one week after signing from Cardiff Corries. He ended up with the County, who had tried to sign him earlier and scored on his debut versus Torquay 30.8.30. He could not appear in the following game and never played in League football afterwards. ˙

MATTHEWS, David Ivor (Dai).

b. Pontygwaith, Rhondda 24.9.21 6'0" 11st 4lbs
6-0 (7-0)
Cardiff C. (Sept 1947) Npt. (Apr 1948) Senghenydd

Dai was a reserve goalkeeper with the County. He played over 20 Welsh League games in 1948-49 before moving into non-League soccer.

MATTHEWSON, Trevor.

b. Sheffield 12.2.63 6'1" 12st 5lbs
73–0 (97–1)
Sheffield Wed. (App., pro Feb 1981) Npt. (Oct 1983) Stockport Co. (Sept 1985) Lincoln C. (cs 1987 £13,000) Birmingham C. (Aug. 1989 £30,000)

A big, awkward defender, whose style did not please all supporters, but who played fairly regularly in the County first side. His uncle had played with Colin Addison at Sheffield United. Trevor would not re-sign in 1985, as he wanted to return North and he was given a free transfer. He was later bought by Lincoln City when they were trying to regain their Football League status. He became their Captain and was then sold to Birmingham, the fee being settled by a Tribunal.

MAYES, Alan K.

b. Edmonton, London 11.12.53 5'7" 10st 10lbs
3–1 (3–1)
Q.P.R. (App., pro July 1971) Watford (Nov 1974) Northampton T. (loan Jan 1976) Swindon T. (Feb 1979) Swansea C. Chelsea (Dec 1980) Swindon T. (July 1983) Carlisle Utd. (July 1985) Npt. (loan Feb 1986) Blackpool (loan Sept 1986, then full-time) Wycombe W.

Alan was an effective striker with good close control and the ability to turn defenders. During a long career he scored plenty of goals, but he was not fully fit when joining the County and was soon discarded.

McBLAIN, Andrew.

b. Bo'ness, West Lothian 11.8.26 5'11" 12st 0lbs
36–1 (41–1)
Grange Rovers Forth Wanderers Npt. (Feb 1947) Trowbridge T. (Dec 1948 £250)

A wing–half, who had been recommended to County by a Scottish scout. Andy played regularly in the 1947–48 season, but was allowed to join Trowbridge the following year. After a season in the West country, he returned to Scotland, and soon after joined his father-in-law's batchery business.

McCOLE, John.

b. Glasgow 18.9.36 5'11" 11st 6lbs
6–2 (7–3)
Falkirk (c 1956) Bradford C. (Sept 1958) Leeds Utd. (Sept 1959 £10,000) Bradford C. (Oct 1961) Rotherham Utd. (Dec 1962) Shelbourne (1963) Npt. (Oct 1964) Cork Hibs (Feb 1965)

John was a very effective centre-forward, who was top scorer in his two seasons with Leeds. Unfortunately he broke his leg in April 1963 and was out of football for a year. After a short stay at Somerton Park he returned to Ireland, where he appeared in the Dublin City Cup Final of 1965.

McCRINDLE, William ("Jock").

b. Hurlford 28.7.23   d. ?Gorleston 20.2.82
5'11" 12st 8lbs
5-0 (8-0)
Falkirk (Apr to Dec 1945) Pollok Npt. (Nov 1948) Gorleston (cs 1950)

A right–back, who spent most of his time in the reserves. "Jock" broke his leg in the promotion Derby versus Swansea in 1949 and was out of action for six months. After that he moved to Gorleston–on–Sea.

McDONALD, Robert William ("Roy").

b. Penarth c 1900   d. Newport c 1970 5'7" 11st 0lbs
8-1 (8-1) (Wales Amateur 1 1923)
Lovells Ath. Barry Npt. (1922) Lovells Ath. (cs 1923)

"Roy" was an amateur international inside–forward, who was a regular goalscorer for County's reserves in 1922–23. He later rejoined Lovells Athletic and was well–known as their Manager from 1939 to the 1950's. He was employed by the Lovells firm as a Buyer. At one time he was a member of the Southern League Management Committee.

McGEADY, John T.

b. Glasgow 17.4.58
2-0 (2-0)
Third Lanark Sheffield Utd. (Jan 1976) California Surfers Npt. (trial Sept 1978)

John was a Scottish forward, who had a very short stay at Newport. His signing was delayed because his contract was held by an American club and he was not retained after a trial.

McGHEE, James W.

b. Motherwell 21.8.30 5'7" 10st 6lbs
10-1 (11-3)
Forth Wanderers Kilmarnock (c 1950) Darlington (July 1952) Dumbarton Barry T. (?cs 1953) Npt. (May 1954) Morton (Aug 1955)

A forward, who scored a lot of goals for Barry Town. At County he was mainly a reserve and scored over 20 goals for the Welsh League side.

McKAY, Robert.

b. Govan, Glasgow 2.9.1900 5'7" 11st 8lbs
16-3 (18-3) (Scotland 1 1928)
Parkhead White Rose Vale of Clyde Parkhead Juniors Neilston Victoria Morton (1921) Glasgow Rangers (June 1925 £1,750) Newcastle Utd. (Nov 1926 £2,750) Sunderland (Oct 1928 p/exchange for Bob Thompson) Charlton Ath (Dec 1930 £1,220) Bristol R. (Nov 1932 £350) Npt. (June 1935)

International forward, who joined the County at the end of a very long and distinguished career. A bundle of tricks, Bobby was good at creating openings. He won many honours in his team. He was in Morton's 1922 Scottish Cup winning side and the Championship sides of Rangers (1926) and Newcastle Utd. (1927). Bobby was always consistent and scored plenty of goals. He was appointed Dundee United Manager in July 1939, but was called up after only 5 games. He became Ballymena United Manager in 1947, but returned to Scotland after a couple of years, and became a Charlton Scout for several years.

McKENNA, Francis Charles (Frank).

b. Walker-On-Tyne 9.12.02 5'7" 11st 7lbs
24-3 (25-3)
Swan Hunter Spennymoor Utd. Wallsend
Grimsby T. (May 1922) Fulham (May 1927)
Norwich C. (July 1928 £100) Npt. (Aug 1929)
Walker Celtic (Aug 1930) Wrexham (cs 1932 to 1933) Walker Celtic

A slightly built but plucky player, a speedy forward with good footwork. Frank scored a lot of goals in his career. He was top scorer in his season with Norwich and was with Grimsby when they won the Division III (North) Championship.

McKENZIE, Francis (Frank).

b. Inverness 5'7" 11st 7lbs
65-0 (75-0)
Inverness Thistle Rotherham County (later United) (1919) Npt. (cs 1924) Scunthorpe Utd. (cs 1926) Gainsborough Trinity Newark Town (May 1928)

Very solid and dependable defender. Frank had spent five years in and out of the Rotherham side, but left after he was refused a benefit. He played

regularly for County over two seasons.

McKENZIE, Frederick Taylor.

b. Lochee nr. Dundee 13.11.03 d. Plymouth
22.11.79 5'10" 12st 7lbs
88-1 (96-1)
Lochee Utd. Npt. (Aug 1924) Plymouth A. (Feb 1926 £1,500) Npt. (June 1934) retired Dec 1934

A cunning and very consistent halfback. Fred actually lost a toe due to blood poisoning, but this did not affect his football. He had been a junior international in Scotland and became a mainstay of the County team. Other large offers were turned down before a record fee was accepted by County from Plymouth. Fred became the Argyle penalty king, only missing one out of twelve. He returned to Somerton Park for a short spell in 1934, but was released from his contract to manage a public house in Plymouth. He spent the rest of his life in Devon.

McLAUGHLAN, Hugh McCann.

b. Galston, Kilmarnock 20.7.01 d. Camden, London mid 1983 5'10" 12st 7lbs
53-0 (58-0)
Kilmarnock Queen of the South Glasgow Celtic Carlisle Utd. (June 1929) Barrow (July 1930) Npt. (Aug 1933 to 1935)

A strong, sturdy defender, who never 'skied' a ball, but always tried to place to a forward. After his arrival in England he spent around five years in League football. Hugh was also an expert golfer.

McLAUGHLIN, Michael Anthony.

b. Newport 5.1.43 5'10" 12st 4lbs
97-2 (108-2)
Nash Utd. Npt. (1959, pro Nov 1961) Merthyr (1962) Barry T. (1965) Lovells Ath. (Mar 1968) Npt. (Aug 1968) Hereford Utd. (at first on loan, Aug 1970 to cs 1975) Cheltenham T. Newport Saracens R.U. Npt. (Mar 1978 to May 1978)

Well-built defender, who began with the reserves, but did not play in the League until his mid-twenties. Mike became County Captain, but left because he wanted part-time football. He had been playing Rugby before returning in a 1978 crisis. He emigrated to America in October 1979, where he has run the Atlanta Renegades Rugby Union side.

McLELLAND, John B.

b. Bradford 15.3.35 5'9"
36-10 (40-10)
Manchester C. (May 1953) Lincoln C. (Sept 1958) Q.P.R. (Sept 1961 £15,000) Portsmouth (May 1963 £20,000) Npt. (July 1968) retired May 1969

Centre-forward or winger, son of the much travelled Jimmy (both scored over 100 Football League goals) and younger brother of Charlie. He always proved a consistent player, with over 100 games for Lincoln and

Portsmouth. John was at the end of his career when spending a season at Somerton Park.

McMANUS, Stuart J.

b. Falkirk 19.3.65 5'11" 12st 7lbs
4-0 (5-0)
Southampton (Juniors July 1984) Npt (loan Aug 1985) Örgryte IS

Stuart is a well-built forward, who scored regularly for Southampton reserves, but made little impact during his loan spell at Somerton Park.

McMILLAN, James ("Jock").

b. ?Seaton Delaval c 1899 5'9" 11st 6lbs
25-0 (26-0)
Seaton Delaval Npt. (Oct 1920 to 1922)

"Jock" McMillan, a former schoolboy international, was one of the County's many North Eastern signings during the 1920's. He arrived on trial, but was then taken on full-time. He was a polished and resourceful right-back, who loved his upfield sorties and was good at the offside game. During his first season he played regularly for the Football League side, but his second spell was in the reserves, for whom he made 30 appearances.

McNAB, Alexander ("Sandy").

b. Glasgow 27.12.11 d. Sept 1962 5'7" 10st 5lbs
3-0 (10-0) (Scotland 2 1937-39)

Tuesday Waverley Pollok Sunderland (May 1932) W.B.A. (Mar 1938 £7,500) war guest for Northampton T., Nottm. Forest & Npt. Npt. (July 1946) Dudley T. (Dec 1946) Northwich Victoria retired cs 1952

A brave and tireless wing–half, who worked as a grocer before turning to professional football. "Sandy" began as an outside–left with Sunderland and was later in their F.A. Cup winning side of 1937. He played for the Football League XI and toured Canada and the U.S.A. with Scotland in 1939. He was Albion's regular war–time captain and spent a short time with the County, but he was over the top by then. He was running "Ye Olde Lyttleton Arms" in Halesowen at the time of his death.

McPHERSON, Kenneth.

b. West Hartlepool 25.3.27 6'0" 12st 0lbs
128-52 (146–59)
Harlepools Utd. (amateur) Notts. Co. (Aug 1950) Middlesbrough (Aug 1953 £15,000) Coventry C. (Nov 1955) Npt. (June 1958 £2,500) New York Americans (June 1961) Swindon T. (Aug 1961 £2,550) retired cs 1965

Red–haired ex–paratrooper, a square–shouldered, high–scoring centre–forward, who made a big impact during his time at Somerton Park. Ken had been understudy to Tommy Lawton at Meadow Lane and was sent off at Somerton while he was with Coventry. He scored with great regularity for County including hat–tricks versus Southampton, Bristol City and Watford and rarely missed a game for the club. He was converted to a half–back at Swindon before retiring to his grocer's shop.

McSEVENEY, John Haddon.

b. Shotts, Lanarks. 8.2.31 5'6" 10st 6lbs
172-51 (192–62)
Carluke Rovers Hamilton Acs. (1948) Sunderland (Oct 1951 £5,000) Cardiff C. (May 1955, with Kirtley and Sheppeard for £9,000) Npt. (June 1957 p/exchange) Hull C. (June 1961 £1,100 to June 1965)

Talented and experienced utility forward, who could score his share of goals including 4 versus Halifax 28.11.59. He had played in Division I for Sunderland and Cardiff and scored twice on his City home debut against his old club. After a long Football League career John has had varied coaching and managerial posts with Hull City, Barnsley, Home Farm, Waterford, Nottingham Forest, Guyana, Dubai, Rotherham United and Sheffield United.

Barry was a well-built inside-forward, who lived a few hundred yards from Dean Court and had two football playing uncles. He played well over 100 Division II games for Bristol Rovers, but left after a dispute over pre-season training arrangements. He played and scored consistently during his time at Somerton Park, but his first love was cricket. Well-known as the Gloucestershire wicket-keeper, he has had a long career as a Test Match umpire.

MELLING, Terence.

b. Haverton Hill, Newcastle 24.1.40 6'0" 12st 4lbs
34-14 (38-15)
Tow Law T. (amateur) Newcastle Utd. (Dec 1965) Watford (May 1966) Npt. (Feb 1967 £2,500) Mansfield T. (Nov 1967 £3,000) Rochdale (Sept 1968) Darlington (Mar 1969) Scarborough (1969-70) Tow Law T.

Physical centre-forward, who could score a few goals and netted a hat-trick for County versus Wrexham 30.9.67. Terry played for Durham schoolboys and captained the British Army XI. He played in the Watford side that held Liverpool to an F.A. Cup draw after asking County for a transfer.

MEYER, Barry John.

b. Bournemouth 21.8.32 5'10" 12st 0lbs
69-27 (78-30)
Bristol R. (Nov 1949) Plymouth A. (Aug 1958 £4,500) Npt. (Feb 1959 £4,000) Bristol C. (Sept 1961 £850) Hereford Utd. (July 1963)

MICALLEF, Constantin (Tarki).

b. Cardiff 24.1.61 5'5" 11st 4lbs
22-2 (30-2) (Wales Under-21 3 1982-83)
Cardiff C. (youth) Tottenham H. (youth) Cardiff C. (App. 1976, pro Jan 1979) Npt. (Sept 1983 p/exchange) Gillingham (Aug 1984 trial) Cardiff C. (Sept 1984) Bristol R. (Sept 1986) Barry T. (cs 1987) AFC Cardiff (cs 1989 to Jan 1990)

A small forward, the son of a Greek restaurateur. Tarki was a Welsh schools, youth and under-21 international. He was voted Cardiff's player of the Year in 1981-82, but left in a multi-player exchange after a row over an unpaid hospital bill. Despite making a fair number of appearances in the County team, he made little impact and departed on a free transfer. He recently left AFC Cardiff because of his work commitments as a scene shifter with the Welsh National Opera.

MILES, Andrew.

b. Tredegar 25.5.61
3-2 (6-2)
Blaenavon Ebbw Vale (1984) Npt. (Aug 1985
non-contract) Ebbw Vale Bath C. (Sept 1985)
Ebbw Vale (Oct 1985) Merthyr T. (Mar 1989)
Ton Pentre (July 1989)

Striker with some ability, who scored
two goals in an away game at
Wolves. He was given few more
chances, however, and has spent most
of his career playing in the valleys.

MILES, Jeffrey M.

b. Caldicot 17.1.49
4-0 (4-0)
Cheltenham T. Npt. (amateur Apr 1966)
Hereford Utd. (loan 1967-68) Gloucester C.
Cheltenham Gloucester C. (c 1980)

Bank clerk, who was on County's
books as an amateur in 1966-67.
Jeff was recalled when Weare and
Timson were injured, but was only
registered on Welsh League forms, so
Alan Wood played in goal. He
helped to knock County out of the
Welsh Cup in one of his games for
Hereford and was last heard of living
in Aberdare.

MILLAR, William.

b. Ballymena 22.3.? 5'8" 11st 7lbs
7-1 (10-1) (Ireland 2 1932-33)
Linfield Liverpool (cs 1928) Barrow (1928)
Npt. (June 1933) Carlisle Utd. (July 1934 to
1935)

Useful forward, although he only
played a few games at Somerton
Park. In his spell with Barrow, Billy
played well over 100 games and
scored over 70 goals, becoming their
only International player. He was
mainly out of the first team here, but
scored 23 goals for the reserves and
played regularly for Carlisle the following season.

MILLER, Paul A.

b. Bisley 31.1.68 6'0" 11st 0lbs
6-2 (6-2)
Yeovil T. Wimbledon (YTS Aug 1987) Npt.
(loan Oct 1987) Bristol C. (loan Jan 1990)

Forward, a Wimbledon reserve, who
played quite well during his loan
spell, but then returned to Plough
Lane.

MILLETT, Glynne.

b. Crickhowell 13.10.68 5'10" 10st 12lbs
23-2 (56-5)
Abergavenny Th. Npt. (YTS cs 1986, pro July
1987) Abergavenny (Nov 1988)

Striker, who looked impressive in his
first few games for County, but
whose later form deteriorated.
Glynne went to Brecon High School
and won mid-Wales caps. He preferred joining Newport to Chelsea
and made his debut as substitute
versus Everton. He found more first
team opportunities after the clearout
of 1988, but after a short time in the
Vauxhall Conference side decided to
move on.

MILLS, Sean D.

b. Ebbw Vale 1.6.68 6'0"
5-0 (13-0)
Sunderland (App. 1984) Npt. (Aug 1986) Bath C. (Aug 1987) Npt. (Sept 1988) RTB Ebbw Vale (1989) Stroud (Nov 1989)

Skilful, ball–playing midfielder, who was only a youngster when appearing in the County's Welsh Cup Final team versus Merthyr. Sean was unlucky to be given a free transfer at the end of the season. He made a brief return to Somerton in the club's Vauxhall Conference season, but could not train properly because of work commitments.

MOFFAT, Adam.

b. Lochgelly, Fife 1.4.41
17-5 (17-5)
East Fife (1958) Npt. (loan Oct 1961) Yeovil T. (Sept 1963)

Fair–haired forward, one of Bobby Evan's imports from North of the border. He was educated at Cowdenbeath High School and was a regular with East Fife. Adam was signed under a "gentlemen's agreem–ent" whilst working as a bricklayer at Spencer Works.

MOGFORD, Reginald W.G.

b. Newport 12.6.19 5'10" 12st 0lbs
20-9 (33-13)
Npt. (Junior late 1937, pro 1939) war guest with Aberaman, Reading, Tottenham H. &

Luton T. Worcester C. (cs 1947) Kiddermins-ter H. (cs 1952)

Centre– or inside–forward, who was mainly a reserve. He was stationed at R.A.F. High Wycombe during the War (he was in the service police), playing rugby for the R.A.F. mid-week, and soccer for Reading at weekends. In the first two post–war seasons Reg scored 58 goals in 45 Welsh League games for County including 5 versus Cardiff reserves. In fairly recent times, he was running a painting and decorating business in Worcester. His son, Bryan, made 163 appearances for Worcester in the 1980's.

MOLLOY, William George.

b. Coventry 28.8.29
3-0 (5-1)
Southampton (Oct 1949) Lockhead Leam-ington (July 1950) Npt. (Nov 1950 on trial, full-time Jan 1951 £100) Lockhead Leam-ington Millwall Rugby T. (Aug 1952) (Mar 1952)

Wing–half or right–winger, who played over 40 reserve games for County, but only made 3 Football League appearances. Billy, had earlier spent a short time at South–ampton after leaving the Army. Later on he became a builder in Coventry, and later played for num-erous non–League sides. His son played soccer for Merthyr T.

MONTGOMERY, Stanley William J.

b. Sidcup 7.7.20 6'2" 12st 2lbs
9–0 (10–0)
Romford (pre–war) Leyton O. (1940) Hull C. (1944) Southend U. (War–time, full–time Sept 1946) Cardiff C. (Nov 1948 £6,000) Worcester C. (July 1955) Npt. (Nov 1955) Llanelli (Oct 1956) Ton Pentre

Talented and commanding half–back, the son–in–law of Jimmy Nelson. Stan was a star of the West Ham Schools XI and had trials with Spurs and Chelsea at 17. He played war–time soccer and captained Southend for three years. He helped Cardiff to Division I and played over 200 games for the City. Stan was trainer at Norwich and Cardiff (1962) and became Bristol Rovers' Youth Adviser, returning to Cardiff in 1985. He played cricket for Essex and Glamorgan.

MOORE, John.

b. Consett 1.10.66 6'0" 11st 11lbs
2–0 (4–0)
Sunderland (app., pro Oct 1984) St. Patrick's Ath. (loan) Npt. (loan Nov 1985) Darlington (loan Nov 1986) Mansfield T. (loan Mar 1987) Rochdale (loan Jan 1988) Hull C. (Aug 1988) Sheffield Utd. (loan Mar 1989) Utrecht Shrewsbury T. (Aug 1990)

Well–built forward who had a brief stay on loan at Somerton Park, but failed to impress and returned to Roker Park.

MOORE, John Frederick Beriah.

b. Cardiff 25.12.19 5'7" 10st 0lbs
121–45 (137–58)
Cardiff Corries (1937) Cardiff C. (amateur 1939, the pro. 1941) war–time with Bristol C. Bangor C. Cardiff C. (1947) Bangor C. (Aug 1949) Npt. (July 1950) Bangor C. (June 1953) Caernarvon T. (to May 1957)

An outside–left, who played war–time soccer for Cardiff City and scored the consolation goal in their 1–10 defeat by Moscow Dynamo. Beriah found the net over 100 times in the war–time matches and played for an F.A. XI. He played regularly and consistently for the County, becoming a firm favourite with the fans. His prematurely bald head glinting in the Winter sun became as familiar a Newport landmark as the Transporter Bridge. He became the only County player to score hat-tricks in the Football League, F.A. Cup and Welsh Cup. Beriah, who also played baseball for Penylan, now lives in retirement in his native Bangor.

MOORE, Kevin J.

b. Blackpool 30.1.56 5'9" 11st 4lbs
140–14 (182–20)
Blackpool (App., pro. Oct 1973) Bury (loan Dec 1976) Swansea C. (June 1977) Npt. (Feb 1979 £12,000) Swindon T. (loan Mar 1983) Burnley (1983)

A very talented and elusive left winger, who played many impressive games for County and seemed to earn a penalty every other game. Kevin was a Lancashire Schools player, who began his professional career with Blackpool, where his father was President. At first he refused to move to Newport, but then Swansea signed Attley. He played in County's promotion and Welsh Cup side. Later he fell out with the Management and reported Addison to the P.F.A. Afterwards Kevin drifted out of League football. In 1977–78 he had only missed 6 games in Swansea's promotion season.

MORGAN, Herbert H. (Harry).

b. Swansea late 1913.
4–0 (4–0)
Cardiff local football Npt. (Dec 1934)

Inside–forward or winger, who had a spell with the County as an amateur, without making any impact at first team level.

MORGAN, Kenneth G.

b. Swansea 16.3.39 5'7" 10st 8lbs
125–43 (141–46) (Wales Under–23 2 1959–60)
Manchester Utd. (Juniors Jan 1955, pro Apr 1956) Swansea T. (Mar 1961 £3,000) Npt. (June 1964 fee) Cwmbran T. (June 1967 to 1970)

One of the cleverest and most accomplished footballers seen at Somerton Park in the 1960's. Normally an inside–forward, Ken was a reserve at Old Trafford, where he made 17 Football League appearances and survived the Munich air crash.

He was a regular County first teamer for three seasons (scoring 4 versus Lincoln C. 26/10/64) and later had a successful time as player–manager of Cwmbran T. He had a pub near Pontypool before becoming a salesman.

MORGAN, Peter W.

b. Cardiff 28.10.51 5'10" 12st 0lbs
22-0 (26-0)
Cardiff C. (Nov 1969) Bath C. (loan c Mar 1974) Hereford Utd. (loan Aug 1974, full–time Oct 1974 to June 1975) Npt. (Mar 1976) Bridgend Sully Cardiff C. (Welsh League 1980)

Peter, who was a full–back, is the younger brother of the former Cardiff City Manager, Richie Morgan, with whom he played a few games in the Cardiff first team. He was out of soccer and working as a fork truck driver when signed by the County as a part–time reserve. He was later with Cardiff City as a coach and scout.

MORGAN, Wendell.

b. Gorseinon 22.4.35 5'7" 10st 8lbs
26-3 (29-3)
Grovesend Cardiff C. (Juniors May 1952) Brentford (June 1954, pro 1955) Gillingham (Sept 1957) Swansea T. (July 1958 £5,000) Npt. (June 1959) Carlisle Utd. (June 1960 to 1961)

Left winger, who had six seasons of League football. Although he played fairly regularly for most of his clubs, Wendell never really settled anywhere. Shortly after leaving his last team he was in Canada.

MORRALL, Alfred Douglas.

b. Duddleston 1.7.16 5'9" 10st 12lbs
28-0 (32-0)
Redditch Northampton T. (1943) Npt. (July 1948 to 1949) retired July 1949.

Half–back or inside–forward, the son of a Hull City player of the same name. He had five years with Northampton, showing his best form during World War II. He played three times in County's famous F.A. Cup run of 1948–49. Alf was an engineer by profession.

MORREY, Bernard Joseph.

b. Liverpool 8.4.27
24-2 (26-5)
Tranmere R. (1944) South Liverpool (Aug 1947) Holywell (1950–51) Llandudno (1951–52) Npt. (trial Sept 1952, pro Nov 1952) Chester (Dec 1953)

Winger, who amassed a fair amount of non–League experience before joining the County. A year later Bernard joined Chester and scored in the 1955 Welsh Cup Final.

MORRIS, Hugh.

b. Hardgate, Dumbartonshire 5'7" 11st 6lbs
22-5 (24-7)
Clyde Manchester C. (Aug 1922) Nottm.
Forest (June 1924) Notts. Co. (1925) Southend
Utd. (Sept 1925) Npt. (July 1929 to 1930)

Hugh was a cool and reliable Scottish winger, who had enjoyed a long career before joining the County. He played over 50 games for Manchester City and more than 100 for Southend. He suffered a leg injury halfway through the 1929–30 season.

MULLEN, James.

b. Jarrow 8.11.52 5'10" 12st 12lbs
19-0 (27-0)
Sheffield Wednesday (app., pro Oct 1970)
Rotherham Utd. (Aug 1980 £25,000) Preston
N.E. (loan Nov 1981) Cardiff C. (loan, full-
time Mar 1982 £10,000) Npt. (p/manager May
1986 £1,500)

A wholehearted, if not polished central defender. Jimmy was a very experienced League footballer, who had skippered three Division III promotion teams and been Coach and Assistant Manager at Cardiff City. After a short stay at Somerton Park, Jimmy left in February, 1987 to join his friend Ian Porterfield in the management set–up at Aberdeen, the Scottish team playing a friendly as compensation. He was afterwards Manager of Blackpool, until resigning 13.4.90.

MURRAY, Donald J.

b. Duffus nr. Elgin 18.1.46 6'0" 13st 0lbs
16-0 (21-0) Scotland Under-23 1 1965)
Burghead Thistle Cardiff C. (pro Jan 1963)
Swansea C. (loan Oct 1974) Hearts (Dec 1974
£15000) Npt. (Oct 1976) Barry T. (Jan 1978
p/exchange) Cardiff C. (Aug 1979, Welsh
League)

Scottish centre–half, who was an institution in the successful Cardiff side of the 1960's, which seemed to play in the European Cup Winners' Cup every season. He was the proverbial tower of strength in the side for over ten years, playing in over 500 League and Cup games. After a short time back in the Scottish League, Don rejoined Jimmy Scoular at Somerton Park. He played reasonably well, but was in the veteran stage and after Scoular had left, he moved on himself. He remained connected with Welsh football and in September 1988 became Coach for Ynysybwl. At present, Don holds a senior management post at a residential special school.

NAIRN, William James.

b. Cowdenbeath 23.8.1898 d. Sept. 1970 5'10"
11st 7lbs
225-13 (246-14)
Cowdenbeath Dundee Ebbw Vale (c 1920)
Npt. (cs 1922 to 1931)

The County Captain and "Daddy of them all". Billy was a superb right- or centre–half, a resolute tackler and accurate passer. By the end of his time with County he had reached the veteran stage and all the youngsters loved to play with him. He played for the Welsh League versus the Irish Free State League in 1928 and was one of the County's most reliable players.

NELSON. James Anthony.

b. Newport 12.4.30 5'11" 11st 7lbs
19–6 (21–8 (Wales Amateur 2 1952)
Npt. (amateur Aug 1950, pro June 1952)
Bristol C. (May 1954) Bournemouth (June 1956 £500) retired 1964

Son of the famous Jimmy Nelson and brother–in–law of Stan Montgomery. He was brought up in Southend, but started in the County reserves. Tony was a centre–forward and had few opportunities because of Reg Parker. He was later converted to centre–half by Bournemouth and played around 200 games for them, afterwards Trainer and Assistant Manager. Tony, who still lives in Bournemouth, is the branch manager of an Estate Agents, and is the manager of the Dorset County X1.

NEWALL, Daniel J.

b. Newport 5.6.21 5'10" 11st 0lbs
233–4 (272–7)
Melrose Stars (of Newport) Npt. (Feb 1938, pro Feb 1939) retired May 1955

Danny was educated at Corporation Road School, winning two town caps and being chosen as reserve for the Welsh Schoolboys. He spent five years in the R.A.F., three in India, where he joined Tommy Walker's football circus. Although he only made one Football League appearance before the War, after 1946 became a regular at left–half in the first team, renowned as a tough-tackling defender. Later he became a licensee, retiring in 1980. He is the brother–in–law of Billy Lucas.

NEWBOLD, Alfred.

b. West Hartlepool 7.8.21
22–0 (23–0)
Ouston W. Coventry C. (1943–44) Huddersfield T. (c 1945) Npt. (Oct 1946 fee) Worcester C. (cs 1947)

Full–back, who was signed by Huddersfield after impressing in an R.A.F. game. Alf played fairly regularly in his one season at Somerton Park, but then moved into non-League football. He was recently living in Birmingham.

NICHOLLS, John Barry L. (Jack)

b. Cardiff 14.12.1898 d. Cardiff late 1970 5'9"
11st 10lbs
11-4 (13-5) (Wales 4 1924-25, Amateur 10 1923-30)
Ton Pentre Cardiff Corries (c 1921) Pontypridd (Aug 1922) Bridgend (1922-23) Npt. (June 1923) Cardiff C. (cs 1924) Swansea T. (Oct 1924) Cardiff Corries (retired Oct 1930)

Son of the Cardiff City Chairman and nephew of the great Rugby Union player Gwyn Nicholls. Jack played as an amateur in Division I and in the full Welsh side – an indication of his ability. He scored twice on his County debut versus Plymouth 15.12.23 and became the first County player to be capped for Wales, but his work prevented him from playing in away games. Merthyr T. tried to sign him in February 1925, but business commitments with Cardiff Council prevented him from playing regularly. After the War he was in charge of Cardiff Nomads, Norwich City's Welsh nursery and kept the "Lansdowne" Pub.

was the record Newport purchase until Dave Bruton was signed. He scored a remarkable number of headed goals for a defender and was the Captain of the promotion and Welsh Cup winning team. He suffered a broken arm in September 1979 and a broken jaw versus Reading in November 1982. Later he became unsettled and eventually moved to Gillingham, the fee being decided by a Tribunal. In 1988 he rejected a move to Somerton, preferring to return to Peterborough. His brother Dennis was also a professional.

OAKES, Keith B.

b. Bedworth nor. Coventry 3.7.56 5'10" 12st 2lbs
232-27 (284-34)
Peterborough Utd. (App., pro July 1973) Npt. (Sept 1978 £15,000) Gillingham (June 1984 £20,000) Fulham (Sept 1986 small fee) Peterborough Utd. (Aug 1988)

A commanding and consistent central defender, who was the cornerstone of the County's successful side. Keith

ODELL, George W.

b. Hoddesdon 5'8" 12st 0lbs
24-0 (25-0)
St. Albans City Northampton T. (July 1927) Wigan Ath. (Aug 1932) Npt. (July 1934 to 1935)

Competent half-back, who had made well over 100 appearances for Northampton, but who just had the one season at Somerton Park.

OGLEY, William.

b. Rotherham c 1896 5'9" 12st 0lbs
39-2 (45-2)
Swansea T. (cs 1919) Porth (1921) Npt. (Apr 1922) Q.P.R. (July 1924) Castleford T. (1925) Denaby Utd.

Strong defender, who joined Swansea T. from the Army and played in their first ever game in the First Division of the old Southern League. After a couple of seasons at Somerton he had a season with Q.P.R. (where he only missed 6 Football League matches) before returning to Yorkshire.

O'HAGAN Patrick J.

b. Llanbadoc 15.3.71
3-0 (3-0)
Coed Eva Cwmbran T. Npt. (YTS Aug 1987) Swansea C. (trial Aug 1988) Cardiff C. (YTS 1988, pro cs 1989) Stroud T. (loan Dec 1989) Cwmbran T. (Aug 1990)

Young YTS goalkeeper, first thrust into the limelight when he made his debut in a friendly against a Brazilian side and played well. When the County's YTS players were sent home, following the club's eviction from Somerton Park, Swansea stepped in to sign him.

O'HALLORAN, Neil.

b. Cardiff 21.6.33 5'9" 11st 12lbs
14-2 (14-2)
Cardiff C. (Aug 1954) Npt. (June 1957) Barry T. (1958) Merthyr T. (1962)

Centre-forward, who started as a left-back. Neil became the first player to score a hat-trick on his debut for Cardiff City (versus Charlton Athletic 10.12.55), but never really established himself and was transferred to Somerton in part exchange for Colin Hudson. He gave up League soccer because of injury, but carried on playing and was the Welsh League's leading scorer in 1960-61. He was later Barry T. Manager and now, being a successful businessman, has had a long spell as Chairman of the club. His father played football for Merthyr, Barry and (war-time) County.

OLDHAM, George.

b. Tintwhistle 20.4.20 5'9" 12st 7lbs
63-0 (66-0)
Mottram Central   Stoke C. war guest for Stockport Co. & Aldershot Npt. (Aug 1946)

A hard-working full-back, who played regularly during his two seasons with County, missing only three games in the only season in Division II. George was a P.T. instructor at Chepstow Cadet College. Later he moved to Hitchin, Herts and wanted to leave. In 1948 he became Hebburn T. coach. He is now living in Luton.

O'MAHONEY, Matthew T.

b. Mullinavar, Co. Kilkenny 9.1.13 6'0" 12st 8lbs
8-0 (8-0) (Eire & Ireland 7 1938-39)

Hoylake Southport (1935) Wolverhampton W. (May 1935 £1,000+) Npt. (Mar 1936, on loan) Bristol R. (May 1936 £175) Ipswich T. (July 1939 £600) war guest for Aberaman, Bristol C., Bristol R. & Tranmere R. Yarmouth T. (Aug 1949)

Talented athlete and skilful half-back. Matt was a long-legged tackler of rare merit, sure-footed and fond of keeping the ball on the ground. He played for Hoylake whilst at St. Edwards' College, Liverpool. After appearing in a North versus South trial he was picked for an amateur cap, then found to be Irish! He signed for Southport three weeks later and by Wolves after a further month. Matt went on the 1938 Eire tour of Europe, and played for an F.A. XI during the War. In recent years he has kept the "Griffin" pub in Norwich.

O'NEILL, Thomas Henry.

b. Spennymoor 5.1.25 d. Newport Apr 1978 5'9" 11st 6lbs
9-0 (10-0)
Spennymoor (Sept 1942) Newcastle Utd. (1942-43) Leeds Utd. (1943-44) Newcastle Utd. (1947) Npt. (Apr 1948 £150) Spennymoor U. (July 1949)

Right-back, most of whose games were for the reserves. He had the misfortune to break a leg versus Aberaman in late March, 1949. He was retained until December 1949, but was forced to give up soccer. Tommy was living in Newport until his death.

ORPHAN, Leslie J.

b. Newport 17.4.23 5'8" 10st 9lbs
1-0 (1-0) (Wales Amateur 1 1949)
Albion Rovers (of Newport) pre-war Girlings (Cwmbran) Npt. (Sept 1948, pro Feb 1949) Lovells Ath. (cs 1950) Pontllanfraith (1953) retired 1956

Forward good enough to play for the Welsh amateur side. He began with the local side Albion Rovers, which his brother helped to found. Luton tried to sign him, but he did not wish to go full-time and spent 46 years working for DeeBee's. Les played 50 reserve games for County before moving into Welsh League football. He played baseball for Wales.

OSBORNE, Lawrence.

b. Stratford, London 20.10.67 5'10" 11st 7lbs
15-0 (18-0)
schoolboy with West Ham Utd., Tottenham H., Arsenal, Chelsea, Norwich C. & Orient Arsenal (July 1985) Huddersfield T. (trial) Npt. (Nov 1987, at first on trial) Wycombe W. (Mar 1988 £1,000)

Midfielder, who played in Arsenal's Combination side. He was a member of the Essex County Schools team and a keen rugby and cricket player. He was pitched into County's first team because of injuries and played quite a few Football League games before being sold with many others to cut the wage-bill.

O'SHEA, Timothy J.

b. Pimlico 12.11.66 5'11" 11st 4lbs
10-0 (13-0)
schoolboy with Arsenal Tottenham H. (App.
c 1983, pro Aug 1984) Npt. (loan Oct 1986)
Leyton O. (cs 1988) Gillingham (loan, full-
time Feb 1989)

Useful, well-built defender, who
made the final trials as an English
schoolboy. He impressed in his
games on loan for County, but the
£10,000 fee Spurs wanted for him
was beyond the means of the hard-
up club and he returned to White
Hart Lane.

OWEN, William ("W.E.").

b. Northwich 17.9.06 d. Newport 26.3.81 5'3"
9st 6lbs
36-2 (83?-8)
Northwich Victoria Macclesfield Manchester
Utd. (May 1934) Reading (Jan 1936) Exeter C.
(Dec 1936) Npt. (May 1937 fee to 1946) war-
time guest for Mansfield T. & Cardiff C.

Nippy little left winger, who was
signed by Louis Page on Newport
Station, while he was waiting to
catch the train to Exeter. He had
scored two goals versus Preston when
Exeter reached Round Five of the
F.A. Cup in 1936-37. Billy was
nicknamed "W.E." (William Exeter)
by Billy McCandless to distinguish
him from "W.M" (William Manchester). He played regularly in his
first season at Somerton Park, but
only twice in the first team in the
promotion year. He played just a
few times after the War and then
became Trainer, before resigning
over the transfer of John Elsworthy
to Ipswich. Billy lived next door to
Somerton Park for a long time. His
younger brother also had a trial with
the club in 1938.

OWEN, William ("W.M.").

b. Llanfairfechan 30.6.14 d. Scilly 14.6.76
5'10" 12st 6lbs
72-5 (166-14)
Northwich Victoria Manchester C. (June
1934) Tranmere R. (Mar 1935 fee) Npt. (June
1936 fee) war-time guest for Cardiff C. &
Lovells Ath. Exeter C. (Oct 1946) Dartmouth
Utd. (1947)

"W.M.", originally a centre-forward,
was later converted to an effective
wing-half, becoming part of the
impressive Owen-Low-Brinton half-
back line. He was one of Louis
Page's best signings and a member of
the promotion side. In the War he
served in the National Fire Service,
for which he played representative
games. He worked for Bowaters at

Newport Docks and later lived in Caerleon.

being the only Newport player to scored 100 Football League goals. Reg was actually brought up in Newport attending Crindau School before the War and learning his football with the Boy's Brigade in Maesglas. He served with the R.A.F. in the Middle East and signed for Cardiff City in Cairo. He was originally a full-back, but was played at centre–forward by County because of his lethal shot. He was at one time an insurance broker, but later went into the licensing trade and was a Barry Town director for many years.

PAGET, William Sidney Thomas.

b. Cardiff mid 1909 5'10" 10st 7lbs
6-0 (8-0)
Cardiff C. (amateur, pro May 1933) Npt. (cs 1934) Clapton O. (Aug 1935) Barry T.

Forward, who never really made it at Football League level, only making 12 appearances during his career. He was mainly a reserve here, scoring 9 goals in 1934–35.

PARLE, James J.

b. Liverpool 1907 5'8" 11st 0lbs
35-8 (37-8)
Bootle Celtic Birmingham (Aug 1928) Chesterfield (May 1929) Walsall (May 1930) New Brighton (Aug 1931) Worcester C. (1933) Yeovil & Petters Utd. (1934–35) Npt. (June 1935) Hereford Utd.

PARKER, Reginald Edwin.

b. Pontyclun 10.6.21 5'9" 11st 0lbs
201-99 (226–110)
R.A.F. Cardiff C. (c 1941, pro Nov 1946) Npt. (Aug 1948 p/exchange) retired May 1954

Popular centre–forward, who was robbed by an abandoned game of

An effective forward, particularly clever with the square pass. Although never more than an average Third Division player, Jimmy enjoyed a long career. He was in Yeovil's 1935 F.A. Cup run (they played Liverpool in Round Three). He came to Newport with Louis Page.

PARSELLE, Norman J.

b. Newport 8.1.70
4–0 (12–0)
Maesglas Utd. Npt (YTS Aug 1986) Forest Green Rovers (cs 1988) Newport A.F.C. (July 1989)

Versatile local player, normally seen in midfield. Because of the County's critical situation in 1987–88 Norman was thrust into the first team on various occasions. He made no great impression and was given a free transfer in May 1988, but later joined the newly formed Newport A.F.C., becoming their captain. Norman, one of A.F.C.'s many postmen, is a keen skittler and baseball player.

PARSONS, John S.

b. Cardiff 10.12.50 5'7" 11st 0lbs
(69–27)
Cardiff C. (schoolboy, app. 1966, pro Dec 1968) Bournemouth (Feb 1973) Npt. (loan Mar 1975, full–time May 1975) Bridgend T. (July 1977) Barry T. (Nov 1978) Sully (1979)

Goalscoring forward, who had been a Welsh Schoolboy international. John joined Cardiff as an apprentice on the same day as Bob Summerhayes. He scored in his first full game for Cardiff and arrived at Somerton Park after a spell in Bournemouth reserves. John proved to be an effective marksman, but was given a free transfer after a close season operation. He played on in non–League football into the 1980's with teams like Taffs Well.

PARSONS, William J.

b. Newport late 1913 d. ?Newport
4–0 (4–0)
Windsor Juniors Npt. (cs 1934) Swansea T. (June 1935)

Bill was a local centre–half from Liswerry. He never managed to establish himself in the County side and failed to make the first team during his time at the Vetch Field.

PASSEY, Peter T.J.

b. Birmingham 13.7.52 5'8" 9st 13lbs
136–2 (150–2)
Birmingham C. (App. Nov 1967, pro Aug 1970) Npt. (loan Jan 1972, full–time Dec 1972 £1,500) Bridgend T.

Although not very big, Peter was a tough and hard tackling back, very popular with the crowd and a bargain signing. He had appeared for England Youth in 1970 and played many fine games for the County. In recent years he has been running a car valeting business in Bridgend.

PATTERSON, Daniel Morrison ("Jock").

b. Leith 1896 5'8" 10st 12lbs
12-1 (13-2)
Loanhead Mayflower Npt. (June 1922) Bo'-ness (cs 1924)

A Scottish centre-forward, whose first team chances were severely limited at Somerton Park. "Jock" scored over 30 reserve team goals in 1922–23, including five hat-tricks, but never appeared in the first team at all the following season. He was once selected to play for the Welsh League, but was not released by County, who needed his services.

PAYNE, Donald.

b. Swansea 18.11.50 5'10" 10st 0lbs
32-0 (39-0)
Swansea T. (Juniors 1969, pro Dec 1970)
Torquay Utd. (June 1971) Npt. (July 1973)
Merthyr T. (cs 1975) Haverfordwest (cs 1980)
Merthyr T. (Sept 1980)

Goalkeeper, who had been a Boys' Club international at left-half. Don was given a free transfer by Torquay when they disbanded their reserve team and arrived at Somerton. After a two year stay he moved into non-League football, where he has spent over ten years, despite cartilage problems. He joined Haverfordwest in 1987.

PAYNE, Irving Ernest Henry (Joe).

b. Briton Ferry 29.6.21 5'8" 10st 10lbs
12-1 (16-2)
Swansea T. (cs 1937) war-time guest for Chester, Wrexham, York C. & Lovells Ath. Npt. (Oct 1949 £5,000) Scunthorpe Utd. (Aug 1950) Northampton T. (Aug 1951 to May 1952)

Winger or inside-forward, who was a groundstaff boy at Swansea, where he played over 50 war-time games. He served in the Army playing football for Western Command and took part in the D-day landings. Joe became the County's record signing, but soon moved on to Scunthorpe, where he played in their first Football League game. The following year Joe joined Northampton and scored a hat-trick in 19 minutes versus the County. He was later employed in various training posts for the Cobblers for many years, seeing them rise to Division I and then fall back again. Afterwards he spent 14 years working for Barclaycard and now lives in retirement in Old Duston.

PEACOCK, Darren.

b. Bristol 3.2.68 6'2" 12st 6lbs
25-0 (51-1)
Bristol R. (Juniors) Npt. (App. cs 1984, pro Feb 1986) Hereford Utd. (Mar 1989) Q.P.R. (Dec 1990 £200,000)

A tall central defender, whose promising career was badly hampered by injury. The captain of the F.A. Youth Cup team, his attempts to establish himself in the County side came to an abrupt halt when a broken leg put him out of football for 18 months. He stayed with the club in its Vauxhall Conference days, but badly broken fingers again put him out of the game for a long spell. He joined Hereford when the County were wound up and won a Welsh Cup Winner's medal in 1990. He recently moved on for a large fee.

PEAKE, Dudley J.

b. Swansea 26.10.34   5'10" 12st 4lbs
129-0 (139-0)
Tawe Utd. Swansea T. (pro May 1956) Npt. (June 1958 £2,000) Romford (cs 1963) Merthyr T. (1964)

An awkward-looking, but effective centre-half, produced by the same junior side as Trevor Ford. After 3 months as an amateur Dudley made his debut in Swansea's Football League side. Dudley, who was with the County for five seasons, was an Economics student at Swansea University.

PEARCE, Cyril.

b. Shirebrook, Derbyshire 28.1.08 5'10" 12st 0lbs
26-21 (30-26)
Shirebrook Welfare (1923) Staveley T. Wolverhampton W. (cs 1929) Npt. (May 1930, with £1,500 for T. Martin) Swansea T. (June 1931 £250) Charlton Ath. (June 1932 £2,250) Swansea T. (May 1937 £400) Frickley Colliery (cs 1938) Shirebrook Welfare

Cyril, who had won numerous awards for professional running, began as an outside-right, being an excellent forager with good distribution. He was later converted to a dashing centre-forward. He was good with his head and, all in all, a prolific goalscorer who was a good replacement for Tudor Martin. After he had found the net five times in a reserve game versus Swansea he made his Football League debut and scored twice (versus Watford 25.10.30). Cyril scored 35 goals for Swansea in 1931-32 and still holds their record today, he won a Welsh Cup winners medal in 1931-32. A broken leg versus Norwich C. 31.3.34 affected the rest of his career. He now lives in Church Warsop near Mansfield.

PEARSON, Horace.

b. Tamworth 6.4.07 5'9" 11st 6lbs
42-0 (50-0)
Nuneaton T. Blackpool (May 1929) Oldham Ath. (1931-32) Coventry C. (May 1933) Npt. (cs 1937) Barry T. Bristol C. (Sept 1938)

A very consistent goalkeeper, who did not miss a game during his only season with the County. Horace was in Blackpool's promotion side in 1929–30, went up with Coventry City and became a 1938 Division III (South) Cup Winner with Bristol City. Before becoming a footballer he worked in the mines and after retiring from the game he settled in Bristol.

PEED, Frank (real name Francisco Enrique GONZALEZ).

b. Venado Tuerto, Argentina 27.7.05   d. 1967
5'9" 12st 10lbs
13-4 (40-28)
Orb Villa   Liswerry Church side   Army Brereton Social Aston Villa (c 1929) Bournemouth (May 1930) Norwich C. (Oct 1930) Npt. (loan Aug 1931, full-time Oct 1932) Barrow (cs 1933) Bath C. (July 1935)

Frank was a brave and bustling centre–forward.   His mother, from Wolverhampton, married an Argentinian, but when he died she returned to Britain and Frank took his stepfather's name. He attended Corporation Road School and developed into an all–round sportsman. At Orb Villa he played as a goalkeeper and centre–half. For six and a half years he served with the South Wales Borderers, whom he joined before he was 16, and represented the Western Command. He was bought out by Villa, but his progress at Villa Park was stopped by "Pongo" Waring. Frank played well at Somerton Park, scoring almost a goal a game in County's Southern League season.

He later appeared in Barrow's record 12–1 thrashing of Gateshead in 1934.

PEMBERTON, Selwyn Robert.

b. Cardiff 13.10.28
1-0 (1-0)
Npt. (amateur, pro Mar 1952) Pontllanfraith (1953)

Full–back, who began with the Colts around 1950.   He played over 40 Welsh League games, but only appeared for the first team on one occasion.

PERKS, Henry (Harry).

b. Cardiff mid–1912 5'7" 10st 7lbs
8-1 (9-1)
Cardiff C. (amateur, pro May 1933) Npt. (June 1934 to cs 1935) Barry T. Milford U. (late 1930's).

Winger, who made 8 Football League appearances for both Cardiff City and the County before drifting back into non–League football.

PICK, William Edward.

b. Danesmoor 5.6.03   d. Clay Cross 27.8.81
5'8" 11st 10lbs
20-4 (20-4)
Danesmoor Rovers Bury (cs 1925) Lincoln C. Portsmouth   Npt. (July 1927) Coventry C. (Nov 1928 fee + Ward) Watford (Dec 1930) Barrow (July 1932) Stockport Co.

Well travelled winger or inside–forward, who had a deadly shot. Bill scored on his County debut versus

Brighton 14.9.27 and found the net on 40 occasions that season. He was selected for the Welsh League versus the I.F.S. League in 1928. On leaving Somerton Park, he had two successful seasons with Coventry.

PIMBLETT, Frank R.

b. Liverpool 12.3.57 5'9" 12st 0lbs
7-0 (7-0)
Aston Villa (App., June 1973 pro Oct 1974) Npt. (loan Mar 1976) Stockport Co. (July 1976) Brisbane City, Australia Hartlepool Utd. (Mar 1980)

Midfielder, who spent a month on loan at Somerton Park, a former England Schoolboy international. After a brief spell with Stockport he spent a few years in Australia before returning to England.

PINCOTT, Frederick C.

b. Bristol 19.3.13 6'1" 12st 3lbs
(14-0) (14-0)
Wolverhampton W. (c 1932) Bournemouth (July 1934) Dartford (June 1939) war-time for Bournemouth, Bristol C. & Chester Gravesend Npt. (July 1947) Bideford T. (1948)

Big, experienced half-back. He was a consistent player, who missed only four games for Bournemouth in four seasons, but was in the veteran stage when coming to Somerton. After a short stay he became Player-coach for Bideford Town.

PLUMLEY, Gareth E.

b. Birmingham 24.3.56 6'0" 12st 0lbs
187-0 (225-0)
Leicester C. (trial Dec 1971, app. cs 1972, pro Dec 1974) Npt (June 1976) Happy Valley (Hong Kong) (Aug 1981) Npt. (Aug 1982) Hereford Utd. (Sept 1982, non-contract) Happy Valley Cardiff C. (June 1983) Npt. (loan Aug 1984) Ebbw Vale (cs 1985) Npt. (c Nov 1985, non-contract) Caerleon (cs 1986) Ebbw Vale (Nov 1986) Npt. (Mar 1987, non-contract) Watford (Apr 1987)

A capable goalkeeper, the son of Coventry and Watford Secretary Eddie Plumley, himself a Birmingham City goalie. Gary proved a popular and consistent signing and was voted Player of the Year in 1976-77. He was a regular member of the County's promotion and Welsh Cup winning side, but was pushed out when Mark Kendall was signed. He had various later spells at Somerton Park during injury crises. He went on tours abroad with Middlesex Wanderers and in 1987 was plucked out of obscurity to play for Watford in an F.A. Cup semi-final. Gary now runs his own wine bar in Caerleon and is married to Olympic horsewoman Debbie Johnsey. He had originally been an outfield player, but was forced to give it up because of his asthma.

POPE, Terence John.

b. Newport 27.1.26 6'0" 11st 0lbs
83-0 (96-0)
Liswerry St. Julian's Girlings Barry T. (c 1948) Bargoed Utd. Npt. (c 1950 amateur, pro July 1950) Bedford T. (Aug 1955)

Goalkeeper, who attended Liswerry School, where he played outside-right. He was with the Army in India from 1945 to 1948, playing versus the R.A.F. Terry joined the County groundstaff in 1949-50 and his second first team appearance was in Round 4 of the F.A. Cup. Later he became Bedford's only full professional and helped them draw with Arsenal in front of a crowd of 55,000.

POWELL, Michael J.

b. Newport 26.4.51 5'10" 11st 7lbs
7-0 (8-0)
Newport Y.M.C.A. (1970) Npt. (amateur 1971, non-contract Jan 1976) Minehead Bridgend T. Npt. (Aug 1984, non-contract)

Enthusiastic and versatile defender, who had a long career in non-League football. Mike played some first team games in 1975-76 on a non-contract basis, being a warehouse

foreman at DeeBee's. Later he came out of retirement to play in the County reserves.

POYNER, Robert Christopher.

b. Maesglas, Newport 25.12.32 d. Llantrissent 31.8.77
2-0 (2-0)
Npt. (amateur 1949, pro Jan 1951) Abergavenny Th. Npt. (Welsh League from June 1954 to May 1956)

Bobby began as a Schoolboy and Youth international, a forward with a defence-splitting pass. He joined the County Colts in 1949, becoming a half-back and despite making few first team appearances, he played well over 100 games for the reserves. Bobby, who was a keen pigeon fancier, owned his own coal business. He was tragically killed, along with two couples, when driving his taxi from the "Greyhound", Llantrissent. Ironically he had been the foreman of a construction gang when the stretch of the A449 was built and it was known as "Poyner's Mile".

PRANGLEY, Samuel.

b. Newport 30.9.24 6'2" 11st 2lbs
7-0 (7-0)
Cardiff C. (1942) Lovells Ath. Npt. (Oct 1946) Lovells Ath. (May 1947) Ipswich T. (c 1948) Hereford Utd. (1949-50) Ebbw Vale Npt. (Welsh League 1954) Aberystwyth (1957-58)

Rugged, but constructive centre-half, who had a long career in non-League football. Sam played 7 games for County in Division II and later came back to look after the reserves, playing over 70 games in two seasons. He retired from playing after leaving Aberystwyth and worked for Standard Telephones. He is still living in Newport, and in recent years has starred as a skittle player.

PRATT, Michael W.

b. Newport 15.1.66 6'0" 10st 12lbs
4-2 (14-2)
Npt. (pro Aug 1983) Bath C. (cs 1985) Mangotsfield Ebbw Vale (Sept 1988) Newport A.F.C. (June 1989) Liswerry (Mar 1991) Clevedon (cs 1991)

Well-built central defender, who was a Youth international versus Ireland in 1984. Mike received few first team opportunities and was then often played out of position at striker. He was given a free transfer, but eventually returned to Somerton Park with Newport A.F.C. He now works for the Post Office, which has occasionally led to him being dubbed "Postman Pratt".

PREECE, Brian J.

b. Hereford 16.2.58 5'5" 9st 11lbs
38-12 (48-13)
Hereford Utd. (schoolboy c May 1974, app., pro Feb 1976) Npt. (loan Mar 1977, full-time July 1977) Trowbridge Minehead (Nov 1978 £1,000) Trowbridge (Nov 1982) Barry T. (1988) Westfields Newport A.F.C. (July 1989)

A punchy little winger, who was signed along with Tony Byrne to stave off a possibly fatal re-election bid. Brian did well, but later lost his form and was given a free transfer. In July 1989 be became one of the first players signed by Newport A.F.C. He works as a rigger with BT International.

PREECE, Paul W.

b. Penarth 16.5.57 5'8" 9st 6lbs
17-0 (23-0)
Clifton Ath. Npt. (App. May 1975, full-time June 1975) Barry T. (cs 1976) Bridgend T. (cs 1981) Barry T. (Nov 1981)

During his days at Somerton Park, Paul was a busy, slightly built utility player. He never really established himself in the first team, but has continued playing for a long time at a lower level and is a non-League international.

PREECE, Ryan.

b. Briton Ferry 10.1.69
7-2 (17-2)
Somerton Youth Npt. (YTS 1986, non-contract Oct 1987) Hereford Utd. (trial Oct 1988) Briton Ferry (1988) Maesteg Park.

Ryan is a versatile left-sided footballer, who can play left-back or striker. He played at Crystal Palace in an injury crisis and received a fair number of Football League opportunities, impressing at times. Seeing little future at Somerton Park, he left. His grandfather was a Football League referee.

PRICE, David William.

b. New Tredegar early 1898 5'10" 12st 7lbs
24–8 (24–8)
Barry (by 1921) Pontypridd Ebbw Vale Npt.
(cs 1926) Barry (Aug 1927)

Billy was a centre–forward with a great deal of experience of Welsh non–League football. His smartness off the mark enabled him to score many goals. He played regularly during his season with County, but left to go into business and joined Barry.

PRICE, Frederick.

b. Brierley Hill c 1894 5'9" 11st 3lbs
27–1 (31–1)
Dudley T. Wolverhampton W. (c 1912) Port Vale (war–time) Sunbeam Motors (1919) Port Vale (cs 1920) Npt. (July 1921 to 1922)

A half–back or right winger, who had been a junior international. Fred enjoyed a successful time with Wolves, being an ever present in 1913–14 and also played fairly regularly during his stay at Somerton Park. By the late 1920's he was the licensee of the "King's Head" in Brierley Hill.

PRING, Keith David.

b. Newport 11.3.43 5'9" 11st 4lbs
61–3 (69–4) (Wales 3 1966–67)
Nash Utd. Npt. (amateur cs 1959, pro Nov 1961) Rotherham Utd. (Oct 1964 £9,500) Notts. Co. (Dec 1967) Southport (July 1969) Wigan Ath. (1970 player–coach)

A fast raiding winger, very much a local product, who joined the County straight from school. Like many others Keith was sold to balance the books and later became a Welsh international. His career was ended by a broken leg in 1970. He is still living in the North–West, where he became a brewery representative.

PRITCHARD, Arthur.

b. Newport late 1917
4–0 (4–0)
Oakdale Npt. (amateur, pro Aug 1936)

Right winger, a product of Welsh Valleys football, who was given a few chances in the County first team. He had impressed against County reserves and scored three in a pre-season trial. He obtained a job in the town and turned professional in his second season.

PRITCHARD, Thomas Francis.

b. Wolverhampton mid 1904 6'1" 12st 12lbs
23–1 (23–1)
G.W.R. Wolverhampton W. (trials Aug 1924) Sunbeam Motors Stockport Co. (amateur) Npt. (July 1926 p/exchange) Wolverhampton W. (Sept 1927 £1,100) Charlton Ath. (May 1929 £700) Thames (Nov 1931–32) Marseilles (1932) Preston N.E. (Aug 1933) Lancaster T. (July 1934)

Very talented half–back, formerly a centre–forward with Stockport, who was excellent in attack and strong in defence. Tommy came from a railway family – his father was a driver who lost his arm on duty and Tommy was an apprentice boiler maker with G.W.R. He joined the County in exchange for Sanderson and after some impressive displays was sold to Wolves. For three years of his youth he had, in fact, been more interested in cycling than football. He was with the ill-fated Thames when they disbanded, then went to France. He became Mansfield Town trainer in June 1935.

PUGH, David.

b. Markham 22.1.47 5'8" 11st 0lbs
73-9 (87-10) (Wales Under-23 2 1967)
Caldicot junior football Npt. (amateur 1962, pro Apr 1964) Chesterfield (Dec 1967 £4,500) Halifax T. (Aug 1973) Rotherham Utd. (July 1976) York C. (Nov 1978) Doncaster R. Goole T. Burton Albion

Captain of the Welsh Youth team in 1963–64. David began as an inside-forward, but later became a defender. He was very much a County product and after establishing himself in the first team, was sold to Chesterfield. He had a very long career in the North and held coaching posts with teams like Doncaster and York.

PUGH, Robert Archibald Lewis ("Jack")

b. Symonds Yat 16.9.09 d. Newport Jan 1986
5'10" 11st 12lbs
66-13 (71-15)
Whitebrook Symonds Yat Chepstow Hereford Utd. (1926) Npt. (amateur, pro Oct 1926) Bury (July 1929) Nottm. Forest (Jan 1931 to 1939)

Robust skilful player and long throw expert, who enjoyed his game. He began as a centre–forward scoring a hat–trick for County versus Merthyr, but later moved to midfield and became part of the famous Forest half–back line of Graham, Pugh and McKinlay. He was signed by County after impressing for Hereford and made his debut a week after turning professional. "Jack" went on the Welsh F.A. tour of Canada in 1929 (they afterwards found he was English) and joined Bury on his return. He was a keen rower and received an award for saving a boy from drowning. On leaving football he obtained a job with the Nottingham Employment Exchange in February 1939.

PUGSLEY, David G.

b. Merthyr Tydfil 15.8.31
1-0 (1-0)
Gloucester C. Npt. (amateur 1952 to cs 1953) Gloucester C. ?Llanelli

Reserve goalkeeper. An amateur, he was given just one end of season chance in the Newport first team.

PULIS, Anthony R.

b. Newport 16.1.58 5'10" 11st 8lbs
75-0 (96-2)
Bristol R. (App., pro Sept 1975) Happy Valley (Hong Kong) (1981) Bristol R. (June 1982) Npt. (June 1984 £8,000) A.F.C. Bournemouth (July 1986) Gillingham (Aug 1989, small fee)

Very cool, polished and professional player, normally a defender. Tony enjoyed a long career at Eastville before arriving at Somerton Park, where he gave two years of consistent service. He was then allowed to join Bournemouth, although he had a year of his contract to go. He is the son-in-law of Bill Stroud. His brother Ray also had a spell with the club. Tony was appointed Bournemouth Assistant Manager in August 1990.

PULLEN, Henry (Harry).

b. Kettering 5'10" 12st 7lbs
21-0 (22-0)
Kettering Q.P.R. (1910-11) Npt. (cs 1920) Hartlepools Utd. (cs 1921 to Mar 1922)

Clever left-back, a two-footed player and a fine tackler. He played for Q.P.R. in their Southern League days and represented the Southern League XI. Harry was reaching the end of his career when arriving at Somerton Park and did not appear in the Hartlepools first team on moving there, due to appendicitis.

RADFORD, Ronald.

b. South Elmsall nr. Cheltenham 12.7.43 5'10"
11st 0lbs
63-7 (75-8)
Sheffield Wed. (amateur) Leeds Utd. (Oct 1961) Cheltenham (1963) Rugby T. (July 1965) Cheltenham Npt. (July 1969) Hereford Utd. (June 1971 £1,000) Worcester C. (July 1974 p/manager) Bath C. (Dec 1974)

Rangy player with a fantastic drive, who was very popular with the Somerton crowd, being voted "Player of the Year" in 1970. Ron joined the County as a full-back, but played in midfield. Later his shot for Hereford in the F.A. Cup-tie versus Newcastle was voted the B.B.C. "Goal of the Season". Ron played for the Southern League XI for 3 seasons and was later player-manager of Worcester. He is a carpenter by trade.

RANDELL, Colin W.

b. Skewen 12.12.52 5'8" 11st 6lbs
15-0 (15-0) (Wales Under-23 1 1975)
Coventry C. (App., pro Nov 1970) Plymouth A. (Sept 1973) Exeter C. (Sept 1977 £10,000) Plymouth A. (July 1979 £60,000) Blackburn R. (Aug 1982 £40,000) Npt. (loan Feb 1984) Swansea C. (July 1985) Preston N.E. (cs 1986) Barry T.

Intelligent midfield player, a good reader of the game. A Welsh Schools and Youth "cap", he went on the 1971 tour of New Zealand. Colin played in the semi-final of the League Cup for Plymouth. He joined Newport on loan after losing his Blackburn place through injury, but was not signed as Rovers wanted £20,000. Recently he became Manager of Briton Ferry, resigning at the beginning of March 1990 to become a P.T. instructor with the South Wales Police.

RATHBONE, Graham C.

b. Newport 22.8.42 6'0" 11st 10lbs
188-7 (218-7)
Npt. (1959) Merthyr T. (1960) Npt. (amateur Aug 1960, pro Dec 1960) Grimsby T. (Nov 1966 £10,000) Cambridge Utd. (loan Feb 1973, full-time cs 1973 for £4,000) Kettering (loan 1973-74) Caerleon (1980)

Tall, lanky stopper centre-half. His father had played for Brookside Athletic before the War along with Billy Lucas. Graham joined the groundstaff and then established himself in the first team, eventually becoming Captain and only missing 13 Football League matches in four seasons. Later he helped Grimsby to win the 4th Division Championship. In 1979 he returned to Newport, living near Somerton Park and working at Llanwern as a joiner. He has coached Liswerry for a few seasons.

RAWCLIFFE, Frank.

b. Blackburn 10.12.21
37-14 (42-18)
Tranmere R. (1936) Wolverhampton W. (pro 1939) Colchester Utd. war-time for Southport, New Brighton, Chester, Crewe A., Stockport Co. & Liverpool Notts. Co. (c 1945) Npt. (May 1946 fee) Swansea T. (June 1947 £3,500) Aldershot (July 1948 £1,250) Alessandria (Italy)(June 1949) South Liverpool Alessandria (Jan 1951)

Rough, no-nonsense centre-forward with a hard shot. In a spell of four reserve games in 1946-47 Frank scored 16 goals. He played for many different clubs in a long career marred by the War, and ended up in Italy.

RAYBOULD, Phillip E.

b. Caerphilly 26.5.48 5'9" 11st 8lbs
5-1 (6-1) (Wales Amateur 7 1966-68)
Cardiff Corries (1963-64) Barry T. (1965-66) Swansea University (1966-68) Bridgend T. Swansea T. (July 1967) Npt. (Aug 1969, at first on trial) Barry T. (June 1970) Everwarm (Bridgend)

A versatile and tireless wing-half, who had a short time with the County. Phil was a Youth international and in an outstanding Cardiff Schools side. He is the brother of the Welsh international rugby player, Billy Raybould and trained as a P.E. teacher. He later emigrated to Australia.

RECK Sean M.

b. Oxford 5.5.67 5'10" 12st 7lbs
15–0 (18–1)
Oxford Utd (App. c 1984, pro Apr 1985) Npt.
(loan Aug 1985) Reading (loan Mar 1986)
Wrexham (July 1989)

A young half–back, who played regularly in his loan spell from Oxford.
The County could not sign him,
although they rated him highly and
he returned after three months. Sean
was in the 1990 Wrexham side which
appeared in the Welsh Cup Final and
qualified for Europe.

REECE, Gilbert I.

b. Cardiff 2.7.42 5'6" 10st 7lbs
32–9 (37–10) (Wales 29 1966–75)
Ton Pentre   Llanelli   Pembroke Borough
Cardiff C. (May 1961) Npt. (July 1963)
Sheffield Utd. (Apr 1965 £8,000) Cardiff C.
(Sept 1972 p/exchange) Swansea (July 1976)
Barry T. (Aug1977)

Gil was a Welsh schoolboy "cap",
who became an outstanding left
winger with the County and a regular
in the Welsh senior side for almost
ten years. He escaped Cardiff City's
net and was sold by Newport to pay
the bills. He spent 7 years at Bram-
all Lane and helped Cardiff to promotion from Division III in 1975–76.
After leaving Swansea he became
Barry youth team coach and set up
his own contracting business. He is
now running an hotel in Cardiff.

REED, Gordon.

b. Spennymoor ?6.5.13 5'9" 11st 4lbs
16–10 (17–10)
Shildon (1929) Spennymoor Utd. Huddersfield T. Everton (Sept 1931) Bristol C. (c
1932) Npt. (Mar 1934) Q.P.R. (May 1934)
Darlington (June 1935) Gateshead (Aug 1936)

Dashing attacker, who scored four
versus Southend 6.1.34 and eventually ended his football career back in
his native North–East. Apart from
his obvious ability to find the back of
the net, Gordon's other claim to fame
was as a competent saxophonist and
he became leader of the band at one
of London's biggest dance halls, in
1939.

REED, Thomas Roland (Ron).

b. Haltwhistle 4.10.34 5'8" 11st 0lbs
2–0 (2–0)
Npt. (June 1954) Altrincham (Sept 1955)

Wing–half, who was spotted at Newport barracks in 1954, whilst doing
his National Service. Ron became a
part–time professional, playing mainly in the reserves. He refused terms
in May 1955.

REES, John F.

b. Bedlinog 3.2.33 6'0"
2-0 (3-1) (Wales Amateur 1 1954)
Bedlinog Welfare Cardiff C. Treharris Ath.
Troedyrhiw Npt. (amateur Aug 1952) Treharris Ath. (cs 1953)

Two–footed centre–forward with a
fine turn of speed, always looking for
a half chance. A youth and amateur
international. John scored 24 goals
in 19 Welsh League games for the
County, but was given few first team
opportunities. He moved on to Treharris and continued scoring goals.

REES, R. Clive.

b. Nantymoel 7.9.37
4-0 (5-0)
Npt. (cs 1962) ?Caerau (1962–63) Ebbw Vale
(1964–65)

Amateur goalkeeper, who took part
in the Welsh amateur trials in 1962–
63. He was a teacher at Cwmbran
and was refused permission to play
versus Crewe by the Monmouthshire
Education Committee.

REID, Anthony J.

b. Nottingham 9.5.63 5'9" 10st 10lbs
74-13 (100-13)
Derby Co. (App., pro May 1980) Scunthorpe
Utd. (loan Feb 1983) Npt. (Mar 1983) Chesterfield (July 1985 fee) retired Nov 1987

Tough, ball–winning midfield player.
Tony had been signed by Addison at
Derby and played fairly regularly at
Somerton Park. He moved on to the
nearer Nottingham, but his career
was finished by injury.

REID, Joseph Edmund.

b. Hebburn–on–Tyne 30.6.1896 5'9" 12st 7lbs
62-1 (67-2)
Hebburn Argyle Manchester C. (1919) Stockport Co. (Oct 1920) Boston (c 1926) Npt. (July
1928) Fulham (May 1930 to 1931)

A reliable full–back, who spent two
seasons with County. He made three
Football League appearances for
Manchester City just after World War
1, then well over 100 for Stockport
in six seasons. Joe was a courageous
and determined defender, good at
clearing the ball.

REID, William Dunlop.

b. Sestlands nr Ayr 13.1.20 5'11" 12st 2lbs
9-0 (11-0)
Morton (1945–46) Glasgow Cumnock Npt. (c
July 1948 to Sept 1950)

Scottish right–half, whose debut was
delayed by illness. He mainly played
for the reserves and returned to Scot-

land at the start of the 1950–51 season to enter the building trade.

RELISH, John D.

b. Huyton 5.10.53 5'8" 12st 0lbs
319–8 (417–10)
Liverpool (trial) Cardiff C. (trial 1969) Chester (App. 1969, pro Oct 1971) Bury (loan) Npt. (May 1974) Forest Green Rovers (Oct 1986) Npt. (non-contract) Newport A.F.C. (June 1989)

Full-back or midfield player, who joined Chester straight from School. When visiting Somerton he once managed to score for both Chester and Newport. Although John's career was confined to the lower leagues, he always proved a whole-hearted performer and excellent clubman. He amassed over 400 appearances for the County, despite a year with a broken leg. Appointed player-manager in March 1986, he helped to stave off relegation, but left to take up a post with the P.F.A. John later played a few games in an injury crisis and in 1989 was appointed the first Manager of the newly formed Newport A.F.C. He helped them to win promotion from the Hellenic League, but has been forced to give up playing because of a leg injury.

RENNIE, Andrew ("Ratty").

b. Baillieston, Glasgow c 1901 d. 5.9.38 5'10" 12st 4lbs
3–0 (3–0)
Paisley Waverley Kilwinning Rangers Luton T. (1925) Npt. (Nov 1935 to Dec 1935)

Andy played just a few games at County at the end of his career, but was a famous centre-forward with a marvellous left foot and the ability to score goals from almost anywhere. He started as a half-back trialist with Luton, but went on to score well over 100 goals for them, topping the Football League scorers with 43 in 1928–29. Known as "Ratty" because of his temper he became more of a schemer in his later career. Andy sadly died of pneumonia at the age of 37.

REYNOLDS, Graham Edward Arthur.

b. Newport 23.1.37 5'10" 10st 7lbs
46–12 (50–13) (Wales Amateur 12 1958–65)
Caerleon Npt. (amateur Aug 1956) Lovells Ath. (Apr 1957) Plymouth A. (amateur) Brecon Corries (1961–62) Npt. (July 1963, pro Jan 1966) Cwmbran T. (Aug 1967) Merthyr T.

Centre-forward, who has long played a prominent part in local sport. Graham first played for County as a St. Julian's schoolboy. He returned to the club in the 1960's and was banned for breeching his amateur status. Now Head of Lower School at Hartridge, he had long spells with Cardiff, County and Spurs as coach and scout, discovering players like Vaughan, Lowndes and Mark Aizlewood. At one time he was a Glamorgan cricketer. He was appointed Newport Cricket Club captain in 1987 after 35 years' connection with the club.

REYNOLDS, Walter.

b. Eccleshall, Sheffield 24.11.06 5'9" 11st 0lbs
59-5 (67-10)
Hathersage Leeds Utd. Sheffield Wednesday Burnley Npt. (July 1933) Accrington S. (Aug 1935) York C. (1938) Rochdale (1938)

A very fast, live-wire raider with ball control and the ability to cut in for goal. Wally had a strong shot, although he was not always the greatest finisher. He was a fine quarter miler and half miler. He was mainly a reserve with large clubs before arriving at Somerton Park and afterwards missed only 2 games in 3 seasons for Accrington, where he played in a famous cup-tie versus Manchester City.

RICHARDS, David.

b. Pentrebach, Merthyr Tydfil 5'9" 11st 6lbs
1-0 (1-0)

Pentrebach Merthyr T. (1926-27) Middlesbrough (Jan 1929) Merthyr T. (Aug 1930) Bolton W. (cs 1931) Wrexham (July 1933) Npt. (1936-37)

Half-back, a good tackler and useful attacker. He had a long career, but was nearly always a reserve. He did make 50 Football League appearances for Wrexham, but only played once in the County first team.

RICHARDS, Leonard George.

b. Barry 13.4.11 d. Newport 27.12.85 5'10" 11st 7lbs
30-0 (62-0)
Tottenham H. (schoolboy) Cardiff C. (amateur 1932 to May 1933) Dundalk (June 1935) Npt. (cs 1938) war-time games for Lovells Ath.

A classy left-back, remembered as part of the County promotion side. Len was a schoolboy international and ended up playing under McCandless at Dundee. He played quite often in 1939-40, when he worked at Newport Docks. After the War he worked at Alcan and was a frequent spectator at Somerton Park.

RICHARDS, Percy.

b. Merthyr 1908 5'9" 11st 7lbs
4-1 (4-1)
Merthyr Vale Cardiff C. (cs 1925) Chesterfield (1928) Tranmere R. (May 1928) Npt.
(trial Sept to Nov 1929) Merthyr T. (Aug
1930) Leicester C. (Jan 1931) Coventry C.
(May 1932) Bath C. (Apr 1934)

An outside–left, who rarely rose
above reserve status. Percy was
signed on extended trial and went
straight into the County first team.
His most consistent spell was with
Coventry several seasons later.

RICHARDSON, George William.

b. East Rainton 5'9" 12st 0lbs
30-14 (36-18)
Horden Athletic Sunderland Burnley (Mar
1921) Derby Co. (May 1923) Hartlepools Utd.
(July 1924) Npt. (Aug 1928) Aldershot (Feb
1930 £125) Blackhall Colliery (Sept 1931)
Horden Colliery

Utility player, who proved to be a goalscorer
for County netting 4 in a Welsh Cup
match versus Swansea 28.2.29. After
being a big club reserve George
dropped into Division III (North)
with Hartlepools and played over 100
Football League games for them. He
was signed from the County by Aldershot in their pre–League days,
when they sold Horton to Millwall
for £1,000.

RICHARDSON, Samuel.

b. Great Bridge, West Bromwich 11.8.1894 d.
c 1960 5'8" 11st 4lbs
127-1 (136-1)
Greets Green Prims Great Bridge Juniors
Great Bridge Celtic W.B.A. (Feb 1913) war-
time for Oldbury T. & Coventry C. Npt. (Aug
1927) Aldershot (c 1931) Kidderminster H.

A strong, but clean tackler, dominant
in the air and an accurate kicker. He
was the brother of William Richardson (W.B.A.). He won a League
Championship medal in 1919-20,
played in the Charity Shield in 1920
and represented the Football League
and F.A. He was unlucky not to be
"capped". He played over 200 games
for W.B.A. Sam became County
captain and a regular at Somerton
Park.

RIGGS, Leslie John.

b. Portsmouth 30.5.35 5'8" 11st 0lbs
110-3 (126-3)
Gillingham (June 1952) Npt. (June 1958
£1,750) Bury (June 1961 £750) Crewe Alex.
(Feb 1963) Gillingham (Sept 1964) Ramsgate
(Oct 1965 p/manager) Margate (1972)

A very consistent, tough tackling
wing–half and long throw expert.
For three years Les was very much a
regular at Somerton Park. After a
long career he moved into non-
League management and later starred
in a TV commercial for a Building
Society. He played for Gillingham in
their 10-1 F.A. Cup defeat of Gorleston and was Manager of Margate
when they were thrashed 0-11 by
Bournemouth.

RILEY, Valentine.

b. Hebburn–on–Tyne 5'8" 11st 7lbs
82–4 (89–4)
Washington Colliery Middlesbrough (Oct
1923) Hebburn Leeds Utd. (Nov 1924) Annfield Plain Npt. (Aug 1928) West Stanley
(Aug 1931) Southampton (Aug 1932) Jarrow

Val was a more than competent half-
back, a wily tactician who was worth
his place in the County side.
Although he never made the grade
with his other Football League sides,
he played regularly during his three
seasons at Somerton Park, but then
the club lost its League status.

ROBERTS, Owen John.

b. Mardy 16.2.19 5'10" 11st 7lbs
7–0 (7–0)
Plymouth A. Aberaman Swansea T. Npt.
(Aug 1948)

Goalkeeper, who played 24 Football
League games for Swansea before
arriving at Somerton Park. After 2
months' trial, however, his contract
was cancelled.

ROBERTS, William Samuel.

b. Bargoed 12.7.08 d. Bedminster, Bristol
22.2.76 5'10" 13st 0lbs
41–0 (45–0)
Army Tottenham H. Bristol C. (cs 1933) Npt.
(cs 1938 to 1939)

Solid full–back, effective but not
known for his subtlety. He had been
a regular for much of his career at
Ashton Gate and won a Welsh Cup

Winner's medal with Bristol in 1934.
Bill was a stalwart in County's promotion season, missing only one
game. In the War he was captured
by the Germans in France. He
returned to County when peace
returned, but soon left to keep a pub
in Bristol. Later he spent a long time
with the Customs and Excise.

ROBERTSON, James.

b. Leith 7.7.40 5'5" 10st 2lbs
29–5 (35–5)
Edinburgh Thistle Aberdeen (May 1960) Npt.
(July 1961) Bath C. (cs 1962) Motherwell
(Aug 1963) Durban City (South Africa)(1965)

One of the Scots brought to Somerton Park by Bobby Evans. A
winger, he had been a reserve for the
Scottish Schoolboy team in 1955.
Although a regular for County, he
was given a free transfer when Evans
left.

ROBINSON, Henry (Harry).

b. Southport 14.9.47 5'6"
39-3 (49-3)
Blackpool (App., pro Jan 1965) Southport (Feb 1966) Burnley (Sept 1966) Npt. (Aug 1967, at first on trial) Worcester C. (cs 1969) Merthyr T. (June 1973)

Enthusiastic right winger, who had been a lifeguard on Southport sands. Harry was recommended by a contact of Les Graham and signed full-time in January 1968. He was a gutsy player, who once had the kiss of life on the pitch.

ROBINSON, Ralph ("Robby").

b. Annfield Plain 1906 5'9" 12st 0lbs
71-0 (78-0)
Towlar Durham C. Huddersfield T. (trial cs 1925) Arsenal (c 1926) Npt. (Aug 1933) Gateshead (July 1935)

Ralph had a most unusual career. He was taken from Huddersfield to Arsenal by Herbert Chapman and did not make one first team appearance in seven or eight seasons there. He was an ideal clubman, who never complained and was associated with five successive Combination Championships. He was the County Captain and the best full-back on their books, a powerful tackler with superb positioning.

RODGER, James McPhail.

b. Cleland, Lanarks 15.9.33 5'10" 12st 7lbs
5-1 (6-1)

Glasgow Rangers (1951) Cumnock (1952-53) Douglas Water Thistle (1953-54) St. Mirren (1954) Npt. (loan, Feb 1957)

A useful forward, who had been a schoolboy "cap" for Lanarkshire and the West of Scotland. Jim had been a University student and was attached to R.A.F. St. Athan as a pilot officer when on loan to the County, for whom he scored plenty of reserve team goals. He played on for St. Mirren into the 1960's and appeared in their record 15-0 win over Glasgow University, when Gerry Baker scored ten goals.

ROFFI, Guido ("George").

b. Matthewston 6.3.23 d. Penrhiwceiber Feb. 1973 6'0" 13st 0lbs
112-27 (125-29)
Arsenal (amateur) Tynte Rovers Npt. (amateur Dec 1946, pro Feb 1947) retired May 1954

George was one of the saddest cases in the County's history. He began in war-time football and had great ability, especially as a header of the ball. He could play half-back or forward (he scored 4 versus Aldershot 2/9/50) and once even took over in goal when Hodge was injured. "George" was so good that Cardiff offered £12,000 for him, but he suffered a mental breakdown around September 1950 and spent his last twenty years in a mental hospital. He was tremendously popular with the Somerton crowd because of his enthusiasm and never say die spirit.

ROGERS, Graham Reginald.

b. Newport 5.9.55 5'9" 10st 7lbs
6-0 (22-1)
Npt. (App. June 1972, pro 1973) Merthyr T. (Aug 1976) Blaenavon Blues Caerleon (cs 1976) Minehead (cs 1979) Blaenavon (Sept 1979) Barry T. (1979–80) Npt. (July 1985, non-contract) Forest Green Rovers Mangotsfield Spencer Works Npt. (Mar 1987) Forest Green Rovers Npt. (non–contract Sept 1988) Newport A.F.C. (June 1989)

Versatile player, who was only 16 when first joining County from Hartridge School, having been a Welsh Schools international. After an eleven year spell in non–League football Graham rejoined the County as a central defender, helping to stave off relegation. He helped Barry to win three Welsh League championships and captained the Welsh non–League international side. He was signed by County as injury cover in 1987 and returned to help the team in the Vauxhall Conference. Now the Assistant Manager of Newport A.F.C., he became their first player to be sent off. A self–employed heating and plumbing engineer.

ROGERS, William.

b. Summer Hill nr. Wrexham late 1905 d. Pen-y-ffordd 14.1.36 5'8" 11st 7lbs
22-3 (25-3) (Wales 2 1931)
Flint Wrexham (1926) Npt. (Aug 1932) Bristol R. (Aug 1933) Clapton O. (Nov 1933)

A right–half or inside–right, who played over 170 Football League games for Wrexham in six seasons and was twice capped for Wales.

Billy went on the Welsh F.A. tour of Canada in 1929. He had only one season with the County, during which he was injured early on, and a few years later died of TB in Meadowslea Hospital at the age of only 30.

ROUND, Freeman.

b. West Bromwich late 1900 5'9" 10st 11lbs
1-0 (1-0)
Abercarn Welfare (c 1920) Rogerstone Npt. (1923-24) Ebbw Vale

An amateur and inexperienced goalkeeper, whom the County were forced to play in one Football League match versus Plymouth 22.12.23. The rest of his career was confined to non–League football.

ROWLAND, John O. ("Polly").

b. Newport 16.3.36 5'9" 11st 6lbs
462-9 (531-9) (Wales Under-23 1 1959)

172

Npt. (amateur 1951 to 1955) Lovells Ath. (pro 1957, after National Service) Npt. (May 1958) Barry T. (May 1969 to 1970)

Welsh Youth "cap", educated at Corporation Road School. A cultured and constructive wing–half, he became a fixture in the County side, setting a record for consecutive appearances, which was only broken by Steve Lowndes in 1981. John played many fine games and would have won numerous senior caps, if he had been with a more fashionable club. He was well–known as the proprietor of a local fish and chip shop before becoming a licensee.

RUSSELL, George H.

b. Atherstone 5'8" 12st 0lbs
16-0 (17-0)
Atherstone T. Portsmouth (cs 1925) Watford (cs 1926) Northampton T. (cs 1927) Bristol R. (1931) Cardiff C. (Dec 1932) Npt. (Aug 1934) Stafford Rangers (1935) Bangor C. (player-manager 1936–37)

A fearless and resolute tackler with a powerful kick. George was a good professional, who was with 6 Football League sides in his time, although he had only one season with the County.

RUTHERFORD, George.

b. Hebburn–on–Tyne 5'7" 11st 0lbs
4-0 (6-0)
Usworth Colliery Npt. (July 1929 to 1930 at first on trial)

One of the County's numerous Geordies of the period. A skilful outside-left, George was eventually signed full–time after first arriving on trial. He made few first team appearances, however, despite scoring four in a reserve match versus Torquay.

RYLANDS, David R.

b. Liverpool 7.3.53 6'0" 11st 7lbs
3-0 (3-0)
Liverpool (App., pro Mar 1970) Hereford Utd. (Sept 1974) Npt. (loan Mar 1975) Hartlepool Utd. (Mar 1976) Halifax T. (June 1976) Bangor C.

Tall centre–half, who did not make a great impact in League football. He was with Hereford for a couple of years, but spent much of his time on loan, including a month's stay at Somerton Park.

SADLER, Joseph.

b. Newport mid 1914 5'7" 11st 0lbs
2-0 (2-0)
Windsor Juniors Npt. (amateur 1933, pro Oct. 1935)

Useful half–back, if a trifle over-weight, who had a spell in the County reserves. A local lad, he used to live behind Somerton Park.

SAGE, Frank Roland.

b. Chipping Sodbury 31.5.24
3-0 (3-0)

Cardiff C. (1944) Npt. (Apr 1948) Chippenham T. (Dec 1948)

Wing–half, who played just three Football League games for the County, but afterwards had a long association with Chippenham.

SANDERS, Peter Charles William.

b. Newport 7.9.42
3–0 (3–0)
Npt. (amateur Apr 1958, pro Oct 1959) Gillingham (July 1961)

Young reserve centre–forward, a Welsh Youth international, who only had a few first team chances with County and a couple more at Gillingham. He was also a useful Rugby Union player with Newport, Newport Saracens and Cross Keys. His son was with Cardiff in the 1981–82 season.

SANDERSON, Frederick Cecil.

b. Seaton Delaval 13.9.02   d. Whitley Bay 26.7.77 5'8" 11st 7lbs
13–0 (20–0)
Seaton Delaval Npt. (June 1923) Stockport Co. (cs 1926 p/exchange) New Brighton (cs 1927) Blyth Spartans (Aug 1928)

One of the County's many North–Eastern signings of the 1920's. He was a well–built right–half or inside–forward, who played mainly for the reserves. Although Fred failed to find the net in a Football League match, he scored 13 reserve team

goals in 1924–25. He played for the Welsh League versus the Irish League in 1925–26.

SAUNDERS, Dennis Frederick.

b. Scarborough 19.12.24
7–0 (8–0) (England Amateur International)
Huddersfield T. (amateur) Npt. (loan Nov 1946) Oxford University (c 1947) Pegasus (1948 to 1963)

Cool wing–half with clever anticipation and wonderful ball control. He was in the R.A.F., then moved on to Oxford University. Dennis was the Captain of the famous Pegasus side which twice won the Amateur Cup. He was the Registrar at Malvern College for over 20 years, then became "Housemaster" of England's new residential football school.

SAUNDERS, John T.

b. Newport 2.10.50 5'11" 10st 12lbs
26–0 (28–0)
Birmingham C. (App.) Npt. (Aug 1969) Leeds Utd. (July 1971 £7,000) Walsall (Oct 1972 £10,000)

Well–built centre–forward, who joined the County in his `teens. He established himself in the first team in 1970 and had ability, but it was something of a shock when he was bought by high–flying Leeds. He never made the first team at Elland Road, but afterwards had four seasons at Walsall.

SAWARD, Leonard Roderick.

b. Aldershot 6.7.27 5'8" 11st 8lbs
25-4 (27-6)
Beddington Crystal Palace (pro. Mar 1949)
Cambridge Utd. (1952) Npt. (Jan 1954 £750)
Brentford (month's trial Feb 1955) Cambridge
Utd. (Oct 1956) Sudbury T. (1958) Newmarket
T.

Len was the brother of the better
known Pat Saward. He was with
Cambridge Utd. in their non–League
days and impressed in a Cup–tie
versus the County. He failed to establish himself after coming to Somerton Park and ended back at Cambridge, where he partnered Wilf
Mannion. Later Len played for small
non–League sides like Pye and Ram-
sey T.

SAXBY, Michael W.

b. Mansfield 12.8.57 6'2" 13st 10lbs
6-0 (8-0)
Mansfield T. (App., pro. Jan 1975) Luton T.
(July 1979 £200,000) Grimsby T. (loan Mar.
1983) Lincoln C. (loan Nov 1983) Npt. (July
1984, trial) Middlesbrough (Sept 1984)

Large and dominant central defender.
Mike had been an apprentice compo-
sitor on a Mansfield newspaper and
within a few years had moved on for
a hefty fee (a Luton record). A serious knee injury put him out of the
Hatters' promotion side. He had
completed 3 of 4 months' trial when
leaving Somerton Park for a more
secure future with Middlesbrough.
He is the brother of Gary, another
professional.

SCOTT, Robert John.

b. Dundee 16.3.37 5'11" 11st 0lbs
18-0 (18-0)
Dundee Violet Cardiff C. (Jan 1957) Swindon
T. (June 1961) Npt. (Nov 1961) Sankey's,
Wellington Southport (June 1963) Boston
Utd. (cs 1964) Germiston Callies (S.A.)(5
years)

Scottish wing–half, who had a modest Football League career, a year of
which was spent at Somerton Park.
Bob was spotted by the brother of
Jackie Mudie, the Blackpool star. He
emigrated to South Africa in 1965
and coached and managed several
teams, including Kempton Park
(Johannesburg). He was last heard of
living in Germiston, Transvaal.

SCREEN, William Robert.

b. Swansea 8.11.48 5'7" 9st 8lbs
137-7 (168-9) (Wales Under–23 2 1968–69)
Swansea T. (Juniors, pro. Mar 1967) Npt.
(June 1972) Ammanford Cwmfelin Steelworks

Very useful full–back, the younger
brother of Tony of the Swans. He
had five years at the Vetch after
playing for Swansea Boys. Willie
was a popular and consistent player,
being voted County Player of the
Year in 1973–74 and 1974–75, and it
was a great blow when he walked out
during pre–season training in 1976.
He played for Ammanford for many
years afterwards.

SEYMOUR, Charles.

b. Hebburn-on-Tyne early 1907 5'8" 11st 7lbs
38-12 (42-13)
Hebburn Colliery Npt. (July 1929 to 1931)

Intelligent forward, who signed full-time after first arriving on trial. Charlie had a good shot (scored a hat-trick versus Bournemouth 1.11.30) and was good enough to spend two seasons at Somerton Park, but then the club lost Football League status.

SHEFFIELD, Laurence Joseph.

b. Swansea 27.4.39 5'8" 11st 10lbs
92-46 (111-56)
Bristol R. (Juniors, pro July 1956) Barry T. (Jan 1959) Npt. (Apr 1962 £1,000+) Doncaster R. (July £5,500 & Alfie Hale) Norwich C. (Nov 1966 £15,000) Rotherham Utd. (Aug 1967 £17,000) Oldham Ath. (Dec 1967 £13,000) Luton T. (July 1968 £13,000) Doncaster R. (Oct 1969 £5,000) Peterborough Utd. (Aug 1970 £5,000) retired 1971

Although not very tall, Laurie was an extremely effective centre-forward and goalscorer. A Welsh Schoolboy international, he later served with the Royal Welch Fusiliers. During a successful time at Somerton Park he scored hat-tricks versus Bradford P.A., Notts. Co. and Torquay Utd. and broke the club's post-war scoring record. He later played for a succession of lower Division sides until an ankle injury terminated his career. He has spent most of the time since as a car dealer, also being involved

with the Doncaster Rover's youth team.

SHELTON, John (Jack).

b. ?Monmouth
3-1 (3-1)
Ynysddu Npt. (amateur Dec 1920) Merthyr T. (trial Aug 1922)

A promising local youngster who, for some reason, never made the grade. He scored on his debut for the reserves (versus Caerau 18.12.20), and for the first team (versus Charlton Ath. 27.4.22)

SHEPPEARD, Howard Thomas.

b. Ynysybwl 31.1.33 6'1" 12st 6lbs
31-6 (35-6)
Ynysybwl Boys' Club (Aug 1951) Sunderland (Dec 1951) Cardiff C. (May 1955 with Mc-Seveney & Kirtley for £9,000) Npt. (July 1956 £1,000) Abergavenny Th. (1958) Tom Pentre (1964) Brecon Corries (1965) retired 1967

Inside-forward, who had played for Ynysybwl with Ken Leek. A hard worker, capable of opening up defences, Howard was a reserve with Sunderland and Cardiff. He played regularly in his first season with County, but then dropped into the reserves where he broke a leg versus Pontllanfraith. Later he had a long spell as Abergavenny Captain and now lives in Pontypridd.

SHERGOLD, William Richard.

b. Newport 22.1.23 d. Newport 25.7.68 5'5"
9st 2lbs
274-48 (305-54) (Wales Amateur 1 1947)
Melrose Stars Wolverhampton W. (amateur)
Darlington (guest 1944) Walthamstow Ave.
Bishop Auckland Npt. (July 1947) Weymouth
(July 1956) Hereford Utd. (June 1958) Merthyr
T. (1960-61) Retired 1961

Pint-sized winger or inside-forward with size 3 boots, who was an institution at Somerton Park in the post-war years. He began as talented schoolboy with Corporation Road and Hatherleigh and made his name as a war-time amateur. He helped Bishop Auckland to reach the Amateur Cup Final and played in Denmark with the Isthmian League. Billy turned down Chelsea to join the County and gave nine years unstinted service at Somerton Park. Sadly his later years were marred by a debilitating disease. His son played for Swindon and Bradford City and his brother Ernie played two war-time games for the County.

SHERLOCK, Steven G.

b. Birmingham 10.5.59 5'9" 11st 8lbs
47-1 (92-1)
Manchester C. (App. 1976, pro May 1977)
Luton T. (June 1978) Stockport Co. (Aug
1979) Cardiff C. (June 1986) Npt. (loan Dec
1986 to Feb 1987), full-time Mar 1987
£2,500) Stroud Newport A.F.C. (Nov 1990)

Steve is an experienced left-back, who was at first signed on loan by the County and later came full-time under John Lewis. Before joining Cardiff City he had played well over 200 games for Stockport. He was one of the few senior professionals not to be unloaded in the great clear-out of 1988. He stayed on to play in the Vauxhall Conference, but then the club folded. Now he is helping Newport A.F.C.

SHERWOOD, Alfred Thomas.

b. Aberaman 13.11.23 d. Llantrisant 11.3.90
5'8" 11st 10lbs
205-21 (228-21) (Wales 41 1947-57, 1 war-time 1946)
Aberaman (amateur) Cardiff C. (amateur late 1941, pro 1942) Npt. (July 1956 £2,000+) New York Americans (guest cs 1960 & 1961) retired May 1961

Superb left-back, master of the sliding tackle and one of the most popular Welsh players of his age, becoming the only County player to captain Wales. His brothers, Cliff and Reg. were also professionals and Alf was a talented schoolboy athlete, being capped at football and cricket. After working in the pits he signed for City at 17 and became an established first teamer from 1942, captaining the Cardiff promotion side of 1951-52. Alf was a useful stand-in goalkeeper and a penalty expert, converting 20 for County out of 22. He later became a security officer with the N.C.B. and died recently while on Llantrisant golf course. At one time

he was the Manager of Barry, but was sacked in the freeze-up of 1963 to save costs.

SIMS, Stephen.

b. Bedminster 11.12.1895 d. Weston early 1973 5'11" 13st 0lbs
4-0 (4-0)
Bath C. (c 1913-14) Leicester Fosse (cs 1914) Bristol R. (cs 1919) Burnley (July 1922) Weymouth (cs 1924) Bristol C. Bristol R. (Sept 1926) Npt. (July 1927 to 1928)

A well-built defender, who started as a centre-forward with Leicester in 1914, but found his true vocation as a centre-half with Bristol Rovers. He was a regular at Eastville for the first three seasons after World War 1, but never found the same consistency afterwards and only made a few appearances for the County. Captain of Bristol Rovers.

SINCLAIR, Colin M.

b. Edinburgh 1.12.47 5'10" 11st 2lbs
29-5 (35-5)
Whitston Star Linlithgow Rose Raith R. (1968) Darlington (June 1971 £5,000) Hereford Utd. (Oct 1976 £10,000) Npt. (Jan 1978 £5,000) Linlithgow Rose (Sept 1979) I.F.K. Vasteras (Apr 1980)

Colin was a striker, a former Scottish schoolboy and junior international, who was the only player bought by Colin Addison during his first spell at Somerton Park. He had scored plenty of goals previously, including

4 for Darlington (versus Torquay) in 1975, but he did not find his best form with County and was given a free transfer in May 1979. In 1968–69 Colin was the leading scorer in the Scottish Division 1.

SINGER, Dennis James.

b. Fleur–de–Lys 30.8.37 5'9" 11st 4lbs
60-32 (63-32)
Hengoed Fleur–de–Lys Npt. (May 1954, pro Dec 1956) Birmingham C. (Sept 1969 £6,000) Bournemouth (Sept 1962 £7,000) Npt. (July 1964 fee)

Very much a local discovery, Jimmy was a penetrative forward whose goalscoring record speaks for itself, although he did not have the best of luck in his career. His early progress was affected by National Service, during which he was posted to Malaya. After scoring well, including a hat–trick versus Reading 20.8.60, he was sold, like many County products of the time. Jimmy later returned to Somerton Park, but was forced to retire because of a cyst on the cartilage. He has since run a restaurant in Caerleon.

SMITH, Alan Frederick.

b. Newport 3.9.49 5'10" 10st 6lbs
87-6 (112-6)
Cromwell Juniors Npt. (amateur cs 1965, pro Sept 1966) Merthyr T. (June 1972) Spencer Works

Alan played for the Newport and Welsh Youth teams and joined the County groundstaff with his brother, Bob. He was a non–playing substitute versus Darlington at 15. He had undoubted ability in midfield, but had difficulties holding down a regular first team place during his six years with the club. He was later player-manager of Spencer Works.

SMITH, Albert Owen Stephen.

b. Bedwellty 18.10.23 6'1" 13st 4lbs
27-0 (29-0)
Blackwood Oakdale Cardiff C. (c Apr 1944) Npt. (May 1947) Tredegar T. (1949)

Well–built goalkeeper, who joined the club at the end of its Second Division season. He played regularly the following season, but then dropped down into non–league football.

SMITH, Edward.

b. Sunderland 22.0.02 5'8" 11st 12lbs
53-2 (61-2)
Robert Thompson's Shipyard (Sunderland)
Hartlepools Utd. (c 1923) Npt. (June 1925)
Portsmouth (Feb 1927 fee) Reading (June
1928) Luton T. (June 1929) Preston N.E. (c
1931) Bristol R. (Sept 1931)

A steady a fearless full-back, who
played regularly for Hartlepools and
the County. He played 12 games in
Pompey's promotion season. Later
he joined a number of other Football
League clubs. Ted played in Hartlepools' record 10-1 F.A. Cup win
versus St. Peter's Albion.

SMITH, George.

b. Connah's Quay 1910 5'11" 12st 7lbs
4-1 (8-1)
Connah's Quay Bristol C. (May 1928) Thames
(June 1930) Bradford C. (July 1932) Npt.
(June 1933) Wolverhampton W. (cs 1934)
Bournemouth (1934) Bath C. (Aug 1935)

A classy full-back, who made his
Football League debut with the
short-lives Thames F.C., playing in
72 of their 84 games (including a 2-
9 defeat by Cardiff City). He was
taken over by the League when they
folded and listed at £1,000. He only
played one game for Bradford City
and never found the same consistency
again.

SMITH, Granville.

b. Penrhiwceiber 4.2.37 5'7" 11st 0lbs
241-38 (277-43)
Bristol R. (c 1955, pro May 1957) Npt. (June
1960) Bath C. (Dec 1967)

Granville was one of the club's most
loyal post-war servants. A winger or
inside-forward, he spent seven years
at Somerton Park, always proving
himself a great trier and overcoming
two broken legs. He has continued
to live in Newport and spent many
years working for Monsanto's. He
was in charge of the County reserves
in 1970 and Manager of Caerleon in
1976.

SMITH, James.

b. Old Kilpatrick, Dunbartonshire 1902 d.
Bridgepoint, U.S.A. 1975 5'11" 12st 7lbs
26-10 (28-10)
Dumbarton Harp Clydebank (c 1925) Ayr
Utd. (May 1927) Liverpool (Sept 1929 £5,500)
Tunbridge Wells Rangers (July 1932) Bristol
R. (June 1933) Npt. (June 1935) Notts. Co.
(June 1936) Dumbarton (p/manager 1937 to
war)

A tenacious centre–forward, who found his way into the record books in 1927–28, when he scored 66 goals in 38 matches for Ayr United. In his first two years at Anfield Jimmy scored 37 times in 58 games, but thereafter his career went downhill somewhat. He was reasonably consistent in his one season at Somerton and bagged a hat–trick at Watford 12.10.35, but at Meadow Lane he was replaced by Hughie Gallacher after 4 games and returned to North of the border. Jimmy emigrated to the U.S.A., where he lived in Bridgepoint, 60 miles from New York.

SMITH, Wilfred Victor.

b. Pucklechurch, Bristol 7.4.18 d. 1968 5'11" 13st 0lbs
9–0 (13–0)
Pucklechurch Bristol R. (1937) Npt. (Dec 1946 p/exchange) Abergavenny Th. (1948)

Well–built right–back or centre–half, whose career was marred by the War. He arrived at Somerton Park in exchange for Ken Wookey and spent most of his time in the reserves. Eventually he drifted into non–League football.

SNEDDON, William Cleland.

b. Wishaw 1.4.14 5'8" 11st 4lbs
18–0 (20–0)
Falkirk Brentford (cs 1937 fee) Swansea T. (July 1939, with Briddon for £3,500) war-time for Brentford, Fulham & Cardiff C. Npt. (Nov 1946) Milford Utd. (June 1947 player–coach)

Capable half–back, who had been a record Swansea signing before the War. Billy became County Captain in their only Division II season, but was over the hill and soon moved into non–League football. Around 1980 he was a publican in the Milford area.

SOLLY, Alfred William.

b. Battersea 6.8.06 d. Chippenham 25.12.54 5'7" 10st 7lbs
38–0 (43–0) (Wales Amateur 3 1929)
Dulwich Hamlet (early 1920's) Arsenal (Aug 1931) Npt. (Sept 1932) Portsmouth (June 1933 fee) Aldershot (trial Aug 1934)

Originally an inside–forward, Alf made his name as a goalkeeper, noted for stopping penalties. A quiet and unassuming player, he was popular with supporters. He was in the South London Schools team which won the English Schools Shield and then joined Dulwich Hamlet juniors. He represented the Isthmian League ten times. Alf impressed against the County and was signed after the club had lost 0–8 to Northampton. He did not make the first team at Fratton Park and had a disastrous trial at Aldershot, when the team lost 1–8 at Exeter City.

SOLLY, Charles Basil (Bert).

b. Battersea 28.3.12 d. 25.10.78
1–0 (1–0)
Wimbledon Npt. (Sept 1932 to cs 1933) Sutton Utd.

Younger brother of Alf. He came at first on trial and scored on his debut versus Corinthians, but had a bad game on his only Football appearance. He was afterwards with Sutton United for quite a few seasons, winning medals for such amateur competitions as the Surrey Charity Cup.

SOUTHAM, James H. ("Jack").

b. Willenhall 19.8.17 5'7" 11st 21bs
8–0 (11–0)
Shornhill Recreation W.B.A. (Mar 1939) wartime with Arsenal, Ipswich T., Bristol C. & Bath C. Npt. (May 1946) Birmingham C. (Oct 1946) Northampton T. (June 1949 to May 1955) Walsall (player/asst. trainer)

Right–back, whose career was marred, like many others, by the War. He helped Albion win the Midland War Cup in 1943–44 and after a brief spell at Somerton Park just after World War II, went on to play just over 150 games for Northampton.

SPRAGUE, Martyn L.

b. Risca 10.4.49 5'7" 10st 0lbs
155–1 (173–1)
Lovells Ath. (c 1965) Npt. (amateur June 1968, pro. Aug 1969) Merthyr T. (July 1974)

Short, but capable left–back, adept at kicking the ball off the goal–line. He had agreed to join Hereford in 1967, but ended up with County the following year. He became a regular and after temporary retirement in 1973 re–signed in the October for the rest of the season. Martyn was a mechanical apprentice when signed.

STANIFORTH, Gordon.

b. Hull 23.3.57 5'7" 10st 7lbs
84–13 (112–13)
Hull C. (App. pro Apr 1974) York C. (Dec 1976 £10,000) Carlisle Utd. (Oct 1979 £120,000) Plymouth A. (Mar 1983 p/exchange) Npt. (Aug 1985, with £15,000 for Steve Cooper) York C. (non–contract Oct 1987) North Ferriby Utd.

Busy forager, in the old inside–forward tradition, who had been an English Schools "cap". A diminutive player, Gordon had been York City's record sale, and appeared in Plymouth's F.A. Cup semi–final team. He came in exchange for Cooper and played regularly for two seasons, without making any lasting impact.

STANSFIELD, Frederick.

b. Cardiff 12.12.17 5'10" 12st 0lbs
21–0 (26–0) (Wales 1 1949)
D. Morgan Rees & Co. (c 1934) Grange Albion Cardiff C. (pro 1942) Npt. (loan Sept 1949, then p/manager and afterward Manager, resigning Dec 1953)

Right–back or centre–half, who began with Whitchurch schoolboys. He played for Cardiff City and later captained their promotion side, missing only one game in the first two post–war seasons, but lost his place through a leg injury in 1948–49. Fred joined the County on loan after Wilcox broke an ankle and later became Manager, resigning during the crisis of 1953. He was afterwards Manager of Bedford T. and later owned his own newsagent's in Cardiff, retiring a few years ago.

STAPLES, Leonard Eric.

b. Leicester 23.1.26 5'7" 11st 7lbs
164–2 (182–2)
war–time for Crystal Palace, Torquay Utd & Leicester C. Leicester C. (July 1947) Npt. (May 1949) Weymouth (July 1957) Nuneaton Borough (June 1958)

Fair–haired full–back, who spent eight years at Somerton Park. An England Schoolboy international, he captained Leicester Boys. He joined the Royal Navy at 18 and played for the Mediterranean Fleet XI. A great trier, he was converted from inside–forward or wing–half to back, by Stansfield, and in a 4–4 draw with Coventry C. scored two goals from the wing after being injured.

STARK, William Reid.

b. Glasgow 27.5.37 5'10" 11st 0lbs
12–2 (17–2)
Glasgow Celtic Glasgow Rangers Crewe A. (July 1960) Carlisle Utd. (Dec 1961) Colchester Utd. (Nov 1962) Doncaster R. (July 1965 p/exchange) Luton T. (Sept 1965) Corby T. (1965–66) Chesterfield (July 1966) Npt. (June 1967) Matlock (1968) Boston Utd. (Jan 1970) Worksop T.

Much travelled inside–forward, who did not show his best form for County. A former Scottish Schoolboy and Junior international, he did the rounds of the lower Division clubs and was in the Crewe side which beat Chelsea at Stamford Bridge.

STEEL, Gregory.

b. Clevedon 11.3.59 6'1" 12st 4lbs
3–0 (3–0)
Clevedon T. (1973) Npt. (trial c Apr 1977, pro. cs 1978) Gloucester C. (1979) Clevedon T. Gloucester C.

Young full–back, who seemed to have some promise, but was eventually given a free transfer. His father, Dick, played for Bristol City and York City. Greg has had a long non–League career, notably with Gloucester.

STROUD, Kenneth A.

b. Fulham 1.12.53 5'11" 12st 0lbs
47–0 (60–0)
Swindon T. (App., pro. Mar 1971) Cardiff C. (trial Aug 1982) Npt. (Aug 1982) Bristol C. (loan Oct 1983, full–time Jan 1984) Bath C. (1985) Newport A.F.C. (July 1990)

Very cool and polished defender, who can play the ball along the ground. Kenny was a regular first–teamer at Somerton but later wanted to leave and threatened to quit football in a row over a loyalty bonus. Later he began running a guest house in Swindon. He joined Newport A.F.C., but was forced to leave by domestic circumstances.

STROUD, William James Alfred.

b. Hammersmith 7.7.19 5'8" 11st 4lbs
63-1 (71-1)
Southampton (amateur Mar 1939, later pro.)
Leyton O. (June 1947, fee & p/exchange) Npt.
(June 1950 £1,000) Hastings Utd. (cs 1953 p/coach) Npt. (Nov 1953 p/coach to May 1956)

Hard working and enthusiastic wing-half and long-throw expert. Bill was a good team player, who learnt his football in Southampton, where he played in the Schools side. He retired through TB in the mid 1950's and was for many years involved with the Southampton team, retiring in 1987. He is the father-in-law of Tony Pulis.

SUGRUE, Paul A.

b. Coventry 6.11.60 5'7" 9st 10lbs
1-0 (25-14)
Aston Villa (schoolboy) Walsall (App. 1977) Nuneaton Borough Manchester C. (Feb 1980 £30,000) Cardiff C. (Aug 1981) Kansas City Comets Middlesbrough (Dec 1982) Portsmouth (Dec 1984) Northampton T. (Mar 1986) Npt. (Aug 1986) Bristol R. (Dec 1987) Bridgend T. (Dec 1987) Finland Npt. (Oct 1988) Kidderminster H. (Mar 1989) Nuneaton T.

Midfield player with a strong tackle, whose career was badly hampered by injury. Paul first made the news when he was signed by Malcolm Allison from non-League football for £30,000. He was out for 11 months during his spell at Cardiff because of a knee, which was completely rebuilt when ligaments were severed. Because of injury he was only able to play a few times in his first stay at the County, but later rejoined the club in the Vauxhall Conference and made a big impression when reverting to striker, scoring three hat-tricks in Cup competitions. He has the ability to wriggle past defenders and score from impossible angles and was quickly snapped up by Kidderminster when the County folded. He turned down the chance of joining Newport A.F.C and became the Manager of Nuneaton.

SULLIVAN, Derek ("Ginger").

b. Newport 10.8.30 d. Newport 16.9.83 5'9" 12st 6lbs
23-0 (27-0) (Wales 17 1953-60)
Temple Street Y.M.C.A. Cardiff C. (1944, pro. Sept 1947) Exeter C. (June 1961 fee) Npt. (June 1962 - with P. Gordon for £1,000) Hereford Utd. (June 1963) Ebbw Vale (1964) Monmouth T. (Oct 1966)

Local Newport product snapped up by Cardiff City. Well-known as half-back, he played in every position for City except goalkeeper. He was a regular Welsh international, having started in the Youth team. Derek was a fixture in the Cardiff first team and helped them win promotion to Division I on two occasions. He joined County at the end of his career and later played for Monmouth with his son, Alan. He worked for Braithwaite's until, sadly, dying of a liver complaint.

SULLIVAN, Maurice J. ("Boy").

b. Newport late 1915 5'7" 10st 7lbs
38–8 (42–9)
Ynysddu Pontyminster Utd. Npt. (amateur 1936, pro. Apr 1937) Derby Co. (May 1938 fee)

Utility forward from Wattsville, who so impressed Derby that they obtained his transfer, part of the deal being a friendly at Somerton Park the following season. He shared digs with Jack Brinton in Derby, but his career was terminated by the War.

SUMMERHAYES, Robert E.

b. Cardiff 8.1.51 5'9" 10st 9lbs
74–4 (90–4)
Cardiff C. (App. 1966, pro. Jan 1969) Npt. (Aug 1972) Sully

Skilful midfield player, who could have gone further in the game. A Wales Schoolboy international, Bob

is the brother of David. He was out for six months after breaking a leg versus Ipswich T. in 1971 and given a free transfer by Cardiff. He played many good games for County.

SUMMERS, William.

b. Burnbank 14.7.1893 d. 23.2.72 5'8" 11st 0lbs
36–0 (40–0) (Scotland 1 1926)
Burnbank Ath. Airdrieonians (1919) St. Bernard's (1920–21) Airdrieonians St. Mirren (May 1921 p/exchange) Bradford C. (Sept 1927) Npt. (Sept 1932 to 1933)

Pillar of the defence, a wonderfully consistent pivot, who could master the man and the ball in tackles and could give a pass out to the wings. He won a Scottish Cup Winner's medal in 1926 and was in Bradford City's Division III (North) Championship side. He also played in Bradford's record 11–1 victory versus Rotherham, 25.9.28. He won his cap when over 30 and was almost 40 when playing regularly for the County.

SUTHERLAND, James Sinclair.

b. Armadale 6.8.18 d. Bathgate 16.9.87 5'10" 11st 0lbs
32–0 (34–0)
Winchburgh Albion Bathgate Thistle Lochgelly Albert Forth Wanderers Npt. (July 1947) Trowbridge T. (Dec 1948) Chippenham T.

Full-back, who was signed from Scottish junior football and became a full-time professional. Jimmy, who had served in the Scots Guards, played fairly regularly in 1947–48, but shortly afterwards drifted into non–League soccer. He soon returned to Scotland, and held down various engineering jobs before retiring through ill-health.

SWAIN, Kenneth J.

b. Cardiff 31.12.54
7-0 (11–0)
Npt. (App. 1970, pro. Aug 1973) Barry T. (to Sept 1976) Cardiff Corries

Full–back, who had been a Welsh Schoolboy international. He spent a couple of seasons at Somerton Park, but had few first team opportunities and moved into non–League football.

SWINDELLS, John (Jackie).

b. Manchester 12.4.37 5'8" 11st 0lbs
23-3 (28–6)
Manchester C. (amateur) Blackburn R. (Nov 1957) Accrington S. (Dec 1959) Barnsley (June 1961) Workington (Feb 1962) Torquay Utd. (July 1963) Npt. (July 1964) Altrincham (Aug 1965 £500)

Inside–forward or wing–half, the son of a former professional. Jackie had the best part of a season here, but his contract was cancelled by mutual consent in March 1965, so that he could go home and look after his sick father. He proved to be a prolific scorer with Altrincham with 250 goals, including 86 in 1965–66.

TALBOT, Robert Curry.

b. North Hylton 20.9.08   d. Wigan mid 1971
6'0" 12st 7lbs
10-0 (11–0)
Hetton Utd. West Ham Utd. Burnley (Sept 1931) West Stanley Npt. (Aug 1932) Wigan Ath. (May 1935) Oldham Ath. (1935)

Full–back, who had been a miner. He was a clever player and delightful to watch, but for some reason always seemed to languish in the reserve teams of his clubs. After a short spell at Somerton he returned North.

TAPSCOTT, Derek J.R. ("Tappy").

b. Barry 30.6.32 5'9" 10st 6lbs
12-1 (15-1) (Wales 14 1954–59)
Barry T. (amateur, pro. Apr 1953) Arsenal (Oct 1953 £2,750) Cardiff C. (Sept 1958 £8,000) Npt. (June 1965) Cinderford (1966) Haverfordwest (1968) Carmarthen (1970)

A leading Welsh personality of the 1950's, but past his prime when coming to Somerton Park. He played for his R.E. unit side during National Service and was then signed by Bill Jones at Barry T. Some of his brothers played for Barry, not surprisingly, as he was one of 16 children! Derek was working on a building site when signed by Tom Whittaker at Arsenal. He scored two goals on his debut and was selected for Wales a few days later. He later scored for Arsenal versus the County at Somerton Park. He helped Cardiff City to Division 1 and scored the 40 yard goal that beat Sporting Lisbon.

He was later player–manager of Carmarthen. Derek is now a sports firm representative and keen golfer.

TAYLOR, David.

b. Cwmbran late 1909 5'5" 10st 7lbs
6–0 (6–0)
2nd Mons. Npt. (cs 1927 amateur, then pro. Nov 1927 to 1929)

Versatile local forward, who was signed as a promising youngster after a trial in 1927. He had few first team chances, but was a prolific scorer for the reserves, with 40 Southern and Welsh League goals in 1927–28.

TAYLOR, Frederick E.

b. Wolverhampton 5'8" 11st 0lbs
34–13 (40–15)
Sunbeam Motors Port Vale (cs 1921) Sunbeam Motors (cs 1922) Npt. (cs 1923) Bournemouth (cs 1926) Gillingham (cs 1928) Shrewsbury T. (Aug 1929)

Goalscoring centre–forward and solid grafter. He made his Football League debut with Newport and was at one time wanted by Plymouth, but suffered from illness in his second season here. After leaving Somerton Park, Fred had three more seasons of League football before dropping down into non–League soccer with Shrewsbury.

TAYLOR, George.

b. Failsworth nr. Manchester ?23.1.08 5'9" 11st 0lbs
11–6 (15–8)
Ferranti Oldham Ath. (1925) Macclesfield (c 1929) Npt. (Sept 1933) ?Yeovil (June 1934)

A robust centre–forward, keen and hard working. After five years in and out of the Oldham side moved into non–League soccer. He scored 40 goals for Macclesfield in 1932–33 and scored quite a few goals for County, but was allowed to leave at the end of the season.

TAYLOR, Robert S.

b. Plymouth 3.12.67 5'9" 10st 10lbs
37–7 (54–9)
Portsmouth (Y.T.S. Aug 1986) Npt. (Mar 1987) Weymouth (Sept 1988) Barry T. (Aug 1989) Torquay Utd. (trial Sept 1989) Dorchester T. (cs 1990)

Young striker, who made a good impression on joining the club, with his ability to beat a man and score. His confidence suffered, however, as he played on in a poor side. Robbie obtained a transfer shortly after his team entered the Vauxhall Conference.

usually with lower Division sides. Pat was last heard of working as a taxi driver.

TENNANT, Sydney David Keith.

b. Newport 6.6.34 5'11" 11st 0lbs
40-1 (46-1)
Npt. (amateur 1950, pro Jan 1955) Barry T. (1960) Ebbw Vale

Wing–half, who was mainly a reserve, being often kept out of the first team by George Thomas. Keith played for Newport Schoolboys and later for Combined Services, whilst serving in Germany in 1954. He has scouted for County and Cardiff in recent years.

TERRY, Patrick Alfred.

b. Lambeth 2.10.33 5'10" 12st 0lbs
55-30 (63-34)
Eastbourne U. (amateur 1953) Charlton Ath. (Mar 1954) Npt. (June 1956 £100) Swansea T. (Feb 1958 £7,000) Gillingham (Oct 1958 £4000) Northampton T. (July 1961) Millwall (Feb 1962) Reading (Aug 1964 £2,000) Swindon T. (Feb 1967 £8,500) Brentford (June 1968) Hillingdon Borough (July 1969) Wimbledon Folkestone (May 1970) Greenwich Borough

Aggressive centre–forward, especially good with his head, who amassed over 200 goals in his Football League career. He had been a reserve with Charlton, but soon started scoring regularly with County and was on his way, through economic necessity. He had 15 years of League football,

THACKERAY, Andrew J.

b. Huddersfield 13.2.68 5'9" 11st 0lbs
53-4 (66-9)
Manchester C. (Juniors cs 1985, pro. Feb 1986) Huddersfield T. (July 1986) Npt. (Mar 1987 £5,000) Wrexham (July 1988 £5,000)

Useful midfielder, with a good cross-field pass. Andy made a good impression when he arrived at Somerton Park, but his form deteriorated as he played in a struggling side. He had been a member of Manchester City's F.A. Youth Cup winning side of 1986 and asked for a transfer in January 1988, because he wanted to return North. He joined Wrexham when County were relegated from the Football League and appeared in the 1990 and 1991 Welsh Cup Finals.

THOMAS, David A. (Dai).

b. Abercregan, Port Talbot 1.8.26 5'7" 11st 6lbs
58-1 (65-1) (Wales 2 1957-58)
Abercregan Juniors Swansea T. (1947, pro. Aug 1948) Npt. (July 1961) Hereford Utd. (1963) Barry T. (1964)

Dai started as an inside–right, but became a Swansea Town full–back, playing almost 300 Football League games for them. He was almost 35 when joining the County and after playing regularly for two seasons was given a free transfer to take up a post with B.S.C. Port Talbot. Nowadays Dai is living in Neath.

THOMAS, George Vincent.

b. Cardiff 25.6.30 5'7" 10st 9lbs
137-0 (153-0)
Cardiff Nomads Cardiff C. (May 1949) Npt. (July 1953) Bath C. (cs 1959)

Competent and consistent wing-half, a product of Cardiff schools football. He was a reserve at Cardiff, where his progress was interrupted by National Service, but a regular at Somerton Park in the mid 1950's and one of the unsung heroes of the County side. George was a strong tackler and whole-hearted player.

THOMAS, Jeffrey.

b. Newport 18.5.49 5'9" 10st 12lbs
206-31 (242-41) (Wales Under-23 1 1967)
Npt. (amateur cs 1965, pro. May 1966) Cwmbran T. (1973) Caerleon (Aug 1979)

Small, but useful inside-forward, who had been a talented schoolboy athlete at St. Julian's and gained Welsh School and Youth "caps". Jeff was Newport's youngest debutant at 16 and the youngest Welsh under-23 player. He went on the Welsh tour of Malaysia in 1971. His League career was terminated by a knee injury, but he continued to play in the Welsh League and managed Caerleon. He is also a keen cricketer.

THOMAS, Peter John.

b. Treforest 18.10.32 5'6" 10st 6lbs
6-1 (6-1)
Cardiff C. (amateur c 1949, pro. Mar 1953) Exeter C. (Dec 1954) Npt. (July 1956) Bath C. (Aug 1958) Weymouth (June 1962)

Outside-right, who spent most of his time in the reserves. Peter scored on his Division 1 debut versus Aston Villa 22.8.53. He also found the net on his Exeter debut versus Crystal

Palace, but struggled to obtain a regular League place. He was a schoolmaster by profession.

THOMAS, Roderick J.

b. Glyncorrwg 11.1.47 6'1" 13st 4lbs
3-0 (3-0) (Wales 50 1967-78, Under-23 6 1967-70)
Gloucester C. Swindon T. (July 1964) Derby Co. (Nov 1973 £100,000) Cardiff C. (Oct 1977 £10,000) Gloucester C. Npt. (Mar 1982) Barry T.

Big defender, who had enjoyed an illustrious career in League football and was a well established member of the Welsh team. His 9 years at Swindon saw him winning a League Cup medal when his team beat Arsenal and he won a League Championship medal with Derby. He joined the County 2 months after leaving Cardiff, in the hope of getting the job of coach. He once worked for Francis Lee's tissue paper firm and now runs a pub in Cheltenham.

THOMAS, William Rees.

b. Port Talbot 20.8.03 5'6" 10st 7lbs
280-53 (330-68) (Wales 2 1931)
Port Talbot Bridgend T. (1922) Lovells Ath. (1926) Npt. (1927) Barry T. (1936) Aberdare (1937) Port Talbot

Along with Jimmy Gittins, Billy was the Club's best pre-war servant. He was a tricky winger, who started as an inside-left. He had a dangerous lob and could score or lay on goals.

Billy lived in his native Port Talbot, where he worked as a commercial traveller in the week. He refused several chances from bigger clubs, but managed to win two caps when Welsh players with English clubs were not released for internationals. He was never dropped until 1936, when it caused a public outcry. He represented the Welsh League. He still lives in Port Talbot.

THOMPSON, J. Trevor.

b. North Shields 21.5.55 5'9" 10st 12lbs
32-2 (45-2)
W.B.A. (schoolboy, app. 1970, pro. Jan 1974) Washington Diplomats (1976) Npt. (July 1978 £7,500) Lincoln C. (Dec 1979 £10,000) Gainsborough T. Worksop T.

A Tynemouth Schools player, who joined W.B.A. as a schoolboy, then apprentice, and appeared in their promotion side of 1975-76. He captained their reserves and came to Newport as part of the deal when

Addison joined W.B.A. Trevor was a tough–tackling full–back, who got "stuck in". Later he became a regular with Lincoln City.

THOMPSON, Richard J.

b. Yate, Bristol 11.4.69 6'2" 12st 1lbs
10-1 (18-1)
Watford (Junior) Bristol C. (non–contract) Yate T. Npt. (non–contract, pro. Jan 1987) Exeter C. (trial Nov 1987) Torquay Utd. (June 1988 £4,000) Yeovil T. (Mar 1989)

Very tall and raw striker, who had been an England Schools trialist. He went to college in Bath to study for a P.E. diploma. Richard had a few first team chances with the County and scored on his debut versus Colchester. He was originally given a free transfer, but was later sold to Torquay for a small fee.

THOMPSON, William ("Rubber").

b. Morpeth mid 1886 d. Byker nr. Newcastle 28.12.33 5'7" 11st 0lbs
17-1 (19-1)
Middlesbrough (1905) Morpeth Harriers (1906) W.B.A. (Mar 1908) Sunderland (May 1911) Plymouth A. (c 1912) Q.P.R. (1912) South Shields (c 1914) Npt. (cs 1920 £250) Hartlepools Utd. (1921–22) Jarrow

Spring–healed winger, nicknamed "Rubber". He was not a prolific scorer, but a clever and speedy player, the length of his career speaking for itself. He made over 50 first team appearances for W.B.A.

and over 100 for Q.P.R. in their Southern League days.

TIMSON, David Yowles.

b. Leicester 24.8.47 5'11" 11st 0lbs
23-0 (27-0)
Leicester C. (app., pro. Sept 1964) Npt. (Oct 1967) retired early 1968

Goalkeeper, understudy to Gordon Banks for three seasons and the youngest Leicester debutant before Peter Shilton. David was a useful player, but became disappointed with his progress and left professional football in his early twenties.

TOONE, Percy.

b. Colchester mid 1883 d. Ealing early 1955 6'2"
1-0 (1-0)
Army Woolwich Arsenal Leyton Southend Utd. (1909–10) Preston N.E. (1911) Barrow (cs 1912) Southend Utd. (1913) Bolton W. (cs 1914) Plymouth A. (Oct 1919) Npt. (Aug 1920 to 1921)

Strapping goalkeeper from the London area, an ex Army man who had spells in the reserves of Preston and Bolton. Percy, who once let in 11 goals versus Northampton, was in the veteran stage by 1920 and was kept out of the first team by Jack Cooper. He performed capably in his one first team game and played regularly for the reserves, appearing at full–back on occasions. He was a well–known Essex cricketer (1912–22), a lower order batsman and right arm bowler.

TUPLING, Stephen.

b. Wensleydale 11.7.64 6'0" 11st 3lbs
30-2 (42-4)
Middlesbrough (App., pro. July 1982) Carlisle
Utd. (loan Sept 1984) Darlington (Sept 1984)
Scarborough (trial cs 1987) Npt. (July 1987)
Cardiff C. (July 1968 £7,500) Torquay Utd.
(loan Sept 1988) Exeter C. (loan Jan 1989)
Merthyr T. (loan Nov 1989) Hartlepool Utd.
(Dec 1989)

Well-built midfield player, who
could look impressive on occasion.
Steve played well over 100 games in
a Darlington side which won promotion and beat Middlesbrough in the
F.A. Cup. He was given a free
transfer by Eastick in December
1987, but stayed on and gave his best
displays as County Captain. He
moved to Ninian Park rather than
play in the Vauxhall Conference, but
was only ever a reserve and soon
left.

TURNBULL, William.

b. Blyth c 1900 5'6" 10st 10lbs
6-4 (6-4)
West Stanley Cardiff C. (Apr 1922) Npt. (cs
1924) Ashington (June 1925) Manchester C.
Chesterfield (1927) Brighton (May 1928)
Ashington (July 1929) Gateshead (c 1932)
Oldham Ath. (May 1935)

Midget winger or inside-forward,
who had scored 28 goals for West
Stanley before joining Cardiff at the
end of the 1921-22 season. Billy
only made one first team appearance
for the Bluebirds, but represented the
Welsh League in 1923-24 and scored
36 reserve goals during his one season with County. He scored regularly for Ashington and Chesterfield on
returning North and was still playing
in the mid 1930's.

TURNER, Charles John.

b. Newport 1.7.19 6'0" 12st 0lbs
37-0 (49-0)
Dewstonians Ebbw Junction Npt. (1938
amateur, then pro.) Swansea T. (Aug 1948)
Yeovil T. (1949 to 1951)

Charlie, who was brought up near
Somerton Park, began by playing
rugby at school. He made one appearance in the promotion season,
letting in five in the last game at
Southend. After being called up, he
spent 4 years in a P.O.W. camp,
having been captured at Boulogne in
1940. He found fame of a kind
when Newcastle put thirteen past
him, but he was a daring, though
modest goalkeeper and often played
brilliantly behind an inadequate
defence. He only played twice in the
Swansea first team and was then
signed by Alec Stock at Yeovil. He
now lives in retirement in Cwmbran.

TURNER, Ian.

b. Middlesbrough 17.1.53 6'0" 12st 5lbs
7-0 (7-0)
South Bank Huddersfield T. (Oct 1970)
Grimsby T. (Jan 1972) Walsall (loan Feb
1973) Southampton (Mar 1974, with Chatt-
erley for £25,000) Npt. (loan Mar 1978) Lincoln C. (loan Oct 1978) Walsall (Jan 1979
£25,000) Halifax T. (loan Jan 1981) Witney T.
Waterlooville Salisbury

Nomadic goalkeeper, whose main claim to fame lies in winning an F.A. Cup Winner's medal in 1976. He also played in the last few games of Grimsby's promotion season. He had been McMenemy's first signing for Southampton. Ian spent much of his career on loan and played a few games for the County in 1978. He has played on in non–League soccer.

TYNAN, Thomas Edward.

b. Liverpool 17.11.55 5'10" 11st 11lbs
168–65 (229–88)
Liverpool (App. 1971, pro Nov 1972) Swansea C. (loan Oct 1975) Dallas Tornado (cs 1976) Sheffield Wed. (Sept 1976 £10,000) Lincoln C. (Oct 1978 £33,000) Npt. (Feb 1979 £25,000) Plymouth A. (Aug 1983 £55,000) Rotherham Utd. (July 1985 £25,000) Plymouth A. (loan Apr 1986, full–time Sept 1986 £25,000) Torquay Utd. (May 1990)

Talented and fiery player, who joined Liverpool following a newspaper competition and topped their Central League scorers for 4 seasons. Tommy became a record Newport signing and a cornerstone of their best ever team. He was at times played in midfield, but scored in County's promotion game at Walsall and found the net three times in the Welsh Cup Finals and twice in the famous away game at Carl Zeiss Jena. He set a Newport post–war scoring record and was joint top scorer in the Football League in 1983. He became a County record transfer when sold, because of the club's financial problems, to Plymouth. Tommy became Plymouth's

record scorer in 1984–85 and played for them in the 1984 F.A. Cup semifinal. He has continued to score with great regularity since. He was put on the transfer list, when he fell out with Torquay after making a rude sign at the Directors' box!

VAUGHAN, Nigel M.

b. Caerleon 20.5.59 5'5" 8st 7lbs
215–33 (280–38) (Wales 10 1983–85, Under–21 2 1982)
Npt. (Ground staff July 1975, app. May 1976, pro. May 1977) Cardiff C. (Sept 1983 p/exchange) Reading (loan Feb 1987) Wolverhampton W. (Aug 1987 £12,000) Hereford Utd. (Aug 1990)

Small, nippy midfielder, who could be inspirational on his day, but sometimes lost his form. He had a trial in December 1974, became an apprentice in 1975 and became a Welsh Youth "cap" in 1976–77. Nigel was an every present in Newport's promotion and Welsh Cup winning side. In 1982 he became the first County international for 25 years. He had four years at Ninian Park after being part of a 5 player deal. He turned down the chance to rejoin County in the Vauxhall Conference after being given a free transfer by Wolves and fought to win back his first team place at Molineux. Nigel broke his ankle shortly after joining Hereford.

VENABLES, Albert.

b. Cardiff ?28.12.1899   d. Barnstaple 1976
5'9" 11st 0lbs
1-0 (1-0)
Cardiff Camerons Npt. (1922-23) Minehead (by 1924) Ilfracombe T.

Unselfish amateur centre-forward and later centre-half, who had a short spell with the County. Albert moved to Minehead, then Ilfracombe (1927), where he became Manager of the National Omnibus Co. depot and later North Devon District Manager. He was elected to Ilfracombe District Council in 1947, becoming Chairman two years later.

VICKERS, John (Jack).

b. Auckland Park 7.8.08   d. West Auckland 24.9.80 5'9" 12st 0lbs
19-0 (22-0)
Bishop Auckland Hull C. (Mar 1928) Darlington (June 1929) Doncaster R. (July 1930) Charlton Ath. (June 1932 £540) Port Vale (May 1933 £200) Npt. (May 1936 to 1937)

A solid, defensive player, who began as a wing-half and was later converted to full-back. Jack partnered Jimmy Kelso at Port Vale before arriving at Somerton Park, where he had just the one season.

VILLARS, Anthony K.

b. Cwmbran 24.1.52 5'8" 10st 8lbs
23-1 (36-1) (Wales 3 1974, Under-23 2 1974)
Cwmbran local Npt. (cs 1967) Panteg (early 1968) Cwmbran T. Cardiff C. (June 1971) Npt. (July 1976) Blaenavon Blues

Useful but inconsistent winger, who was originally on County's groundstaff. Tony worked as an electrician and played Welsh League soccer before returning with Cardiff City and scoring the goal which kept them in Division II. Later he returned for a brief spell at County before drifting out of professional football. Tony now runs a milk business in Newport.

VINTER, Michael.

b. Boston 23.5.54 5'9" 11st 0lbs
30–6 (44–10)
Boston Utd. Notts Co. (Mar 1972) Wrexham (June 1979 £150,000) Oxford Utd. (Aug 1982 £25,000) Mansfield T. (Aug 1984 £15,000) Npt. (Aug 1986, trial then full–time) Gainsborough Trinity (cs 1987)

Very capable forward, who had enjoyed a long career and scored plenty of goals. He signed for the County after impressing on trial, but was suffering from a persistent pelvic injury, which restricted his mobility and forced his retirement from League football.

WADDLE, Alan R.

b. Wallsend 9.6.54 6'3" 13st 0lbs
19–7 (33–7)
Wallsend B.C. Halifax T. (Juniors, pro Oct 1971) Liverpool (June 1973 £50,000) Leicester C. (Sept 1977 £45,000) Swansea C. (May 1978 £24,000) Npt. (Dec 1980 £80,000) Gloucester C. (July 1982) Mansfield T. (Aug 1982 £1,000) Hong Kong Hartlepool (Aug 1983) Peterborough Utd. (Oct 1983 £6,000) Hartlepool (Jan 1985, non–contract) Swansea C. (Mar 1985) Finland (cs 1985) Barry T. (cs 1986) Port Talbot Maesteg Park Bridgend T. (Nov 1989) Llanelli (Dec 1989)

A strapping striker, Alan was the County's record signing. This put the club firmly on the downward trail and helped Len Ashurst to get the sack. After being sold by Halifax for a record sum, he played in Liverpool's first team and later scored in Swansea's final promotion game of 1979. He played relatively few games for County, often being ham-

pered by injury, and was eventually sacked in April 1982. He was later with Swansea City when they were liquidated and has since played for a succession of clubs from Hong Kong to Llanelli. Alan is the cousin of Chris Waddle.

WAITE, Thomas John Aldwyn.

b. Pontllanfraith 3.8.28 5'9" 11st 8lbs
57–1 (64–1)
Npt. (amateur, pro Dec 1951) Llanelly (1954) Abergavenny Th. (1954) & other Welsh League sides, retiring 1964

A local product, whose brother was also on the groundstaff. Aldwyn was an attacking wing–half, sometimes drafted into the forward line. He had a couple of years with County's first team before going with Welsh League football and later ran his own plumbing business.

WALDEN, Richard F.

b. Hereford 4.5.48 5'11" 12st 9lbs
151–3 (193–3)
Aldershot (App. 1964, pro May 1965) Sheffield Wed. (Jan 1976) Npt. (July 1978 £3,500) Farnborough (1982)

Very polished right–back, who was a regular member of Newport's promotion and Welsh Cup winning side. He played for over 20 years, starting as Aldershot's youngest post–war debutant. Richard played over 400 games for the Shots missing only 3 in 1972–73 promotion season, and 100 for Wednesday. The fee County paid was one of the first to be decided at a Tribunal, Sheffield having asked for £20,000. He lived in Fleet and travelled to Newport for games. He was later a rep. for a sports firm and Captain of Farnborough.

WALKER, Andrew McQ.

b. Dalkeith c 1892 5'10" 12st 1lbs
75-14 (84-15)
Dundee   Chelsea (cs 1913) Npt. (cs 1920) Accrington S. (cs 1922 to 1923)

A bit on the cumbersome side, but a very able player. Andy had two seasons as centre-forward with Dundee. He was mainly a reserve at Chelsea, where he was converted to a goal-scoring half-back, but won a F.A. Cup Winner's medal in 1915. He only missed nine games in two seasons at Somerton Park before going North. Andy had turned down the chance of playing abroad to sign for his second season. He was the County captain and a successful penalty taker, who could also score from 30 yards.

WALKER, Frank.

b. Newport mid 1906 5'7" 10st 7lbs
6-1 (6-1)
St. John's Npt. (amateur 1924, pro 1927 to 1928)

Local wing-half, who began as an amateur and spent most of his time in the reserves. He scored on his

Football League debut versus Brentford 16.4.27.

WALKER, Ronald L.

b. Kingsbury 2.9.52 6'2" 13st 8lbs
88-5 (104-7)
Carshalton Arsenal (trial) Watford (schoolboy, app., pro. Aug 1970) Workington (Aug 1971) Aldershot (Mar 1973, loan) Swansea C. (trial May 1975) Darlington (July 1976) Npt. (July 1976) Minehead (Oct 1979) Barry T. (Feb 1981) Bridgend T. (Apr 1982)

Big centre-half, who was never more than a lower Division player, but gave some solid performances and only missed three games in 1977-78. Ron had been with Darlington for only two days before coming to Somerton Park. He became surplus to requirements when Oakes was signed and moved into non-League soccer, later managing Bridgend Town.

WALKER, Shane.

b. Pontypool 25.11.57 5'9" 11st 4lbs
27-2 (36-2)
Arsenal (App. 1973) Bristol C (trial Feb 1975) Hereford Utd. (Mar 1975) Sligo Rovers (Feb 1977) Npt. (Aug 1977) Trowbridge (1978) Caerleon (cs 1980) Pontllanfraith Forest Green Rovers Ebbw Vale Pontllanfraith (Mar 1986) Ebbw Vale (cs 1987) Trinant Npt. (Sept 1988)

Mainly a midfield player, Shane was a regular member of the County first team in 1977-78, but did not seem to make the most of his ability. He drifted into non-League football, but made an exceedingly brief return to the County during the Vauxhall Conference season. Before joining the County, Shane had been one of Wales' most capped schoolboys with Oakdale Secondary School, and with Sligo he won a Championship medal and toured America.

WALSH, John **Brian**.

b. Aldershot 26.3.32 5'8" 10st 4lbs
27-3 (28-3)
Chase of Chertsey Arsenal (pro Aug 1949) Cardiff C. (Sept 1955, p/exchange for Tiddy & Nutt) Npt. (Nov 1961 £2,500) Guildford C. (June 1963 £200)

Brian was a tricky right winger, whose talents were not always appreciated by the crowd. He had been a sprint champion over middle distances and later played for Cardiff City in Division I. He made over 200 appearances for the City and his exploits included missing a penalty in their 16-0 Welsh Cup win over Knighton. He had a brief stay at Somerton Park and there was a row when Bobby Evans wanted to drop him after six games. Brian is a qualified chartered accountant. He retired following an injury in the 1963-64 season.

WALTERS, George.

b. Wolverhampton 21.6.35 5'10" 11st 10lbs
80-2 (95-2)
W.B.A. (1952) Jenks & Cattell (Wolverhampton)(1956) Shrewsbury T. (Feb 1957) Npt. (Sept 1963 £2,000) Cinderford (May 1965) Npt. (Aug 1967) Abergavenny Th. Cinderford

Very cool and polished full-back. His early progress was affected by National Service, during which he played football in Hong Kong. George joined Shrewsbury in 1957, making his debut versus County, and only missed 21 Football League games in his last five seasons there. He was County Captain until 1965, when he went part-time, studying at a Cardiff College. A groin injury affected him, but he returned to captain the reserves in 1967. He still lives locally and has worked for IMI Santon for around 20 years.

WARD, David.

b. Barry 19.7.01 d. Barry late 1959 5'8" 11st 0lbs
6-1 (7-1)
Pentrebach Harriers Merthyr T. (c 1924) Aberaman Barry T. (1926-27) Coventry C. (1927) Npt. (Nov 1928) Barry T. (cs 1929)

A very good centre-forward and excellent marksman. He made his Football League debut with Merthyr Town in 1924 and played 10 games for Coventry three years later. He was signed by County as part exchange for Bill Pick and scored on his first appearance versus Southend. Then he had a long spell at Barry, where he played with Bill Jones. He was the father of Welsh international Dai Ward. He worked for Western Welsh for most of his life, ending up as a fitter in Ely. He represented the Welsh League between 1927 and 1932.

WARD, Robert.

b. Glasgow 27.10.58
2–0 (4–0)
Blantyre Victoria Glasgow Celtic (cs 1976)
Blantyre Victoria (loan 1976–77) Celtic (cs 1979) Npt. (Jan 1980 £3,000 to Mar 1981)

Midfielder, mainly a reserve with County. He had a five day trial with Arsenal and was offered terms, but preferred to join Celtic. He could have gone to Wigan Athletic, but signed for County in 1980. He was late starting the 1980–81 season because of arthritis of the hip and was later given a free transfer.

WARDELL, Albert ("Nippy").

b. Bliston 12.1.08 d. Pestatyn March 1987
5'7" 11st 3lbs
43–9 (46–9) (Wales Amateur 1 1927)
Newport Amateurs Npt. (amateur c Apr 1924, Pro. Oct 1928) Chelsea (loan) Wolverhampton W. (loan) Darlington (Aug 1930) Npt. Hereford Utd. (Aug 1931) Shrewsbury T. (July 1933) Taylor Bros. (Manchester)(p/manager)

"Nippy" was a sturdy winger, who could dash down the wing like a greyhound. His parents moved to Newport the day after he was born and he joined the County as a talented amateur before returning professional. He had been a Welsh Schoolboy international at soccer and rugby and in 1929 went on the Welsh F.A. tour of Canada. Later he worked at Manchester Power Station, then ran the "King's Head" in Eccles. He was the Manager of Prestatyn in the 1960's and early 1970's and died after a spell of poor health. "Nippy's" brother Bill, who also died fairly recently, was also on the County groundstaff and Andy Higgins became his brother–in–law. His father was the Mayor of Newport.

WARRINER, Steven W.

b. Liverpool 18.12.58 5'7" 10st 0lbs
28–2 (42–2)
Liverpool (schoolboy, app. 1974, pro Dec 1976) Npt. (trial July 1978, pro Aug 1978) Rochdale (Aug 1981) Tranmere R. (Feb 1983)

Midfielder or full–back, who was a Lancashire Schools player and appeared for Liverpool reserves, but suffered from cartilage problems. Steve never really established himself at Somerton Park, but his progress was not helped by a cartilage operation. He was given a free transfer and returned to Lancashire.

WATERSON, Archibald Rutherford.

b. Mussleburgh, nr. Edinburgh 13.10.02 d. Tranent, East Lothian 13.5.82 5'10" 11st 7lbs
43–36 (45–36)
Mussleburgh Bruntonians (1922) Leicester C. (July 1923) Cowdenbeath (cs 1926) Npt. (July 1927 £50) Southampton (Dec 1928 £1,000) Tranmere R. (July 1929) Southport (Oct 1930) Doncaster R. (July 1932) Aldershot (July 1934) Edinburgh City (1935)

An astute leader of the attack, well–built and able to use both feet. Archie scored well over 100 goals in the lower Divisions and was normally his club's top scorer. He scored almost a goal a game for County, but asked for a move when the club signed Ward. Archie had scored 4 versus Charlton and hat–tricks versus Luton, Coventry and Gillingham. He returned to Musselburgh, where he spent 30 years at Brunton's Wire Mills.

WATTS, Farewell.

b. Sheffield 10.3.04   d. Sheffield mid 1970
5'11" 12st 0lbs
5–1 (7–1)
Gainsborough Tr.   Portsmouth (July 1927)
Npt. (July 1928) Tranmere R. (Aug 1929 to 1934)

Farewell had no first team chances with Portsmouth and few with County, but played well over 100 Football League games for Tranmere Rovers. He was converted to an inside–right by them and was known as one of the most dangerous forwards in Division III (North), finding the net 27 times in 1930–31.

WEALE, Robert Henry.

b. Merthyr 9.11.03 d. Merthyr early 1970 5'7"
11st 6lbs
26–8 (30–10)
Troedyrhiw Luton T. (trial) West Ham Utd. (pro. Mar 1925) Swindon T. (June 1927, trial) Southampton (c Dec 1928 £1,000) Guildford C. (1930) Cardiff C. (Aug 1930) Boston T. Guildford C. (Aug 1931) Merthyr T. (trial cs 1932) Npt. (Aug 1932) Wrexham (Mar 1933) Glentoran (Aug 1935) Cheltenham T.

Speedy goalscoring winger, who won several medals as a sprinter. He was a Welsh schoolboy "cap" and after an unsuccessful trial with Luton started with West Ham's Combination side. He was in and out of League Football for ten years and his brother Tommy was also a well–known player.

WEARE, Leonard.

b. Newport 23.7.34 5'11" 12st 0lbs
525–0 (607–0)
Temple Street Y.M.C.A. Wolverhampton W. (trial 1949–50) Bristol R. (amateur c 1951) Npt. (amateur Jan 1955, pro. June 1955) retired May 1970

Possibly the best–known goalkeeper in County's history. Len is the son of Arthur and brother of Jack (Bristol Rovers, West Ham and St. Mirren). Len, who was educated at Hatherleigh School, had an eight month spell with Wolves, whose Manager wanted him to turn prof–

essional at 17. He was demobbed in 1954 and became a part–time professional, also running a painting and decorating business. He played in many notable games over a long career and the County turned down good offers for his transfer. In 1958 he was a reserve for the Welsh World Cup squad and he is the holder of Newport's appearance record. Len emigrated to South Africa in 1970, but returned after a few years and still lives in Newport.

WEAVER, Reginald William.

b. Clutton, Somerset 14.9.05   d. Gloucester 16.7.70 5'9" 11st 9lbs
52–21 (54–21)
Llanhilleth Utd. Npt. (amateur Oct 1926, pro. Jan 1927) Wolverhampton W. (Nov 1927 £1,100) Chelsea (Mar 1929 £5,000) Bradford C. (June 1932) Chesterfield (1933) Npt. (Sept 1934 to cs 1935)

Reg began and ended his Football League career with County. He had moved to Newport with his family and proved to be a prolific goalscorer (including a hat–trick versus Brighton 14.9.27) and expert penalty taker. He was very fast and won the Welsh Powderhall sprint in 1931. County were forced to sell him because of falling gates and Wolves suffered the same fate. He had an unsuccessful spell at Chelsea, where he was replaced by Hughie Gallacher.

WEBB, Harold.

b. Fulham 5'11" 12st 0lbs
54–3 (66–5)
Park Royal   Walthamstow Ave.   Fulham (1930) Exeter C. (Mar 1933) Coventry C. (cs 1935) Npt. (July 1936) Bristol R. (cs 1938)

Although described as an "ungainly stopper", Harold was a useful and effective utility player. He could play centre–forward, all half–back positions and settled down at right–back. He was a fairly regular first teamer in his spells with Exeter and the County.

WEBB, John Armstrong (Jack).

b. Southwick, Sunderland 19.5.08   d. Derby 11.1.84 5'11" 11st 6lbs
33–0 (88–1)
Sunderland Co–op Wednesday North–Eastern Marine Blues Apprentices Southwick Juniors Derby Co. (1928) Npt. (June 1937) war–time for Swindon T., Lovells Ath. & Bristol C.

Solid full–back, who played 13 games in County's promotion season. Jack was a former miner, who played mainly in Derby's Central League side. He became an Auxiliary Fireman in 1939 and made a brief return to Somerton Park after the War. He left in 1946 to join Derby's ground–staff. Jack was still living close to their ground more than 30 years later. He played for Derbyshire Cricket Club's second team, and became the club's masseur.

WEBSTER, Colin.

b. Cardiff 17.7.32 5'9" 11st 2lbs
31-3 (39-5) (Wales 4 1957-58)
Avenue Villa   Cardiff Nomads   Cardiff C.
(amateur, pro. May 1950) Manchester Utd.
(May 1952) Swansea T. (Sept 1958 £6,000)
Npt. (Mar 1963 £4,000) Worcester C. (July
1964) Merthyr T. Portmadoc (1965)

Forward developed by Cardiff. He
won an Army Cup Final medal, but
was given a free transfer by the City
and was spotted by a Manchester
United scout. Colin played in their
first post Munich match versus Sheffield Wednesday and appeared in
their Cup Final team. He had just
over a year with County at the end of
his career and then moved into non-
League football.

WELSH, William.

b. Douglas Water, Edinburgh 2.5.1898   5'8"
12st 4lbs
6-1 (6-1)
Douglas Water Thistle   Hearts (cs 1922)
Dundee Utd. (late 1925) Charlton Ath. (May
1927 £1,000+) Wigan Borough (Dec 1928
£50) Southport (Feb 1930) Npt. (June 1930)
Connah's Quay (Nov 1930) Wrexham (Jan
1931) Gateshead (cs 1931) Hartlepools Utd.
(mid 1933-34) Jarrow (July 1936)

A well-balanced goal scoring forward, whose footballing travels took
him on a tour of England and Wales
in a career of over 10 years. He only
made 6 appearances in the County
first team, but was a regular with
some of his other clubs. He had
studied mining at the Technical College, Lanark and was the cousin of
James Welsh M.P., the Scottish poet
and author.

WETHERBY, Thomas.

b. Worcester 5'10" 12st 8lbs
40-3 (44-3)
Plymouth A. (amateur) Royal Navy Npt. (c
Apr 1924, at first on trial) Crystal Palace (June
1928 to 1931)

Full-back, who arrived at Somerton
Park on trial and spent four seasons
here, mainly as a reserve. He once
played in goal for the reserves and
saved a penalty. He was something
of penalty expert and had played in
the same Royal Navy XI as Jack
Davis. Afterwards Tom made over
60 Football League appearances for
Palace. He played for the Welsh
League in 1927.

WHARTON, John E. (Jackie).

b. Bolton 18.6.20 5'5" 10st 6lbs
74-10 (78-12)
Plymouth A. (amateur Oct 1935, pro. June
1937) Preston N.E. (July 1939, with James
Hunter for £5,500) war time for Carlisle Utd.,
Liverpool, Blackburn R., Bolton W. & Rochdale   Manchester C. (Mar 1947 £5,000)
Blackburn R. (June 1948) Npt. (Feb 1953,
with Graham for £4,000) Wigan Ath. (cs 1955)

Jackie was a nippy, enthusiastic little
left winger, who began in Bolton
schools football. He joined Plymouth
before the War and scored in the first
minute of his debut. He later played
in Blackburn's 1952 F.A. Cup semi-
final and gave the County a boost

when joining with Les Graham, becoming a regular first-teamer for two years. He is the father of Terry Wharton of Wolves' fame.

WHEELER, George Harold.

b. Newport 19.2.10 5'8" 11st 2lbs
60-1 (86-1) (Wales Amateur 2 1931)
Npt. (Juniors 1925, amateur 1928, pro Aug 1931) Lovells Ath. (1933)

A local full-back, at first an amateur with the County, then a part-time professional. His father, of the same name, was a former player, referee and County director. George was the first Newport Schoolboy "cap" and also represented the town at rugby. He was a more than useful performer and played for the Welsh League, but he eventually became fed up with the County's efforts to sell him. He turned down a move to Wolves and was persuaded to join Lovells by his friend Eddie Jenkins (not the County player). He concentrated on his trade with Lysaght's and moved to Port Talbot with the firm. Around the beginning of the War he gave up football following a nasty operation. He is the older brother of Jim and still lives in Port Talbot.

WHEELER, James Arthur.

b. Newport 7.6.16 5'10" 12st 10lbs
7-0 (11-0)
Lovells Ath. (c 1932) Npt. (cs 1937 to 1939)

A talented young right-back, the brother of George. Jim played for Corporation Road and Hatherleigh Schools and captained the Welsh Schools. He played in the Welsh League side versus Ireland and was at one time sought by Arsenal. He worked at the Orb steelworks, and gave up football in war-time because he was working 12 hour days in the brass foundry. He now lives in Porthcawl. His son played for Welsh R.U. versus the All Blacks in 1967.

WHITE, Andrew C.J.

b. Caerleon 6.11.48 5'7" 10st 6lbs
225-25 (279-28)
Caerleon (1964) Npt. (amateur, pro. Aug 1969) Yeovil (1977) Minehead Caerleon Npt. (reserves Sept 1984) Spencer Works

Tricky little left winger, with a useful turn of speed, who twice had trials for the Welsh amateur side. He was at first signed on three months' trial, but soon became established as a

202

fixture in the side, staying for eight years. He might have gone farther in the game, but kept on his trade as an electrician. He was eventually forced out of first class soccer by knee problems. Andy recently had a spell as Spencer Works Manager. He is the brother-in-law of Graham Rogers.

WHITE, Frank.

b. Nuneaton 30.6.10 5'8" 11st 3lbs
17-1 (18-1)
W.B.A. Coventry C. (May 1931) Npt. (July 1935) Dudley T. (Aug 1936)

Right winger or inside-right, who was quick on the ball and a good passer. He played over 100 Football League games for Coventry and scored 27 goals, but only managed one in his single season with County.

WHITE, Harry.

b. West Bromwich Feb 1902 d. mid 1927 5'7" 11st 0lbs
1-1 (1-1)
W.B.A. (Mar 1923) Npt. (Aug 1924 to 1925)

Inside-forward and brother of Tom, who had joined the County earlier. He went from the Birmingham Combination to W.B.A., where he played in the reserves, later fracturing an ankle. He scored on his only first team appearance for the County versus Q.P.R. on 27.12.24, but broke his kneecap at Taunton the following month. Harry contracted a lung dis-

ease and died a few months after having to give up the game.

WHITE, Thomas.

b. West Bromwich 5'8" 11st 0lbs
48-0 (59-0)
Notts. Co. (war-time) Birmingham (cs 1919) Worksop T. (cs 1921) Npt. (Sept 1922) Kidderminster H. (cs 1925)

Talented full-back, who was a wartime discovery, playing many fine games for Notts County with the international Jesse Pennington. He was at Somerton Park for three seasons before returning to the Midlands, where he looked after his brother, who was terminally ill.

WHITE, William W.

b. Kirkcaldy, Fifeshire 1911 5'9" 12st 4lbs
19-3 (21-3)
Mussleburgh Bruntonians Reading (cs 1927) Bristol R. (cs 1928) Southport (c 1929) Charlton Ath. (July 1930) Gillingham (Dec 1930) Aldershot T. (June 1932) Carlisle Utd. (June 1934) Npt. (Nov 1934) Bristol C. (May 1935) Lincoln C. (Dec 1936) Hull C. (June 1938)

An enthusiastic, 90 minute player with a strong shot. He did not really establish himself until he left Charlton (to cut their wage bill) and joined Gillingham. Thereafter he scored goals for a variety of Football League clubs, but only spent just over 6 months with County.

WHITEHOUSE, Charles Henry ("Chookie").

b. Newport 12.11.10 d. South Africa 1957 or 1958
42-1 (48-1)
Windsor Juniors Npt. (amateur 1933, pro. 1934) Lovells Ath. (c 1936 to c 1946)

Able wing-half, a product of the Newport and District League. Charlie stayed with the County for a few seasons and could have played at a higher level, but preferred to concentrate on his career. He had a powerful right foot and later played at centre-forward with Lovells, for whom he scored 30 goals in 1936-37. Charlie's brother Harry also played for the County and Lovell's.

WHITTON, Percival A.

b. Taunton c 1896 5'9" 12st 7lbs
79-6 (90-7)
Eastville F.C. Bristol R. (1918 to 1920) Aberaman Npt. (cs 1922) Brentford (cs 1925 to 1927)

Hardworking utility player and penalty expert, who began in Bristol Rovers' side in the old Southern league after being released by the Army. Percy played regular first team football in his three seasons at Somerton Park before moving on to Brentford.

WILCOX, Caradoc.

b. Treharris 8.11.23
31-0 (37-0)
Npt. (Oct 1946, amateur) Treharris Cardiff C. (May 1949) Npt. (July 1952)

Defender and younger brother of Ray. Crad played as an amateur for the County in 1946 whilst in the Forces and had a spell as a Cardiff reserve, scoring twice in the Welsh Cup game versus Milford T. He was a miner at Treharris during the week, playing part-time. Crad left the County after a couple of years, he was wanted by Bedford T., but was badly injured at work in June 1954 when a wire rope fractured his skull. He spent 25 years as a motor fitter with the ambulance service, retiring in 1985, and now lives in Pontypridd.

WILCOX, Raymond.

b. Treharris 12.4.21 5'10" 11st 8lbs
488-0 (546-0)
Treharris Derby Co. (1936) Npt. (May 1939) war-time for Lovells Ath. & East Fife retired 1960

The cornerstone of the post-war County side. With a more fashionable side Ray would surely have won many caps at centre-half, but was only ever selected for the Welsh League team. Before Len Weare, Ray held the record number of appearances for the club, despite the intervention of World War II. He was first on the books of Derby County, despite never visiting the Baseball Ground, and in 1939 joined the R.A.F., touring India with Tommy Walker's "circus". Ray stayed with the County so long that he received two benefits and later became Trainer. When he left in 1970 he had spent over 30 years with the club. He later worked for Girling's and is still living in Newport.

WILKINS, Ronald.

b. Treherbert 21.12.23
1–0 (20–4)
Gwynfi Boys' Club Npt. (cs 1945 to Nov 1946) Aberaman (1946) & other Welsh League retired 1951

Young centre–forward from Gwynfi, who was picked to face Fulham in the League (South) on the basis of his performance versus County reserves a few days previously. Ron only made one Football League appearance before disappearing into Welsh League football.

WILLIAMS, Alan.

b. Bristol 3.6.38 5'10"
64–3 (79–5)
Bristol C. (Juniors, pro Sept 1955) Oldham Ath. (May 1961 £1,000) Watford (July 1965) Npt. (Nov 1966 £2,500) Swansea T. (Oct 1968 £1,500) Gloicester C. (June 1972) Keynsham (p/manager June 1975)

Very talented fair–haired half–back, who made a big impression at Somerton Park. Alan was selected for the England under–23 side in 1959, but the game was postponed. He played in Bristol City's record 11–0 Cup victory versus Chichester 5.11.60. He enjoyed many seasons of League football and was Captain of Watford and Swansea. Alan had a few disciplinary problems with Newport and was allowed to depart despite his obvious ability. Later he became the publican of the "White Horse" in Bedminster. His son, Gary, has played for Bristol City and Oldham.

WILLIAMS, Benjamin David.

b. Penrhiwceiber 28.10.1900 d. Bridgend Jan 1968 5'9" 11st 5lbs
18–0 (20–0) (Wales 10 1928–35)
Penrhiwceiber Swansea T. (Mar 1925 £25) Everton (Dec 1929 £7,500) Npt. (June 1936)

One of the most polished full–backs of his time, a dedicated professional, who never knew when he was beaten. Ben was a talented schoolboy boxer and considered it as a career. He became famous as the Everton Captain (being known as "Khyber" because of his birthplace!)

He captained their 1931 promotion side, 1932 Championship side and only missed a Cup winner's medal in 1933 because of injury. He never really overcame a cartilage operation and came to Somerton Park, where he became Trainer cs 1937. Ben went back to the mining industry at the outset of war and stayed until his unfortunate mental breakdown. He sadly spent his last two years in an institution.

later released because of disciplinary problems. He became an asphalt layer, but enjoyed a glimpse of glory when, having helped to defeat County in the Welsh Cup Final, he scored Merthyr's winner versus Atalanta in the European Cup Winners' Cup.

WILLIAMS, David Samuel.

b. Newport 1.3.42 5'7" 11st 0lbs
302–2 (355–2)
Nash Utd. Npt. (amateur, pro Nov 1959)
retired Sept 1973

WILLIAMS, Ceri.

b. Tonyrefail 16.10.65 5'7" 9st 2lbs
19–2 (35–3)
Npt. (App. Apr 1982, pro June 1983) Merthyr T. (Nov 1984)

Slightly built winger, who had been developed in Rhondda Schools football and been a Youth "cap". Ceri showed early promise and scored on his Football League debut versus Exeter C. at the age of 16, being

Nippy and consistent full–back, who suffered through injuries, including a broken leg in April 1967 and a severe facial injury at Darlington in October 1972. He was very much a local find, having played for Corporation Road School and the town team. David played in the County first team for over 10 years. After retiring he had a few seasons with Spencer Works, but has spent most of the time at Somerton Park, normally in a coaching capacity. Dai became acting Manager when Eastick was sacked in March 1988, but resigned in the May and reverted to Coach. He stayed with the club until they were liquidated and then took a job at the Orb works. He was a Director of Newport A.F.C. and is still associated with the Club.

WILLIAMS, Grenville Rees.

b. Swansea 30.6.21 5'10" 11st 8lbs
5–0 (5–0)
Arsenal (1938) Canterbury Waverley Norwich C. (1945) Npt. (May 1949 £400) King's Lynn Yarmouth T. Lowestoft retired 1959

Half–back, who was mainly a reserve with the County. He played for Swansea and Wales Schoolboys and afterwards served in North Africa and Italy with the Royal Fusiliers. Grenville was ready to sign for Cardiff City when Cyril Spiers invited him to sign for Norwich. He was always interested in electrical engineering and started up as a contractor. He is now living in Norwich.

WILLIAMS, Harold

b. Briton Ferry 17.6.24 5'4" 9st 4lbs
85–17 (101–18) (Wales 4 1949–51)
Briton Ferry (1935–38) war–time for Cliftonville Ferry Athletic (1946) Npt. (amateur Nov 1946, pro 2 weeks later) Leeds Utd. (June 1949 £3,000 & Depear) Npt. (Mar 1957 £750) Bradford P.A. (June 1957)

Quick and elusive winger, who made a big impression despite his size 5 boots. Harold started as an inside–forward and captained Briton Ferry Schools. He was on destroyer escort duty in the Atlantic during the War. Swansea Town turned him down and he was on his milk round with his horse and cart when signed by Tom Bromilow. He impressed in the 1948–49 F.A. Cup run with his pace and ball control and was transferred to Leeds afterwards. After seven seasons in the Leeds side Harold returned to Somerton Park for a brief stay. He went into the licensing trade and retired a short time ago. He is now living in Morley, Leeds.

WILLIAMS, Herbert J.

b. Cwmbran 19.6.25
2–1 (2–1) (Wales Amateur 1 1949)
Weston's F.C. Npt. (amateur cs 1948) Weston's F.C. (Sept 1949) Yeovil T. Whitstable (Sept 1956)

Welsh amateur international, who worked and played for Weston's Biscuits. He was a left-footed inside-forward with the hardest shot in local football, but somewhat out of his depth at Football League level. Bert fairly recently emigrated to Edmonton, Canada.

Full-back, who joined the County as a promising youngster, playing several reserve games at the end of the 1948-49 season. Mostyn, who had been a miner, returned to non-League soccer after a few seasons. He had a spell in America, but returned to Cwmfelinfach and died at the age of 61.

WILLIAMS, Mark.

b. Hereford 17.9.57 5'4" 10st 0lbs
59-8 (78-10)
Arsenal (App June 1974) Bromsgrove (cs 1975) Kidderminster (trial) Npt. (Welsh Lge. Mar 1976, pro July 1976) Hereford Utd. (loan May 1978) Telford Utd. (Nov 1978) Yeovil T. (Nov 1979 £300) Gloucester C. Trowbridge Westfields (1985)

Small, but enthusiastic midfield player, a former Arsenal apprentice, who spent a couple of years with County before disappearing into non-League football. Mark is the son of Roy, who played for Southampton and Hereford, scoring 265 League and Cup goals for the latter. Mark now owns an industrial supplies company and is Manager of Westfields.

WILLIAMS, Mostyn.

b. Cwmfelinfach 2.10.28 d. Ynysddu c 9.5.90
5'8" 11st 0lbs
28-0 (30-0)
Ynysddu Welfare Npt. (amateur 1948, pro Dec 1949) Gloucester C. (July 1952) Abergavenny (1953)

WILLIAMS, Paul A.

b. Sheffield 8.9.63 6'2" 12st 9lbs
25-3 (29-3) (N.Ireland 1 1991)
Distillery Leeds Utd. Arcadia (Pretoria)(1986) Grinaker Rangers (Johannesburg)(1986) Nuneaton Borough Preston N.E. (Dec 1986) Carlisle Utd. Npt. (Aug 1987) Sheffield Utd. (Mar 1988, loan full-time June 1989 fee) Hartlepool U. Stockport Co. (c.s.1990) W.B.A. (Mar 1991, £250,000)

Very big player, who came to Somerton Park as a centre-half. He moved to live in Lisburn, Northern Ireland, when 6 weeks old and later won 2 caps at youth level. He also played hurling and gaelic football. Paul was not an apprentice, but worked in the family coal business and as a part-timer played 200 games for Distillery. As a defender he was prone to some comical mistakes and proved himself master of the Alehouse Ball, but he showed improved form as a sticker, using his weight. He is the son of the leader of the Peace movement, Betty Williams. He was suspended three times with the County and was known to disagree with his own side. In the clear-out of 1988 he joined

Sheffield United on loan on the understanding that they would pay £17,000 if he proved satisfactory. Paul recently joined W.B.A. for a hefty fee and is now a member of the Northern Ireland Squad.

WILLIAMS, William.

b. Llantwit Vardre 5'9" 10st 7lbs
6-0 (6-0) (Wales 1 1925)
Abercanaid Argyle Pontypridd Cardiff C. (cs 1919) Northampton T. (Aug 1921) Npt. (Aug 1927)

Left-half, who could play in the forward line in emergencies. His thin and frail physique belied his tremendous stamina. Billy joined the Army at 18, becoming a member of the R.F.A. football team. He played for Cardiff City in their Southern League days and then became a fixture at Northampton Town, where he played almost 200 Football League games. He left the Cobblers after missing the 1926–27 season through injury and had a brief stay at County, where he was also crocked.

WILLIAMSON, David Leonard.

b. Llanelly 5'9" 11st 0lbs
7-0 (8-0)
Swansea local football & Swansea T. "A" Npt. (1934) Guildford C. (Aug 1936)

Len joined the County as an amateur in their Southern League side, but soon became a professional. He was small for a goalkeeper. The oppos-

ing side scored six on his debut versus Charlton Athletic, and another six on his farewell performance versus Crystal Palace, although in the later match he was injured and replaced in goal by Billy Burgess.

WILSON, Charles W.

b. Whitburn 5'8" 11st 0lbs
2-0 (3-0)
Whitburn Sunderland (amateur, trial cs 1920) Carlisle Utd. Npt. (July 1926) Lovells Ath (cs 1927) Whitburn Villa

Wing-half from the North, who did not make a great impact during his season with County. Afterwards he had a very short spell at Rexville.

WILSON, Joseph.

b. Workington 6.7.37 5'8" 11st 6lbs
42-0 (54-0)
Workington (Juniors 1955, pro Jan 1956) Nottm. Forest (Mar 1962 £8,000) Wolverhampton W. (Mar 1965) Npt. (May 1967) Workington (p/coach cs Sept 1968)

Craggy and vastly experienced full-back, who had played for Forest in Division I and helped Wolves to win promotion. He was made County Captain, but was allowed to rejoin Workington at the start of his second season. In 1973 Joe emigrated to Melbourne, Australia, where he coached George Cross in the Victoria League. Ten years later he was still there, coaching Keilor Austria.

WITCOMB, Douglas Frank.

b. Cwm 18.4.18 5'7" 11st 4lbs
25-0 (31-0) (Wales 3 1947 & 7 war-time 1939-45)
Cwm Villa Tottenham H. (amateur) Northfleet Enfield W.B.A. (Oct 1937) war-time for Grimsby T., Leicester C., Lovells Ath. & Npt. Sheffield Wed. (Feb 1947 £6,000) Npt. (Nov 1953) Llandudno (Jun 1954 p/coach)

Stylish and talented half-back, who had started with Ron Burgess at Cwm Villa and enjoyed a distinguished career before joining County in the veteran stage. Dougie became Sheffield Wednesday Captain in 1950-51 and helped the team to win promotion in 1950 and 1952. He was one of the experienced players signed by Lucas during his spell as player-manager. These days Dougie is living in Redditch.

WITHERS, David.

b. Llwynypia, Rhondda 28.4.67 5'8" 11st 7lbs
7-1 (39-5)
Bristol R. (YTS 1983) Cardiff C. Bristol R. Npt. (non-contract, pro Oct 1986) Ton Pentre (c Nov 1987) Npt. (non-contract Apr 1988, full-time Jan 1989) Barry T. (Mar 1989) Ton Pentre (cs 1991)

Young forward or midfield player, who arrived from Bristol Rovers with Tony Pulis. He was voted "Young Player of the Year" in 1986-87, but was later given a free transfer by Eastick, in order for him to to sign other players. In the County's player crisis of April 1988 he agreed to play at full-back for nothing and returned early in the club's Vauxhall Conference season. On the County's liquidation he moved to Barry Town.

WITTON, Joseph.

b. Newport 14.12.08
14-5 (15-5)
Npt. (amateur cs 1927, pro Sept 1929 to 1931) G.P.O. (early 1930's to 1939)

Versatile and energetic forward from the local Leagues, who had a few seasons in and out of the County first team. Joe could also be a keen tackling wing-half, when required. He later moved to London and played for the G.P.O. He is now living in Cowes, Isle of Wight.

WOLSTENHOLME, Arthur.

b. Middleton 1889 5'8" 12st 0lbs
29-8 (31-8)
Tonge Oldham Ath. (1907) Blackpool (1910) Gillingham (1912) Norwich C. (1913) Lincoln C. (1914) war-time for Nelson Oldham Ath. (cs 1919) Npt. (June 1920) Darlington (July 1921) Nelson (May 1922 to 1925) retired

Well-known for his goal scoring prowess, but a versatile player able to fill almost any outfield position. Arthur was signed for County by Harry Parkes, but only spent one season at Somerton Park, as he did with most of his sides. He played in Darlington's first Football League team and was a regular in Nelson's promotion side of 1922-23.

WOOD, Alan H.

b. Newport 13.1.41 6'1" 12st 0lbs
149–5 (183–6)
Central Y.M.C.A. Lovells Ath. Bristol R.
(Oct 1962) Merthyr T. (1963) Npt. (May 1965
to 72)

A tall and competent centre–half,
who was initially with Bristol
Rovers. Alan, who played with contact lenses, started off with the
County as a part–timer, but became
a full–time professional in July 1967,
staying for another five years. In
recent years he has had spells at
Somerton Park in charge of the youth
team. A keen cricketer, he is currently Fixture Secretary of the Newport Athletic Club and still performs
as an umpire.

WOOD, Arthur Basil.

b. Southampton 8.5.1890 d. Merton 17.5.77
5'10" 11st 1lbs
13–3 (14–3)
St. Mary's Ath. Eastleigh Ath. Fulham (Apr
1911 to 1915) Gillingham (1918) Hamilton
Acs. (cs 1922) Npt. (Nov 1922) Q.P.R. (1923
to 1925)

A big, robust forward, Arthur scored
on his County debut versus Q.P.R.
18.11.22 and joined them the following season. He had started as a Fulham reserve before World War I and
then played 80 Southern and Football
League games for Gillingham.

WOOD, Thomas.
("Smokey" or "Splinter")

b. Wednesbury, Staffs April 1908 5'8" 11st
8lbs
104–25 (122–34)
Wednesbury Shrewsbury T. (1925) Aston
Villa (Feb 1930, fee) Npt. (Nov 1936) war-
time football for Walsall

A great utility man, with genuine
skill and resource. Tommy, who
moved from half–back to inside-
forward, had a powerful shot and was
an expert penalty taker. Although a
long time Villa reserve, he became a
mainstay of the County first team and
was a regular in their promotion side.
He returned to Birmingham to live in
1939 and by the end of the War he
had reached the veteran stage.

WOODALL, Harry.

b. ?Newport c 1900
1–0 (1–0)
Npt. (by Sept 1920)

A young amateur, who played just
one game for County, when they lost
1–5 in a snowstorm at Watford. He
played only eight Welsh League
games for County, scoring two goals.

WOODRUFF, Robert J.

b. Wolverhampton 11.3.65 5'10" 10st 6lbs
9–0 (14–1)
Cardiff C. (youth) Npt. (pro Aug 1983) Swindon T. (loan May 1984) Cork City (cs 1984)
Menen (Belgium)

The son of Bobby, Robert showed early promise, winning Welsh under-15 and 18 caps. He was not offered professional terms at Cardiff. Although well-built he failed to make the most of a run in the County first team and show the form which had brought him 34 youth team goals in 1982–83. He has since performed abroad, however, and managed to score 22 goals in the Belgian League in 1987–88.

WOODRUFF, Robert W.

b. Highworth, Wilts 9.11.40 5'11" 11st 4lbs
52–7 (63–11)
Swindon T. (Juniors, pro May 1958) Wolverhampton W. (Mar 1964 £40,000) Crystal Palace (June 1966 £35,000) Cardiff C. (Nov 1969 £25,000) Npt. (1974) Bridgend T.

Bobby was an attacking wing-half, noted for his enormous long throw, which eventually caused his retirement through back trouble and a nine month stay in hospital. He was a well respected professional with a long career, making over 100 appearances for Swindon, Crystal Palace and Cardiff and helping Swindon and Palace to win promotion. He became Jimmy Scoular's most expensive signing at Ninian Park. After retiring he did some coaching for Cardiff and played the odd game for Bridgend. In a County versus Bridgend Welsh Cup-tie, he played against his son. Bobby had a four year spell as a representative for a sports firm and is now working with young offenders in South Glamorgan.

WOODS, Edward.

b. Pentre 29.7.51 5'11" 10st 10lbs
149–55 (175–60)
Ferndale (amateur 1966) Bristol C. (Sept 1971) Folkestone (loan c 1973) Scunthorpe Utd. (loan Oct 1973) Npt. (loan Aug 1974, full-time 1974) Bridgend T. (1979) Ton Pentre (Jan 1981) Ferndale (p/manager)

Eddie was a skilful striker, an outstanding header of the ball who also had a good drive. He is still remembered by Newport supporters for scoring the goal which knocked West Ham out of the F.A. Cup. He scored many goals for the County, including hat-tricks versus Rochdale and Scunthorpe, and could have gone further in the game, but preferred the security of his job as a draughtsman. He left County because of a ligament injury, but played on in Welsh League soccer and netted the goal which won the Championship for Ton Pentre in 1982. He is now living in Llantwit Fardre and selling specialist machinery.

WOOKEY, Kenneth George.

b. Newport 30.12.46 5'9" 10st 4lbs
57–5 (69–5)
Npt. (1962, pro Jan 1964) Lovells Ath. (loan 1963) Port Vale (July 1969) Workington (July 1970) Yeovil T. (July 1971) Salisbury Barry T. (cs 1973) Westland Sports

A winger or centre–forward, the son of Ken Wookey Snr. Ken joined the County straight from school and although rarely a regular in the first team, he was always a trier and never gave less than 100 per cent. He was a reserve for the Welsh under 23 side in 1968. Now living in Yeovil, he finished his non–League career with Chard Town and Glastonbury and is currently Manager of Shaftesbury Town.

WOOKEY, Kenneth W.

b. Newport 23.2.22 5'7" 11st 7lbs
14–2 (57–7)
Npt. (Juniors c 1938) Bristol R. (Dec 1946 p/exchange) Swansea T. (Nov 1948) Hereford Utd. (cs 1950) Ipswich T. (Oct 1950, retired May 1951)

Lively and talented winger, a Welsh Schoolboy international in 1936, who at one time worked in the Per Way Department at Newport Docks. The War interfered with his career, though he later made over 50 Football League appearances at Eastville. A local boy, bought up in Slade Street, Ken is still living in Newport.

WOOLLISCROFT, Arthur.

b. Salford 17.2.04 d. mid 1977 5'11" 11st 0lbs
15–0 (19–1)
Manchester Ship Canal Manchester C. (by 1927) Caernarvon Leicester C. (cs 1929) Watford (Jan 1930) Npt. (Sept 1933) Northwich Victoria (July 1934)

A dainty inside–forward, capable of beating three or four opponents. Arthur had played over 60 Football League games before arriving at Somerton Park, but his over elaborate style did not find favour with the supporters. He was at one time a dock worker.

WORTHY, Reginald Francis ("Wacker").

b. Newport 1903 d. Newport 29.8.58 5'8" 12st 2lbs
3–0 (5–0)
Brookside Ath. Cwmbran Npt. (1929 to 1931)

Local centre–half, who joined the club as an amateur in the late 1920's. Reg, who worked for a timber firm, only had a few first team opportunities.

WRIGHT, Harry Fereday.

b. West Bromwich late 1888 d. West Bromwich Sept 1950 5'9" 11st 7lbs
17–3 (18–4)

West Bromwich St. Mark's West Bromwich Wednesbury Ath. W.B.A. (Nov 1906) Stourbridge (cs 1909) W.B.A. (June 1910) Wolverhampton W. (Nov 1919 £600) Npt. (July 1920) Chesterfield (Sept 1921 to 1922)

Swift and energetic utility forward, who filled all five positions during his long stay at West Brom. He won a Division II Championship medal in 1911 and played in the 1912 F.A. Cup Final in opposition to Jack Cooper. After a short spell at County, Harry was signed by Chesterfield, who wanted an experienced player to bring on their youngsters.

YOUNG, Herbert.

b. Liverpool 4.9.1899 d. Lancashire mid 1976 5'7" 11st 0lbs
64–6 (68–9)
Everton (c 1922) Aberdare Ath. (cs 1923) Brentford (1925) Bangor C. Npt. (June 1927) Q.P.R. (July 1929) Bristol R. (Aug 1930) Swindon T. (1932 to 1933)

Bert was a fast and forceful left winger, born close to Anfield. Although he did not find the net very often, he was a consistent performer who was a first team choice for most of his clubs, including the County. He scored an F.A. Cup hat–trick versus Woking 24.11.28.

YOUNG, Robert George.

b. Newport 5.1.50 5'8" 10st 5lbs
90–6 (113–7) (Wales Under–23 1 1970)
Cromwell Juniors Npt. (amateur Mar 1967, pro July 1968) Hereford Utd. (cs 1972) Merthyr T. Barry T. Cinderford

A ball playing inside–forward, who was unmistakeable with his jogging run and shaggy hair. George joined the groundstaff on leaving school and had five years in and out of the County side. He still lives in the area and in recent years has played for and still manages Ellwood.

AFTERWORD.

This book has told the story of the players, managers and trainers of Newport County up to the time of its winding up in Court. They were in many ways the lifeblood of the Club, but many others gave varying amounts of their time to it, from Chairmen – who volunteered to endure the slings and arrows of outraged supporters – to humble programme sellers. There were many backroom staff who made their contributions over the years, such as Keith Saunders – Secretary 'off and on' from 1946 – barman Paddy Gordon – who over the years quenched many thirsts – and Ann Pring, who helped to keep the commercial side ticking over.

The sadness and feeling of humiliation caused by the County's slide from the Third Division, and from the European Cup Winner's Cup to extinction, soon gave way to a certain degree of optimism. There was an apparent attempt, taken with a pinch of salt by most supporters, to resuscitate the team, and play in Division 2 of the Vauxhall League. As things turned out, the team was expelled by that League 48 hours before kick–off, when none of the outstanding bills had been paid. In the meantime, the basis of a new team, to be known as 'Newport A.F.C.' had been formed by old County supporters, based largely from the Lifeline Society. The County had actually got a side together for the new season, under John Mahoney, so at one time there was the possibility of two teams representing the town.

What happened at the beginning of the 1989–90 season is now history. It was Newport A.F.C. who turned words into reality, kicking off in the Hellenic League. The team which included various ex-County performers, played its way to the top of the League, and performed with distinction. That it played at all was a rare achievement, for the team – opposed by the local Council – was forced to play at Moreton-in-Marsh. The opposition of the Welsh F.A. had meant that an alternative Welsh Ground had been an impossibility. During the course of the season, A.F.C. bought the rights to the name of Newport County from the liquidators, but decided against using it.

The path of Soccer in Newport has never been easy. As the County's Founder – Chairman Bert Moss – stated in May 1920, when the Club was heading for the Football League:

" In the first three years the Directors were initiated into the secrets of how Writs and Court summons' were issued and served. I hope we have seen the last of those days, and we look forward to brighter days. Let us hope the Club will be a credit to the good old town of Newport................ "

The supporters fervently hope, like the County's founder, that after the thunderstorms of the recent past, there will be brighter skies ahead.

YORE PUBLICATIONS.

Yore Publications is led by Dave Twydell, who is the author of a number of books, including:

'Defunct F.C.' – which contained detailed histories of five defunct non–League Clubs – this book is now out of print.

'More Defunct F.C.' – contains the histories of a further six non–League Clubs that also fell by the wayside, and includes Lovell's Athletic, the Newport 'Works' Club (of which there are a number of references to, in this, 'The Ironsides' book) Copies of this book are still available at:

£6–75p plus £1–00p post and packing.
(230 pages, A5 format, softback)

'Rejected F.C. (Volumes 1 and 2)' – contains the histories of all the Clubs that were 'rejected' (i.e. resigned or were voted out) of the Football League..... of particular local interest are the Aberdare Athletic and Merthyr Town Clubs of pre–war days. The books are profusely illustrated, and although now out of print, reprints will be available in 1992.

'Albania F.C.' – is a somewhat lighthearted (but factual) account of football – with an emphasis on the Grounds – in this little known country, which followed a visit by the Author in 1989.
A few copies remain, priced £2–50 incl. P/packing. (48 pages)

'Football League – Grounds For A Change' – is a comprehensive study of all the former Grounds on which the current Football League Clubs once played. The 424 information packed pages include around 250 illustrations, and the book is casebound with a full colour dust jacket. (Published Summer 1991)

Price £13–95 plus £1–80 P/Packing.

Cardiff City F.C. – *The Official History of the Bluebirds (Author John Crooks)* – *will be available from February 1992. This book will appeal to many former County supporters since the two Clubs often competed with each other, particularly in Welsh Cup encounters, and of course there were many players transferred between the two. John Crooks is the Club's Historian, and this large format (A4) sized book contains the full history of the Club. The text section (with illustrations) gives the written history, while the 'easy to read' statistics contain all the match details (including team line–ups) from 1910 to the 1990/91 season. An Additional chapters include, a 'Who's Who' of the prominent players who appeared in the Club's colours, and an unusual feature which relates the Club's History through the players eyes. The book contains over 300 pages and is casebound with a dust jacket.*

Price: £16–95 plus £3–00 P/packing
(Subscribers list, at reduced cost, closes 31st December 1991)

'Rejected F.C. of Scotland' – *will be available in early 1992, and will follow similar lines to its English equivalent. 'Volume 1 – Edinburgh and the South', will contain the well illustrated histories of ten former Scottish League teams.*

'Rejected F.C. – The Video' – *will appeal to a wide variety of football fans, and is a professionally produced, 90 minute long video for home viewing. In addition to extensive Ground views and interviews, it contains some remarkable archive footage, including .... Ashington versus Aston Villa (F.A.Cup 1924), pre–war New Brighton, and of particular relevance to former County fans – footage from the last home match of Workington (versus Newport County in May 1977). This unusual but highly entertaining video is now available at:*

£12–99p plus £1–00 post/packing.

Further Titles – *Other Club Histories, reprints of pre–war football books, and others with a historical content are planned for 1992. A S.A.E. will bring you the latest 'Yore Publications' Newsletter, and the above books can be obtained from:*

YORE PUBLICATIONS,
12 The Furrows,
Harefield,
Middx. UB9 6AT.